PENGUIN BOOKS



# CRIME SCENE

Esther Mckay served in the NSW Police Force for seventeen years, attaining the rank of Detective (technical) Senior Constable. She worked in Forensic Services for fifteen years, specialising in crime-scene examination and vehicle identification. She has a Diploma of Applied Science in Forensic Investigation (NSW Police) and was awarded the National Medal for service in 2001. Esther lives in Sydney with her two children.

Further information about the author may be found at www.esthermckay.com

# CRIME SCENE

## TRUE STORIES FROM THE LIFE OF A FORENSIC INVESTIGATOR

ESTHER MCKAY

PENGUIN BOOKS

PENGUIN BOOKS

UK | USA | Canada | Ireland | Australia
India | New Zealand | South Africa | China

Penguin Books is part of the Penguin Random House group of companies whose addresses can be found at global.penguinrandomhouse.com.

Penguin
Random House
Australia

First published by Penguin Group (Australia), 2005



Cover design by David Altheim © Penguin Random House Australia Pty Ltd
Text design by Lynn Twelftree and David Altheim © Penguin Random House Australia Pty Ltd
Cover photograph by Joel Rogers/Getty Images
Typeset in Minion by Post Pre-press Group, Brisbane, Queensland
Printed and bound in Australia by Griffin Press, an accredited ISO AS/NZA 14001 Evironmental Management Systems printer.

NATIONAL LIBRARY OF AUSTRALIA

A catalogue record for this book is available from the National Library of Australia

ISBN: 978 0 14300 529 2

penguin.com.au

To my mother Valerie

and my two children Robert and Alice

## Praise for *Crime Scene*

'I was amazed and inspired by your book. I read it in a day. I couldn't put it down. At times I was absolutely horrified at the situations you faced. You are an amazing and incredibly strong woman. Your thoughts and situations made me feel like I was experiencing the same situations as you. An incredible book.'
**M., police officer**

'Once I started reading, I couldn't put it down. I was amazed by your determination and stamina and also appalled by the lack of support you received. It is obvious you did a great service to Sydney. The book was an unbelievable insight into my chosen career and I thank you for it.'
**Lynn, female Year 12 student going on to study forensic science**

'Outstanding book. You make the reader feel as though they are standing next to you throughout. You have inspired me to return to the police force.'
**Mark, male police recruit**

'*Crime Scene* was by far the best book I have had the pleasure of reading. Not only do the events in your book captivate you so much that you cannot put the book down for one moment, it also takes you there, visualizing each scene as if you were there. I didn't want the book to come to an end and I just wanted to keep reading. You truly are a remarkable woman and author. No book has ever had such an impact on me. You are an inspiration to all women.'
**Betty, female reader**

'I am absolutely addicted to your book! I've always been interested in reading about forensic science and your book is by far the best.'
**Sarah, female reader**

'Wow, an amazing book! It's by far the best book I have read. I'd like to thank you because since reading your book I have been interested in reading. Although nothing compares to *Crime Scene* so far!'
**Elisha, female Year 10 student**

'I found the book riveting. The balance your book strikes between police work and the psychiatric problems it caused you is precisely right for a general audience.'
**Fred, information scientist, USA**

'Thank you for a marvellous book. It took me all of eight hours to read it. It is thought provoking, terrible, mind-jarring, with constant reminders of what ordinary people have to do.'
**Gordon, former military serviceman**

# Acknowledgements

I'd like to thank my mother, Valerie Ross, for total commitment, feedback and brilliant editing skills. I'd also like to thank her for her love and support throughout the writing of this book. Thank you to my husband Ken for listening, and for giving me the courage to face my demons. Thank you also to my wonderful family and close friends, whose encouragement and guidance helped make this book possible; and to my former colleagues – you have been an inspiration and it was an honour to work with you.

To Dr Selwyn Smith, you guided me forward when I was at my lowest. Your reassurance and care encouraged me to tell my story, and I thank you for being with me every step of the way.

I'd like to express my gratitude to Jock Blair, who gave up his time to give me advice.

Thank you to the Australian Society of Authors, especially the mentorship program, for allowing me the privilege of working with Gabrielle Lord. Gabrielle's amazing strength, wisdom and skill helped to polish the book.

My thanks to my publisher, Ali Watts, for her compassion and understanding, it was a pleasure working with you. I'd like to thank Belinda Byrne, my editor, for her advice, gentle coaching and friendship throughout the editing process. To the wonderful team at Penguin books, I can't thank you enough. It has been a delight to work with you all.

# Contents

# Foreword by Gabrielle Lord

'My name is Esther Mckay,' I read in a letter in October 2003. 'I am a former Detective Senior Constable of the NSW Police Force, retiring Medically Unfit, Hurt on Duty, in March of 2001. I have a Diploma of Applied Science in Forensic Investigation (NSW Police). I have been working on an untitled manuscript which follows my career as a young policewoman . . . [and] my appointment to the Scientific Investigation Section as a Crime Scene Examiner . . .'

This was my introduction to the author that accompanied her application for a Mentorship with the Australian Society of Authors, a system which teams new writers up with professional writers. Despite the fact that I was far too busy working to a looming deadline with my publisher, I decided to have a tea break and sit down with the sample Esther had sent to support her application.

From the moment I started reading, I knew I was in the presence of a powerful, original voice with a story to tell. These three factors – power, originality and a story to tell – are for me, the necessary ingredients of gripping narrative. They are the hallmark of a genuine writer.

As I read Esther's eyewitness account of the fatal car crash in which two young brothers lost their lives, I started to forget everything except that slippery road, and the dying boy whose eyes seemed to look into mine through Esther's words. Esther Mckay writes not only from the perspective of a police officer – her professionalism is unquestionable – but also from her heart, that place of our common experience. How would I feel, I couldn't help thinking as I read, if I were the young woman knocking on that front door to tell the mother that her boys would not be coming home that day, not then, not ever. I looked up from my reading, my eyes filled with tears, seeing the scene unfold, that mother's scream resonating through me. Without further hesitation, I accepted the honour of being Esther's mentor.

Esther and I had quite a bit of work to do. Her writing, although very strong, was raw. Also, there were years of Esther's own training in objective reporting to overcome before she could reclaim her normal writing voice. She needed to replace unnatural police constructions like 'juvenile male person' with ordinary words, she needed to tighten and edit her own writing, and most importantly, structure the book so that her own personal journey formed the ground on which the dramatic incidents proceeded.

Esther took to this job with the intelligence of a natural who just needs to be given the right set of tools. As the book progressed, so did our acquaintance. Often I found that when I made some observation about a scene, Esther would tell me that it was just what she herself had been feeling or thinking at the time. 'Then write it,' I'd say. 'Put it in. Readers will want to know who you are. Not just the incidents you attended.'

Esther's writing is the more powerful for her own unconsciousness of her personal attributes. Alone and unsupported, labouring through the dark hours of the night with her camera and her notebook, and with a full day of work yawning ahead of her as well, Esther attended horrific scenes, bringing to these wretched places – as any astute reader will see – the light of her own grace and dignity. Young officers like Esther work in the hell realms, where the horror of what human beings do to each other is simply 'all in a day's work'. Most of us don't come into contact with violent crime in a lifetime – these folk deal with it day by day. They are supposed to be 'objective' and 'detached' when the proper response is grief and anger. There is little or no support for these young men and women, who do the work none of us would want to do.

This book will remind you that behind every crime scene or accident reported in the daily news, people like Esther Mckay are there before you read the summary of the tragedy, dealing with the bloody aftermaths, securing the scene, doing what they can to comfort survivors and relatives, going into people's homes to tell them the worst news we can ever hear. These aren't skilled grief counsellors with long years of dealing with human suffering; more often than not these are young officers, scarcely out of their teens. They are expected to do this work as part of the job and they do it, unquestioningly. But the demands made on them take their toll. Without wise supervision and understanding support, as Esther reveals in her book, years of trying to suppress strong, natural emotions results in a huge build-up of unexpressed feelings. One day the inevitable happens. It happens to any human being who is forced to practice an inhuman way of living.

Often on call twenty-four hours a day, with constant court appearances interrupting their case work, these people find the backlog of cases building and building as new calls come in all the time. Long hours of overtime cut into family life and social life and even then, there's never enough time. When the stress levels build, as they must, often they are told to 'go and have a few drinks'. Alcohol cannot relieve an impossible workload, only workplace support and good organisation can achieve that. But with superiors also stressed and pressured by those in higher ranks to clear cases quickly so that they're not in strife, compassionate understanding is rare. No wonder they say 'the job's fucked'.

With her usual humility, Esther wrote in her application that her book might appeal to 'readers with an interest in crime or policing in Sydney and/or human interest.' I think any reader will agree that what interests the reader first and foremost is the story of one woman's journey from naivete to maturity, a journey to hell from which some people don't return. Fortunately for us, Esther not only returned, but brought back with her, and writes from, her new knowledge and awareness. She offers the depth of someone who has seen the worst and yet continues to choose life in spite of this. Readers will be riveted by her emotional and spiritual growth, which I felt was perfectly captured at the end of the book as Esther finally lays to rest the case that, years before, cracked her heart open.

It was a delight to work with Esther. She is a keen and experienced horsewoman and somehow, an equine metaphor seems apt for the track work we did together on her book. Really, all I had to do was show her the hurdle course, and Esther did the rest.

# 1 Induction – 1985

*Standing there in the hot January sun I can feel a bead of sweat running down my face. I'm twenty-one years old and I'm about to face the most frightening thing I've ever experienced. Beyond that mortuary door lie nameless bodies. I'm trembling inside but I compose myself, determined to prove I can handle this or anything else I'm about to encounter. Paul, Sharan and I have just graduated from class 207 at the Goulburn Police Academy and we have all been posted to Campbelltown Police Station in Sydney's south-western suburbs. We huddle close together for support as the old sergeant opens the door and ushers us into the morgue. In that instant the sense of death hits me with full force, and to this day I have never forgotten it. The smell of death hangs over us as we stand in the doorway. It is cold, hard and pungent. To my left I see a wall of steel doors, and through a doorway on the right I see an old cement slab. The morgue attendant's face is cheery and bright. I can tell he loves his job.*

*'Got a few new recruits, Sarge? Any of you blokes seen a dead body before?'*

*'I don't think so,' I say, looking at Paul and Sharan, who nod in agreement.*

*'I've got a stillborn baby in fridge two, just came in this morning. Give me a sec and I'll bring it out for you to have a look at.'*

Does it have to be a baby? *I think. A friend of mine is in the maternity section of the hospital at this very moment.* Please God, don't let it be her baby.

*The morgue attendant opens the door and pulls out a steel trolley. There on the trolley lies a tiny bundle wrapped in hospital sheets. My heart pounds as I stare at the bundle. The attendant opens the sheets to reveal a doll-like creature, perfect in every way. Its little hands are clenched as if every ounce of strength it possessed was in those tiny fingers. Am I the only one feeling so horrified? I look at the others and I see the horror in their eyes, too. It's a sight I am to encounter many times during my career.*

*The morgue attendant breaks the silence.*

*'Well, now you've seen your first body. Soon enough you'll be back here for a post-mortem. Any questions?'*

*'What do we have to do at the post-mortem?' I ask.*

*'Don't worry about that now, we'll show you next time. We're very much a hands-on morgue here and you'll get the hang of things soon enough.'*

*Back in the car, the old sergeant explains what's expected of us for the remainder of the induction but I'm sure no one is listening. The picture of the baby is frozen in my mind and I can't stop wondering how the family is coping with their loss. My mother had told me many years before that the worst thing that can happen to a parent is to lose a child. Was it possible that the morgue attendant had been showing off, I wonder? Had he used the death of a baby for* shock value?

*The sergeant pulls the Falcon into a small one-man station in the rural coalmining town of The Oaks. He tells us we'll be meeting the lock-up keeper. As we get out of the car, a stocky blond-haired senior constable comes striding out to greet us as if he has something important to say. Before we can be introduced he flies into words.*

*'Sarge, got some young'uns, eh? Two birds as well. You blokes have got no idea what this job's about. All I can say is, "The job's fucked".'*

*I am speechless. It is our very first day in the job and I am full of enthusiasm. It's been such a struggle to gain entry to the police force. Each step of the recruiting process presented a challenge and I constantly feared I wouldn't make the cut, let alone pass the gruelling three months of training I've just completed. I am proud to be wearing the uniform of a probationary constable, and I plan to pursue a long career with the force. They warned us at the academy about the 'disgruntled senior constable' syndrome, but I am not prepared to deal with it so early in our induction. I have absolutely no idea what to say to someone who is so obviously bitter and burnt out. We are ushered into the station while the sergeant reprimands our new acquaintance. We never meet again but I hear some time later that he's been transferred. I hear the saying*

*'TJF' many times after that first day; usually from disgruntled senior constables. I never think I will agree, but as time passes and I, too, become a senior constable, I begin to feel the same way.*

* * *

I always had a strong sense of justice. Originally, I had worked towards a career in law and was bitterly disappointed when my HSC results were below the required entry level for university. After leaving school I worked at the *Star* newspaper in Campbelltown as a 'Girl Friday'. I was interested in journalism, but after the newspaper was bought out by Kerry Packer, new staff were brought in and I found myself on the retrenchment list. The next day I applied for a position at the Australian Consolidated Press Library in the city, and started there the next week. It was funny really – Packer had retrenched me from one job and then re-employed me in another position the following week. But travelling into the city from Douglas Park, a semi-rural township on the outskirts of the far south-western suburbs, was draining. An hour and a half each way on the train after a half-hour drive to Campbelltown station began to take its toll. I realised that the mundane work of the press library was nowhere near fulfilling enough and I wanted a job that presented challenges and the possibility of promotion. So I set my sights on joining the police force. My family were shocked and a little worried that I was considering such a dangerous career, though they still gave me their full support. Once they got over their initial concern, they were very much involved in helping me prepare for the recruitment process. Later, when I began general duties, my family and friends were very supportive and took an active interest in my work, often asking me how it was going.

When I first went to police headquarters to sit the recruitment test, I was turned away because I was half a centimetre below the regulation height of five foot six inches (167 cm). Feeling rejected and disappointed, I took the elevator back down to the foyer and as I walked past the sergeant on the desk he asked why I was leaving. Because I wasn't tall enough, I told him.

With a smile he said, 'Don't worry, love, just go down to the Domain and hang by your legs for half an hour, then come back and have another go, you'll be right.'

He seemed confident that his stretching method would work so I decided to take his advice. While working for Australian Consolidated Press I had learned that there was a gym in the basement of the building used by a lot of the employees. I decided to walk over to the gym and tell them I worked upstairs in the press library, hoping they would help me. The plan worked and a gym instructor gave me several stretching exercises to do. But he was worried that by the time I walked back across the park in my high heels I would shrink again, so I walked barefoot.

Back at headquarters I told the desk sergeant I had gone away and stretched. With a big smile he wished me luck and I again took the elevator up to the recruitment level. I stood in the doorway and announced that I was now the regulation height. A young policewoman came to the door and reluctantly agreed to re-test me. Although I was slightly taller, I was still on the borderline so she called in another constable for a second opinion. My stomach churned as I waited for their decision – this was my chosen career and I was determined to pass the test. What could I say that would make me look like a good candidate for policing? All of a sudden I blurted out, 'I've got a Rotary Youth Leadership Award!'

The young male constable said, 'All right, we'll let you in. I'll give you one hundred per cent for persistence.'

I was so thrilled that I'd passed the height requirement, I didn't care that I'd missed the bus to the police academy for the fitness test. I was told I'd have to come back later for that, but I could sit the IQ test before I went home. Afterwards, I had to sit and wait for what seemed an eternity while it was marked. Finally the policewoman returned and told me I had just passed by the skin of my teeth. It seemed I was scraping in on all counts that day, but I didn't care. As long as I was accepted into the police academy, that was all that mattered.

I didn't realise it at the time, but this was all part of a manufactured, military-style attitude that police put on for each other. Right from the start I was made to feel inadequate and told I should think myself lucky to be one of the chosen ones. It never crossed my mind to think that perhaps my test results weren't that bad, or that, in fact, I might have a lot to offer the police force. Throughout my training and later career there were many instances where I was put down by my so-called colleagues who were exercising their hierarchical right to do so. But after my experience with the height requirement, whenever anyone asked me how tall I was I would always say with a laugh, 'Five foot six inches, regulation height.'

Back at the station on my very first day in the job, we were taken around to all the sections and introduced to the various police we would be working with. A big office on one side of the building housed the detectives and as we entered, a group of men were sitting at desks, banging away on typewriters. Just inside the doorway we were approached by the boss and a couple of the younger blokes.

I was introduced to a very tall, fair-haired man by the name of Ken. I didn't know it then but our paths would cross eight years later, and this man would have a significant impact on my life. At the time he turned to his mates and commented, 'I didn't know the academy was allowing schoolgirls to wear the uniform now.' The others chuckled in agreement. He looked at me and asked how old I was but before I could answer he turned to the others and spoke as if I wasn't there, saying, 'She looks fifteen to me.'

My appearance and, in particular, my size, were obstacles from the very start. At the age of twenty-one I thought I was more than old enough to wear the police uniform, but I certainly did look younger than I was. Later, when I was working out on the truck, I was often harassed because of the way I looked, but the fact remained that I had the powers of arrest, and I often got the last laugh when I threw some protesting crook into the back of the paddy wagon.

After our introduction to the detectives we went to the charge room where we were shown the dock and the fingerprint area. Leaning behind the charge table was the charge sergeant.

'Got plenty of good-looking fellas here for you, love,' he said as he looked at my hand and saw the engagement ring on my finger.

'I'm not here to meet fellas,' I replied. 'I'm here to do a job.'

As we walked out to look at the cells I could hear him sniggering.

It hadn't entered my mind that perhaps I'd be looked at as a potential partner by the single men I'd be working with, and once it was established that I was engaged it wasn't an issue at all. I was obviously committed to my fiancé, Greg, and we were happily planning our future together. Greg had supported my decision to join the police force from the beginning. He was comfortable with me working odd hours as he was a shift worker in the coalmines. It was hard being away from each other while I was at the police academy, but we both took it in our stride. After nearly two years together Greg and I had announced our engagement at my twenty-first birthday party, and we planned to marry in eighteen months' time. Joining the police meant I would be earning double the salary of my previous job, which gave us the benefit of two good incomes. We immediately pooled our money and had started looking for our first home.

Out in the cells, we were approached by a tall policewoman named Paula. She was affectionately known as Big Bird and over time she would become a great friend and mentor. But now she was about to search a female prisoner and she thought it was a good opportunity to show the girls how it was done.

The men left and Sharan and I followed Paula into one of the cells. Here we were introduced to our first prisoner, a drug addict, who was filthy dirty and ready for a fight. Sharan and I stood back as Paula put on the rubber gloves.

'This is how it's done,' she said.

The prisoner refused to undress and instead swung punches, forcing Paula to restrain her by holding her up against the back cell wall with one hand while strip-searching her with the other. The prisoner struggled and screamed abuse the whole time but the job seemed effortless to our experienced colleague. I was shocked that I would have to deal with people who were so unpredictable and aggressive. I wondered if I could do the job as easily. I was a smaller build than Paula and Sharan, and although I was extremely physically fit, I was well aware of the need for brawn in some circumstances. One thing I was not, however, was a coward. I was determined to prove that I would at least have a go if a job got rough. I hoped my fitness and mental attitude would make up for my size.

That afternoon, Paul, Sharan and I were split up and each of us was assigned to a member of the highway patrol. I was introduced to Dave, a seasoned highway patrolman, whose easygoing nature helped me to relax a little. We went down to the basement car park and got into a Holden Commodore V-8. From the minute we took off I knew it was going to be the ride of my life. The car had an enormous amount of power and the surge of the accelerator literally drove my head back into the headrest. We went straight out to the freeway where Dave demonstrated how the radar worked. Suddenly the radar alarm sounded, picking up a speeding motorcycle going in the opposite direction. I hung on to the side of my seat as Dave did a U-turn. The car flew at 180 kph in hot pursuit as we closed in on the cyclist. It was a pure adrenaline rush weaving in and out of traffic, lights and sirens blazing. The sound in the car was deafening. The bike had been clocked at doing 135 kph in an 80 kph zone and as we drew closer I could see it had a 'P' plate dangling precariously from the back. The rider pulled over and we got out of the car and approached. As he slid off the bike I could see the boy's whole body trembling. He knew he was in a lot of trouble. He had sufficiently exceeded the speed limit to warrant an arrest and, to make matters worse, he was also riding an unregistered and uninsured trailbike. Dave told the young man that he would be charged with driving in a manner dangerous. We put him in the back of the car and returned to the station where his parents were contacted and he was charged. As the boy was standing in the charge dock he began to cry and I felt sorry for his stupidity. Should I feel sorry for someone who has broken the law? After my first arrest I had mixed feelings. Was it necessary to make the arrest and bring the boy back to the station to be fingerprinted and charged? It seemed harsh, but then I was new and just learning the ropes.

After the boy had been processed we again headed off in the direction of the freeway. This time we actually made it to the northbound lanes before the radar siren went off. Dave put his foot to the floor and once again I was hanging on to my seat with the deafening sound of the sirens above. We made our U-turn across the grassed strip between the north and southbound lanes and continued in hot pursuit. It happened so fast that I didn't even know what type of car we were chasing. As we ducked in and out of the traffic at close to 200 kph, I heard an enormous bang and a large plume of smoke rose from under the bonnet. Dave swore and banged his fist on the steering wheel. The car stalled and we pulled over to the side of the road. 'Shit, the bloody motor's blown!'

I started to laugh and we both became quite hysterical as the car limped back to the station doing about 5 kph. I spent the rest of the shift staring into the back of a typewriter while Dave banged away on the antiquated machine, trying to explain in triplicate how and why police equipment had been damaged. Every man and his dog from various sections around the station came into the highway patrol office to find out what all the fuss was about.

The next day we were introduced to our buddies, the officers who were to be our sole partners for the next six weeks. In the mid-80s, the buddy system was in full swing. Each probationary constable was paired off with the senior constable who was considered to be the most likely match. Personalities, age and gender were all taken into consideration. My buddy was a stocky man in his late twenties called Doug. I soon learned that Doug was a man of few words – if I wanted to know anything, I had to ask. His method of teaching was simply to demonstrate the correct procedure. I stood back, watched, learned, and kept my mouth shut. Questions were asked back in the truck or later at the station. I found Doug's answers were always short and straight to the point. He didn't give me any indication of what he thought of my progress but after two weeks I knew he considered I was ready to pull my weight the day we were called to a break and enter.

We were standing at the door and Doug was talking to the victim. After a short silence he turned to me and said, 'You do this one.'

That's how I learnt, sink or swim. One bit of advice Doug did give me was to tell me to be careful of a couple of the blokes working in the station. If I was ever rostered on with them, I was to let him know. I wasn't sure what he meant but it was obvious that I didn't need to know. We spent days, afternoons and nights together, sometimes sitting in the truck nearly all night as we drove around the streets at a snail's pace looking for trouble. In those first six weeks we often had to guard Family Law Court judges, which meant sitting in a car together for hours on end. As there was very little conversation it was often hard to stay awake and it was agony trying not to drift off to sleep. We rigged a small black-and-white telly up to the cigarette lighter and I remember watching endless episodes of *Bonanza*.

During those early weeks I was very quiet, especially in the duty room where we did our paperwork or around other police. I felt quite intimidated as, before I joined, I'd only ever spoken to a police officer at the scene of a car accident. One day several constables came up and said, 'You can speak to us, you know.'

After that I tried to be a little more relaxed around the other officers and slowly I started to feel like one of the team. Loyalty was of the utmost importance and once it was established I could be trusted, I was accepted. One of the staff from the rotating general duties team approached me when my buddy training was over to apologise for what had been said about Sharan and me before we started at the station. We were the first female police to be sent to Campbelltown in five years and the blokes thought it was a joke. Some of them had even refused to work with us. I was oblivious to discrimination and hadn't thought anything of it when I joined the police, but women were still relatively rare in the force in the mid-80s and it was a big thing for two women to be sent to a station at one time. We had obviously proven ourselves, to merit the apology.

I had spent my high school years at Presbyterian Ladies College at Croydon. There, all the girls were encouraged to strive and achieve in any chosen field. The subject of sex discrimination had never arisen during my time at school and I had no idea that women could find a particular career path more difficult than their male counterparts. I simply had no opinion on the subject of discrimination – my view was that we all got stuck in to get the job done. In many respects my high school education prepared me extremely well for policing, even though at the time I had no idea I would pursue a career in the police force. I found my high school days at PLC stricter than the Police Academy, and couldn't understand why many of the police trainees complained about what seemed to me trivial matters. My belief was that you listened and did what you were told, it was as simple as that. I was amazed at how many trainees took a completely different view. Some would argue and complain at every opportunity and found themselves being noticed for all the wrong reasons. These recruits tended not to make it in the end; either they dropped out during training, or were weeded out later on.

It was a sad time when the first six weeks ended and my buddy training was over. I felt safe with Doug and by now I knew what he expected. I realised it took a special type of person to take on a buddy; in essence, Doug had put himself at risk by working with a probationary constable. I now knew how vital it was to work with a reliable partner who could back you up if things got rough – that support could mean the difference between life or death. Before starting my buddy training I had no idea how dangerous policing really was. Campbelltown had five separate housing commission estates within its patrol and the work was dangerous and tough. It took both courage and devotion to take on a training role. It was also vital to the future because what I learnt in those first six weeks shaped the way I performed my duties for the rest of my career. It was an extremely important learning experience.

Even though I would still work with Doug from time to time, it was like starting all over again when I fronted up for work after my buddy training was over. All of a sudden I was thrown out among the other thirty or so rotating members of the general duties team, and with that came different personal styles, ideas and expectations. I still didn't know everyone I'd be working with so it took time to assimilate to the new and varied circle of workmates. Each time I worked with a new partner I'd stand back and take it all in until I felt comfortable with what was required and once I'd worked out their expectations I felt confident to work as a team. It was a good, hard-working team of police at Campbelltown and I was lucky to have such a strong grounding in my first year.

# 2 Dead'uns, rapists and a mad woman

'Who wants to go to a dead'un?' called the station sergeant. 'It's an overdose.'

There was a chorus of 'Not me, Sarge.'

After a silence, my buddy Doug yelled, 'I'll do it.'

At the house we were met at the front door by a young man who was the dead man's son. Feeling apprehensive, I followed closely behind my buddy as we were shown to the master bedroom. The dead man was lying face up on the bed with a photograph over his eyes. Doug explained general duties police are never to touch a dead body; if the body needs to be examined, scientific should be called. After viewing the scene Doug determined that this death was straightforward with no suspicious circumstances. The man had written a suicide note saying that he couldn't live without his wife, who had died of cancer six months before. Doug picked up the photograph, a picture of the dead man's wife, and placed it on the dressing table with the letter. In the lounge room I listened as Doug spoke with the man's two sons. It taught me a lot about how to deal sympathetically with relatives in these kinds of situations. This was in contrast to Doug's authoritarian manner when dealing with criminals. The boys were twins in their late teens, and obviously very distressed. I thought how hard it was for them, losing both parents.

Back at the station we did the paperwork required by the Coroner and made arrangements for the post-mortem. At the morgue the next day, we identified the body to the pathologist and I stood back and watched him slice and cut the body as he examined all the relevant parts. I was intrigued by the layer of yellow body fat beneath the skin, the thick fatty tissue attached to flesh; though brighter in colour, it was similar to the fat on meat you'd buy from the butcher. As time went on, I would find it increasingly difficult to wipe out the image of decaying flesh from my mind when eating or preparing meals. The dead man's organs were weighed and then replaced into the body cavity while the attendant washed the blood away with a hand-held hose. Blood ran along the concrete slab through a hole and on to the cement floor where it was washed down a drain. Although the body was not decomposed it still gave off a pungent odour. My sense of smell has always been acute, and even when I was a small child I'd be the first to describe a smell whenever I came across one. Even though the visual aspects of the post-mortem were distressing, it was the smell I really struggled with. It seemed to invade my whole body, and I longed to get a breath of fresh air.

I had been warned about the procedure where the skull is opened by a circular saw but I wasn't prepared for how bad it actually was. Now, when I hear a chainsaw start up I immediately go back in time and relive seeing a skull being cut open for the first time. Tiny fragments of bone flew up into the air.

No doubt while I was standing there I was inhaling a fine mist of bone and whatever else was in the atmosphere. No one wore a mask. In fact, sometimes the morgue attendant or the pathologist didn't even wear gloves. At the completion of the examination the body was sewn up with hessian string, washed down and wheeled back over to the fridge.

As I walked out of the dark morgue into the bright sunlight I squinted as the sun's harsh rays hit my eyes. It was like walking out of a cave. Somehow the smell of the morgue gets into your clothes and up your nose. I could smell it on my uniform throughout the rest of the day. Back at the station we were constantly berated by other police who immediately recognised the smell of death and commented, 'You've been to the morgue!'

I was a little apprehensive before attending my first post-mortem but after it was over I felt that it really wasn't that bad. It was interesting in a clinical sense and I was amazed at how the body worked and what the organs looked liked. Doug had warned me that I might be sick but it didn't affect me in that way at all; I felt I coped quite well.

One Sunday night a few weeks later, while I was watching TV at home, the sergeant on duty at the station rang. A young woman had been viciously raped and the detectives required the assistance of a policewoman. The victim had to be taken to Westmead Hospital for an examination and would later give a detailed statement. At the time, only policewomen were allowed to take statements from female victims, the men could only coordinate the victim's statement, but in this particular case the victim was refusing to talk to any of the male detectives handling her case. She was extremely traumatised and she needed special care. It was going to be difficult to gain her confidence.

Although I had no experience in this type of duty I was keen to do the job. There wasn't one trained policewomen available within the whole division, so I was it.

When I arrived at the station I was met by the same fair-haired detective who had made the comment about my age on my first day at work. He was now in a position where he needed my help and I had a chance to prove that I could do the job with a little guidance. He explained the situation and what I was required to do. The victim was extremely distressed and her fiancé was also at the station making matters worse. She had been waiting in her car for her fiancé to finish work when a man had forced his way inside and made her drive at knife point to an isolated bush area where he raped her repeatedly. She was left naked by the side of the road, screaming and crying until she found help. The woman was due to be married the next weekend and she was terrified the offender would contact her, or worse, turn up at her wedding. After he dumped the stolen car, the rapist had taken her handbag, which contained her personal details as well as the wedding arrangements.

After we were introduced, I drove her to Westmead Hospital. I took this opportunity to gain her confidence. I was horrified when I heard of her ordeal and immediately felt compassion for her. Even though I had never spoken to a victim of such brutality before, I had no trouble understanding how she felt. She cried on and off for most of the journey but by the time we arrived at the hospital she had calmed somewhat and was prepared for what she had to endure. The sexual assault examination is often traumatic as the victim must submit to an internal examination which involves the taking of several upper and lower vaginal swabs. In some cases the victim has suffered severe bruising and the examination can be painful.

Afterwards the victim is counselled and asked if she wishes to be given the morning-after pill to prevent a possible pregnancy. The complete examination can take up to three hours. While I waited in the nurse's meal room, I filled the time by drinking coffee and talking to the nurses who had come in for their break.

Finally the woman's examination was over and we walked out into the cold night air towards the police car. We made the hour-long journey back to the station discussing her version of events. She told me how utterly terrifying the whole ordeal had been, but in the back of her mind she had known that if she studied her attacker, there would be a better chance of an arrest. She could see the tattoo on his fingers and took special note of the letters which spelt out 'FUCK'. She also described to me how helpless she felt as she had no control over the attack. At one stage she thought he was going to kill her and remembered thinking that she would never see her family again. Finally she fell asleep and I woke her when we arrived. By this time she was exhausted but insisted she was up to giving the statement.

The detectives gave me a crash course on how to take the statement and we went into one of the small interview rooms off the main office. I typed her version of events on an old manual typewriter in triplicate using carbon paper. Each time I made a mistake I had to liquid-paper each copy and then retype the word. It was a far cry from the technology available today. There was no such thing as a computer of course. There wasn't even an automatic corrector on the old manual typewriters. It made hard work of the simple job of typing a statement or report. The concluding part of a statement always involves a description and we discussed at length her best recollection of what the offender looked like. Finally at 4 a.m. the statement was completed and after signing each copy I handed it over to the detectives. As the woman left I wished her luck with her wedding. The following week the detectives went to the wedding and mingled with the crowd but the rapist didn't turn up and is still at large.

After that night I was often recalled to take rape victims' statements and I soon became accustomed to the procedure but I never got used to hearing the victim's versions of events. At times I interviewed women who had fabricated their stories for various reasons, but by the end of the interview they had usually admitted to making some or all of it up. These complainants, usually attention seekers, wasted a lot of police time. Regardless, all complaints had to be investigated fully and were given the benefit of the doubt.

After working at the station for a couple of months I became familiar with a woman who had become known as a vexatious complainant. She was constantly racing into the station demanding to see the detectives. Her complaints were usually of a sexual nature. She was a rather large-breasted women and always wore low-cut garments that revealed ample cleavage. Her appearance was dishevelled and she had the misfortune of being cross-eyed. She appeared to be quite mad and some of the detectives had become frustrated when dealing with her.

I was summoned to the detectives' office while on afternoon shift one night by a burly detective whom she had bailed up in the corner of the room. While he was interviewing her regarding a complaint that a solicitor had sexually assaulted her, she suddenly grabbed at her chest and said, 'I shouldn't come to the police station without wearing a bra!'

Anticipating he was going to be next on her list of complaints he jumped out of his chair, calling for help from the station. When I arrived she told me she felt her dress was too revealing and wasn't comfortable talking to the detective. I had a bit of a chuckle to myself; I knew this incident would be doing the rounds of the station. I agreed to talk to her in an interview room and four hours later emerged with an eleven-page statement which was unbelievable to say the least.

By this stage I had taken quite a number of statements and was becoming fairly proficient. But when I took this particular account, I found it hard to keep a straight face. She claimed she had first met the alleged offender in a friend's coffee shop. She had chatted to him while he ate lunch. A couple of months later she was sitting in a bus shelter when he approached her and asked if she needed a lift.

In the car he said, 'You've got a nice set of boobs there.'

At which she replied, 'Oh! Thank you.'

The conversation turned to whether the victim would be interested in having an affair.

Some months later the victim went to meet the solicitor at his office in relation to a legal matter. She was told by his secretary that he was at a council luncheon and was not likely to return that day. Later that night the woman went to the local community centre where the function was being held and, sure enough, the solicitor was there, one of the last few drunken stragglers. They had a heated discussion during which he accused her of trying to compromise him. When the last of the guests left, the solicitor took her by the arm, led her into a vacant room and forced her to stand against a wall where he reached under her dress and pulled at her pantyhose. As the woman recounted her story it became apparent that she was not mentally stable. She went on to say that they went back to his office where she went to the toilet and, while she was inside the locked cubicle, the solicitor burst through the door and hit her on the bottom with a cane. He then told her to go to another room and take all her clothes off. After a few minutes she returned to find him fast asleep and snoring loudly, slumped in a chair behind his desk.

After completing the statement I handed it to the burly detective who had been patiently waiting outside the interview room. We sat in silence while he read over the details and when he had finished he looked up at me and said, 'What the hell–?'

We both knew of the solicitor involved as he worked locally. It appeared that some parts of the alleged incident were indeed true but that there were also discrepancies to be investigated. We decided to visit the solicitor in person the following day, and that if charges were to be proceeded with, he should be summonsed rather than charged. The alleged offender was horrified when he was informed of the woman's complaint but was happy to explain his side of the story. He *had* been involved with the complainant, but soon realised that she was unstable and had tried to end the brief affair. The woman had then begun a campaign of stalking and harassment. The solicitor felt that *he* was the victim, and requested that the police issue an apprehended violence order to keep the woman away from his legal practice.

The matter then went back and forth between the two parties as they complained and counter-complained about each other. I was attending a separate matter at court one day and saw them arguing outside the courthouse. The argument turned into a physical altercation, which had to be broken up by the police. I'm not sure what the eventual outcome was for the solicitor but the woman's husband finally left her and that then turned into a separate police matter.

I was called to the former matrimonial home by the woman when her husband came to collect his belongings and she refused him entry to the property. The case of the feuding couple had been attended to by police several times already that week. I went to the job with my former buddy, Doug, who was getting exasperated by the whole scene. When we arrived we were confronted with an hysterical woman screaming abuse at her estranged husband. He was a small, unassuming man and was obviously distressed. She had changed all the locks on the house and garage and was refusing to let him take what was rightfully his. The stand-off was occurring in front of the garage where she had stored all of his possessions. As my buddy tried to negotiate with her she picked up a pile of empty ice cream containers and started hurling them at us, screaming, 'Get off my fucking property!' When Doug approached her and tried to stop her throwing the containers, she took a swing at him. As he ducked she flew around in a spin and fell over. My buddy grabbed her by the arm to help her up but then she began struggling and yelling that he was assaulting her. She screamed at us that she was going to her solicitor's office to make a complaint of police brutality, and with that she ran down the drive, jumped into a clapped-out Holden wagon and drove off like a madwoman.

My buddy said to the estranged husband, 'Right, get what you need, we'll leave you to it.' Then he hastily turned to me and said, 'Let's go, I want to see where she's going.'

We ran down to the truck and took off in hot pursuit. Soon enough we came across her old car literally dumped beside the roadway in the main street, the front tyres in the gutter and the back portion of the car jutting out into the traffic. We pulled up beside the car and Doug jumped out with the infringement book and slapped a ticket on her windscreen for 'Not Park Close and Parallel'.

He flew back into the truck and said, 'Let's get out of here before she comes out.'

Laughing, we both imagined the sight of her coming out of the solicitor's office and finding the ticket. We drove back to the station to attend to the paperwork involved in the domestic dispute and while we were standing behind the station counter she came racing in. We ducked down behind the counter before she saw us and hid there while she demanded to see the supervisor. She yelled, complaining about her parking ticket, demanding to have it retracted. When she was told it would not be cancelled and that she could go to court and have her say as to why she didn't deserve it, she ripped it up and threw it on the floor. With that she stormed out of the station.

A couple of months later, while working in the station one morning with my old academy mate Sharon, I received a call about a kombi van parked in a paddock up near the local hospital. The van had been there for several days and the hospital staff were suspicious. We had extra staff on the shift, so the senior member on the crew took Sharon and me out in the police truck. When we found the kombi van the first thing we saw was a mass of blowflies caught between the van window and a curtain. It didn't look good as we walked around peering in the windows. I could see the figure of a man lying face down and we banged on the van door to try and wake him. When there was no response we realised that we had a dead'un on our hands. All the doors were securely locked but finally we forced the three-quarter window in the front of the van and were able to get in. As the side sliding door was opened, blowflies swarmed out, making their escape. I furiously swiped them away from my face and looked around the van. There, lying face down on a mattress at the rear of the van, was the body of a young man who had apparently committed suicide. It was a hideous sight. He had a snorkelling mask over his face and the mask was attached to a small gas bottle. Our senior crew member took it in his stride, issuing instructions to Sharon and me. He wanted to search the van for a suicide note so he asked if one of us could get inside the van and crawl around the back of the body to open the rear hatch door. We decided to get in the van together as neither one of us wanted to be near the dead body on our own.

Standing with our heads bowed under the low roof, we made our way to the back of the van to release the lock. The next thing I heard was the sliding door slamming shut and we were both trapped inside the kombi van with the flyblown body. Our colleague went to the rear window where he waved his arms about and doubled over in fits of laughter at the sight of us locked in the van with the corpse. We were not impressed and yelled out to him to stop being so stupid. Finally, after getting his cheap thrill, he unlocked the rear door and opened the hatch, sticking his head inside to inquire sarcastically how we were feeling? After he let us out we walked away from the van, refusing to come back and help him look for the suicide note. We stood well back and watched as he did all the searching. Under the body he found a handwritten note that described the bitter split between the dead man and his girlfriend. He wrote that he couldn't live without her so he decided to end it all.

As a young policewoman I found it hard to accept suicide. I attended many such senseless scenes and I became angry at how selfish it seemed to kill yourself. It wasn't until much later, when I had endured so much heartache in my work, that I started to empathise with the dead. I began to understand how the feeling of utter despair can engulf you so that the idea of living another day, minute or second seems impossible to bear. It's like time itself stands still and there is no prospect of the future, only a desolate feeling of hopelessness that commands the moment. Yet I know only too well that the impact of suicide is devastating to family and friends.

After this incident I developed a kind of paranoia relating to kombi vans. I couldn't stand the sight of them and would definitely never get in one. To me this type of van now represented death and I felt quite superstitious about them.

# 3 Father's Day

The weekend of Father's Day, two-thirds of the way through my first year, I was rostered to work with Brad, a young constable who was suffering from terminal cancer. It was Saturday morning and we attended the usual jobs: stolen cars, break-ins, shoplifters etc. The weather was absolutely perfect, a beautiful spring day. While taking our lunch break we heard a call over the radio for assistance from the other car on the morning shift. They were at a scene of a fatal abseiling accident and needed help with taking witness statements. We jumped in the police truck and headed out to the bush area where the accident had occurred. When we got there we were faced with a tragic scene.

A group of abseilers were under instruction as they climbed a large rocky outcrop near the Wedderburn Gorge, an hour south-west of Sydney. The instructor climbed to the top first and prepared the descending rope by placing it in the ready position. A karabiner, a springloaded metal clip, is used to anchor the rope to a secure point. The instructor only had one, so he told the group to wait at the top until everyone had completed their climb. Then he would transfer the karabiner over from the ascending rope to secure the descending one. One member of the party, who happened to be the instructor's son, was among the first of the group to reach the top. Without thinking, he took hold of the descending rope and began his descent. Whether he had not heard his father's instructions, or whether he became momentarily confused, will never be determined, but in leaping out from the top of the rock he fell to his death when the rope gave way.

He was a dark-haired boy of about nineteen and standing there looking at him I thought how sad it was that he had died so young. His injuries were severe; he had lost a huge amount of blood which had seeped into the ground around the body. I was shocked by how white he was. His father was sitting on the ground nearby and he looked completely desperate.

'How am I going to tell his mother that our son is dead?' he said.

My colleague offered to take the news to the heartbroken man's wife but he insisted it would be best if he did it himself. Taking down their account of the accident was difficult as members of the group were very distressed. The sun slowly disappeared behind the cliff face as we interviewed everyone. An eerie quiet fell on the afternoon, the scene became cold and dark.

In the truck on the way back to the station there wasn't much said. Perhaps Brad was considering his own situation. I wanted to reassure him but I didn't know how. Six months later, I stood at his funeral and witnessed his family going through the same pain I'd seen in the family of the abseiler.

The following day was Father's Day and I was happy to be

rostered on the morning shift because I was looking forward to a family dinner that night. My parents had separated when I was fourteen. Family gatherings now meant my father, his new partner and her children. I was also looking forward to catching up with my brother, Peter, who was two years older than me. He worked as a sound technician and had been away with a band on tour. We had been very close as kids and had spent hours playing in the bush together during school holidays. Peter loved motorbikes the way I loved horses and we would set out side by side, him on his bike and me on my horse, to explore the local bush. We would fossick for hours, picking our way through the dense scrub and swimming in the river while our parents were at work. As we grew older we were still close, but busy with our work commitments.

My partner for the shift was Roger, the constable in charge of the abseiling incident the day before, and we talked about it in the truck as we went about our jobs. Around midday we were called to investigate a dog attack in which a young girl had been severely bitten on the leg by a German shepherd. She was hospitalised and received a number of stitches to the wound. As we approached the house we could hear the dog growling in the backyard at which we had a bit of a laugh and decided to go back to the truck and get our batons. The whole time we were there the dog continually growled and barked and was jumping up at the gate. At the door we discussed the dog attack with the owner. I was surprised at her lack of concern. Roger was not amused and warned her that if she didn't keep the dog under control we would take it and have it put down. I was shocked when Roger threatened her with this course of action. To our amazement, she said it was a stray and she was frightened of it, adding that she would appreciate it if we would take the dog now. My immediate reaction was, what the hell are we going to do with the dog? How were we going to restrain it and how were we going to avoid being bitten ourselves?

Roger had been a dog handler in his previous job so he removed his inner belt and wound it around his baton to make a muzzle. I went to the back of the truck and opened the cage door while Roger and the owner went to the backyard to corner the dog. I could hear it raging around the yard as it growled and barked from behind the fence. All of a sudden Roger came flying around the side of the house with dog in tow, wrestling it all the way to the rear of the truck. It was almost as if the dog had a sixth sense and somehow knew what we were going to do with it because when the animal saw the police truck it went completely berserk. Roger threw the dog into the truck and as the door slammed shut I heard the dog hit the rear door as it leapt towards its only means of escape. The truck began to rock back and forth as the dog went crazy inside the back of the paddy wagon. With all the noise, neighbours began to line the street to see what all the commotion was. We couldn't get out of there fast enough.

Typical of Roger, he wasn't worried; he had a plan. He told me to drive the truck to a bush area in a far part of the patrol where I backed the truck down a dirt track into the bush. The whole time we could hear the dog jumping around in the back, fiercely growling and barking. We went to the rear cage door where Roger gave me instructions. Plan 'A' was that I was to hold my baton up in the ready position and open the cage door when I was given the command. Roger was standing at the ready with his gun pointed toward the cage door and would shoot the dog as it jumped from the rear of the truck. If plan 'A' didn't work I was to go to plan 'B', which was to hit the dog on the head with my baton. On the count of three I swung the door open, the dog leapt out and Roger shot it in the head in mid-air. It was dead before it hit the ground. As it landed it sprayed blood all over my shoes and legs and onto the back of the police truck. With my ears ringing from the gunshot, we both dragged the dog into the bush and left it where it wouldn't be seen.

Later, I wondered why we didn't take the dog to the pound. I also realised how dangerous it was to shoot the dog in mid-air with me standing less than a metre away. At the time my adrenaline was pumping and it was a case of doing what had to be done so we could get to the next job. It hadn't occurred to me to think about the danger, or what could go wrong, as I had full confidence in Roger's ability. It showed the constant pressure we were under; when jobs were piling up, critical decisions had to be made in a split second. But I felt almost invincible. Wearing the blue uniform protected me from danger and I had no fear.

Back at the station I drove the truck straight around to the wash bay so we could wash the blood off the back and I could clean my shoes. I had a preoccupation with having clean shoes and would spit polish them at night as I sat in front of the TV. I was quite upset that they were now looking the worse for wear and hosing them off had not done the leather any good.

The morning had been beautiful, crisp and clear, but as we cleaned the truck I could see huge black clouds descending over us. The afternoon was turning foul and the light was fading even though it was only 2.15 p.m. Before I could get into the station, huge raindrops began to fall and I could hardly see in front of myself as I ran up the station steps. In that short distance I was completely soaked and I was greeted by an outburst of laughter as I ran into the duty room looking like a drowned rat. Roger and I sat down to complete our paperwork but as we prepared to finish our shift an urgent message came in. There had been a fatal accident on Bulli Road, Appin. We dropped everything, ran to the truck and, with sirens blaring, drove the twenty-minute journey to the scene.

At the bottom of a steep hill on King Falls Bridge, we could see the scene of the accident. A Toyota Dyna truck with a campervan fitted to the rear was stopped in the westbound lane. Further up the road, in the same lane, I saw an almost unrecognisable Gemini sedan. This car was so badly damaged that its axle had been torn away and was wedged underneath the truck. Smoke was pouring from the rear of the sedan and as we ran to the car I saw three boys trapped inside. The young man behind the wheel was dead and another boy in the passenger seat was pale and not breathing. The boy in the back was alive but unconscious and appeared to have suffered severe neck and head injuries. Roger cut this boy free from his seatbelt while a female motorist who had stopped to help gave him support. She held the boy's head in her arms which allowed us to go to the aid of the front passenger. Roger found a weak pulse and immediately started mouth-to-mouth resuscitation. The threat of fire loomed as smoke was still billowing from the car. I watched on as my partner tried in vain to save the trapped young boy. It was extremely difficult to resuscitate him through the broken window with the dead driver lying across the seat, his head behind the front passenger. All four doors of the car were jammed and Roger yelled at anyone to help us get the boy out. We both yanked at the door, trying to pull it free, when Roger went berserk, ripping at the door with all his strength. But it wouldn't budge.

'It's hopeless, we need rescue,' I yelled.

Roger continued with resuscitation but with each breath there was no sign of life and as I watched on in hope, I eventually saw the boy open his eyes. That was the instant he died. I saw the terrible look in his eyes. I'll never ever forget it. I knew he was dead but Roger was still desperately trying to get him to breathe. It went on and on until eventually, I grabbed his arm and shook him.

'Stop it!' I screamed. 'He's dead, he's dead.'

Roger continued to blow air into the boy's mouth, but it came out again like steam rising from a heated pool. I could see there was nothing else that could be done. Finally Roger stopped. He stepped back from the car window and looked at me. His face was desperate, he was devastated and I felt completely defeated. His voice was hoarse from his desperate cries for help.

'No, no, we have to save him!' he cried. 'He'll be all right, if the ambos get here soon, everything will be all right.'

'No,' I said, 'it's too late, everything isn't all right, it's not going to be, he's dead.'

We stood there, shoulders hunched, surrounded by smoke, looking at the scene. Two boys dead and a third boy in the back who might also die. I could hear the distant wail of sirens and finally the ambulance and fire brigade arrived. After checking both boys in the front for any sign of life, the ambos went to the boy in the back as the firemen voiced their concerns. It was confirmed, both boys were dead. There was nothing that could be done.

A helicopter was called to take the boy in the back seat. As we were releasing him I heard a man yelling and looked up to see him running down the road. Someone said it was the father of one of the boys and I ran to him before he could see the horrific scene in the car. Gently steering him to the side of the road, I asked him if he knew where his son had been sitting. He said his son was in the back seat, and his son's two friends, brothers of thirteen and seventeen, had borrowed their mother's car to go down to Wollongong for a surf, picking his son up on the way. I told him his son was alive but he was going to be airlifted to Westmead hospital; it appeared he had a broken neck. As we walked over to the ambulance I explained that the other two boys had died. He let out a cry. I tried to comfort him by reassuring him his son would be okay, that he needed to have hope for his own critically injured son. As I spoke to him I could see his look of fear and agony turning to shock.

The ambulance took the boy and his father to Appin Oval where the helicopter was waiting. Shortly after, I heard the distant sound of its engine as we continued taking witness statements at the scene. All the statements pointed to the same scenario. As the sky opened up and rain began to fall, the boys had approached the curved decline leading onto the bridge. Travelling too fast in the wet conditions, the inexperienced young driver had lost control, aquaplaning violently and hitting the steel railing of the bridge, then spinning into the path of the campervan travelling in the opposite direction. The impact threw the boys around inside the small sedan as it bounced off the bridge safety rail. In the other vehicle, a young boy, sleeping in the front bunk over the driver's compartment, was thrown through the front window. Miraculously he sustained only slight bruising. As he recounted the accident, his parents stood with their arms around him holding him tight. He was one of the lucky ones.

The scientific officer arrived and once we had spoken with

him and organised scene preservation, we were free to go. Roger was insistent that we leave as soon as possible as he didn't want the parents of the dead boys finding out about the accident from some other source. I hadn't even noticed the blood on Roger's face until we got into the police truck where he wiped it away with his handkerchief. His shirt was also stained with dark-brown dried blood. I looked down at my own shirt and saw that it, too, was bloodstained. Roger called in to say we were on our way to Campbelltown Hospital to complete the witness statements and to ask for the address of the parents. They lived in Tremlow Crescent, the same street where my father had lived a year before. Now the storm had passed, the sun was shining again in a perfect blue sky and the world was serene as we made our way to reveal an almost unthinkable fate.

After attending the hospital, we drove the short distance to the parents' address. We pulled up outside the house and I climbed out of the truck, my heart dead and my legs heavy. Roger knocked on the front door. When it opened, the mother of the two boys let out a scream. I had never been greeted with such terror and foreboding before. Later, I wondered if it was the looks on our faces or our bloodstained uniforms that had instantly conveyed to her the awful realisation that the two people standing at her door were covered in her sons' blood. Behind her stood an elderly man and he pulled her back into the house as we followed her in. Roger asked her to sit down which she did immediately. She sat huddled over on a large three-seater lounge. Roger crouched down in front of her holding her hands on her knees.

'Is your husband home?' he asked.

She couldn't speak but the elderly man told us he was at work in their bottle shop.

'What is it?' she cried.

Looking up into her eyes, Roger spoke slowly, 'It's really bad, really, bad.'

As he held her I saw a young girl who had come out of her bedroom standing in the living room. Later, I was to discover that she was the dead boys' sister.

'It's really, really bad,' Roger continued. He said it over and over and finally, 'They're both dead.'

The mother screamed. It was the most horrific sound I'd ever heard, a sound so awful that I will never forget it. It took all my strength to stay standing and I leant against the dining room table, biting my lip, trying not to cry.

Roger held her as she rocked back and forth in his arms and screamed, 'No! No! Not both of them! No.'

'Yes,' he had to repeat. 'Yes. They are both dead, your boys.'

The young girl ran from the room, down the hall and into her bedroom, slamming the door. I could hear her sobs behind the door. I saw an elderly woman standing by the dining table; both grandparents appeared to be in shock.

I said, 'I'll go to her.'

'No,' they replied. 'Leave her, she's better on her own.'

The house was full of the sound of sorrow. The elderly couple went to the dining table and sat down, indicating to me to sit with them. It seemed best to leave Roger with the mother and I sat down opposite the grandfather, looking at the carpet. I couldn't hold it any longer and the tears ran silently down my face.

Roger turned to me and said, 'We need to get her husband home.'

The elderly gentleman replied, 'I can give you his phone number but I can't ring him, could you do it?'

Roger made the call. 'This is Senior Constable Mayer, I'm ringing from your house. I'm here with your wife and parents and I need you to come home straight away.'

He hung up and went back to the lounge room where he sat beside the sobbing mother. I looked at the elderly lady and asked her to go to her daughter-in-law. She sat down beside her and they embraced, crying and rocking back and forth.

The mother kept repeating, over and over, 'How can I live without them?'

As we waited for her husband to come home I spoke with the grandfather.

'We were just sitting here at lunch time,' he said. 'All of us for a Father's Day lunch, the boys were right here.' He indicated the seats they had sat on for their Sunday meal.

'After lunch they wanted to go to Wollongong and try out their new surfboards. We thought it was a bit late in the afternoon for them to go but they were persistent until eventually they were allowed. They rang a couple of their friends and they set off in their mother's car. That's the last time we saw them, they were laughing and joking as they set off.'

I had noticed at the scene that the car had 'P' plates on it so I asked him how long the eldest boy had had his licence.

'Only two weeks,' he replied.

The man suddenly looked at me and asked, 'What about the other two boys?'

There had only been one other boy in the back seat and I explained to him that he was critically injured and had been flown to Westmead Hospital. Many years later I met the boy, since grown into a man, who was to have been the second back-seat passenger. His father had refused to let him go in the car, and he felt lucky to be alive.

The mother on the lounge had become silent except for the occasional sigh, her head buried in the elderly lady's shoulder. The front door opened and I looked over to see the boys' father enter the room. He went straight to the lounge and embraced his wife. She let out a loud cry, her voice distorted.

'They're both dead, our boys!'

The father was silent and I could see his body crumble as she spoke. He looked up towards Roger for confirmation.

'Yes, it's true,' Roger nodded.

'How can that be? They were just here not long ago. We sat and had lunch together.'

'I'm sorry,' said Roger, leaning over and putting his hand on his shoulder, 'we tried to save your younger son but it was too late, I tried everything to revive him but it just wasn't possible.'

The father rose from the lounge. 'Where's my daughter?'

'She's in her room,' said Roger.

The father walked off down the hall and we could hear her cries as he comforted her.

Roger went to the grandfather and explained that we needed to go to Liverpool Hospital to formally identify the bodies.

'Is it possible that it may not be them?' the grandfather asked.

'It's possible,' Roger replied, 'but unlikely. We are pretty sure they are your grandsons but there's always that slight chance that there could be a mistake, that's why we have to do a formal identification so that the Coroner can be sure we have the correct details of the deceased person. It would be of great assistance if you could come to the hospital with your son for support. Are you up to it?'

The man didn't hesitate, assuring us that he would come to the hospital, then disappeared down the hallway to tell his son what was required. That faint glimmer of hope had given them a chance of getting their boys back, though I knew it was not to be. Finally the two men came back into the lounge room and told us that they were ready. The mother stood up and grabbed her husband by the arms and begged to go to the hospital.

'I want to see them.'

She repeated this over and over through her tears. Her husband stood firm, it was not for the best, she wasn't up to going to the hospital and he really didn't want her to be further distressed. Roger asked if he had the phone number of their family doctor. Roger dialled the number and explained the situation. He spoke to the father in the hallway where he told him that the doctor was on his way.

We filed out of the house into the afternoon sun, not a hint of the storm left in the sky, the two men following close behind the police truck in their sedan. Roger and I were silent for some time. Through the windshield I looked up into the perfect blue sky, the colour was striking as the sun with its orange halo melted into the horizon. How could it be so beautiful after such a tragic day? I couldn't relate the scene we had left with what I was seeing now.

I broke the silence. 'Roger are you okay?'

'Yeah, I'm all right, but I'm not looking forward to doing the ID. It's going to be as hard as telling their mother.'

'Neither am I,' I replied.

Roger continued, 'It's all right. I'll handle it. I'll check that the hospital has cleaned the bodies before they look at them and that will make it a bit easier on their dad.'

We turned off the freeway and made our way through the back streets of Liverpool towards the hospital, eventually parking at the rear of the casualty department. We stood behind the truck until the two men parked and came over to stand with us. Roger went and made inquiries as to whether the bodies were ready for viewing. Then we all filed through the automatic doors with Roger leading the way and the two men following silently, the older man resting his hand on his son's shoulder. It was like walking towards the gas chamber, with no way out and nothing but pain and suffering at the end.

We were ushered into a small room containing a couple of chairs in either corner and a large window covered by a drawn curtain on the other side. Roger asked the men if they were ready.

'Yes I am,' said the father. 'But I want to know exactly what happened to them before I see them.'

Roger explained the accident scene and how the small car had been buffeted on the safety railing of the bridge as the car had spun out of control, eventually hitting the oncoming truck and coming to rest further along the bridge. He explained how the boys were positioned in the car when we arrived and that the eldest son had been killed instantly. He painfully described how he had tried to resuscitate the younger boy.

The father nodded and simply said, 'Thank you.'

Roger reassured him that the boys were not disfigured and that they had most likely died from internal injuries. Both men stepped up to the window and Roger let the morgue attendant know that we were ready for the viewing. Roger stood on the father's left and the older man on his right, both men with their hands on his shoulder for support. I looked on from behind, using all my strength not to cry. The curtain was drawn back and behind the window were the two boys lying side by side. They were together and looked peaceful in their never-ending sleep, their brown curly hair thick and tangled.

'Yes, they're my boys,' said the father, saying their names.

As is required during an identification, Roger asked him if he was absolutely sure.

'Yes,' he replied, 'I am sure.'

Roger nodded to the morgue attendant to indicate that the viewing was finished, the curtain was slowly drawn over the window and we stood in the dimly lit room until Roger moved towards the door.

'A post-mortem will have to be performed on both boys before their bodies can be released; this could take a couple of days. It's standard procedure so that we can determine the actual cause of death, and it will give you a little time to make funeral arrangements. If you need any help with anything at all, please ring me at the police station. If I'm not there I can be contacted at home, you can ring me any time.'

Both men nodded. 'Thank you. Is that all that has to be done here?'

Roger got out his notebook from his top pocket and explained that he needed a signature from the father to prove that the identification had been done. As the father signed the short paragraph relating to the positive identification of his two sons, Roger told him that it was for the Coroner.

We silently filed out of the viewing room and back along the long corridor, which we had just come down, all walking with downcast eyes as if the grey lino floor was of great interest. Back at the truck we shook hands and said our goodbyes. Roger and I sat in the truck and watched the sedan drive away. Then Roger called in to let the station know we were returning. It was 6.30 p.m. I kept thinking, if I was the boys' mother I would just want to go back to yesterday and then everything would be all right. I felt a wave of desolation engulf my body. It was the first time I had felt such unbelievable pain; it was both physical and emotional. It started from the pit of my stomach and made my throat tight, a feeling of heaviness taking hold of my entire body. Yet I wasn't suppose to feel this way, was I? There was no rule book to consult in situations like this.

'Why Father's Day?' It wouldn't matter what day it was but the fact that it was Father's Day made it seem extra cruel. Each year, the celebration of fatherhood would be a day of mourning for this family. For me, also. I think of the accident every Father's Day, and now that I am a mother I am terrified by what that mother went through. My eyes often fill with tears at the memory of that day. Each year I remember how old the boys – then thirteen and seventeen – would have been and what their mother has missed out on and I wonder how she is coping. Sometimes I say a prayer or light a candle. My heart goes out to her.

Back at the station we attended to the mountains of paperwork required when there is a multiple death of this kind. But first we contacted Westmead Hospital to find out how the other boy was doing. He had just come out of surgery and although he was in a critical condition, he was stable. He had suffered a broken neck, broken leg and abdominal trauma. The hospital staff were quite sure he would survive but it would be a long road to recovery. The news of his certain recovery lifted our spirits enormously. We kept up with him over the next couple of months, and each progress report would be entered on the occurrence pad where I would check any news on his condition. Many months later I arrived at the station for afternoon shift to discover he had been released from hospital. This caused excitement around the station because many of the staff had been following his progress – it was the result we had all been waiting for.

I rang my father and explained that I wouldn't be attending the arranged family dinner. He argued the point, declaring that surely I could finalise my work and still make it in time. I felt his total lack of understanding put unnecessary pressure on me to fulfil my family obligations, a commitment that seemed trivial in the light of what had happened that day. But how could I expect him to understand what I was facing? He had never suffered such a loss and couldn't know the impact of such an event. I learned later that he was of the firm belief I would not be doing frontline policing and had scoffed when my mother had voiced her concern that policing was a dangerous job. He told her that it was most likely I would be relegated to menial tasks such as chauffeuring commissioned officers around in the latest departmental sedan during their station inspections. I wasn't told about his attitude initially but later I gathered it came from his view that women weren't up to the job of policing, or at least should only be used in areas suitable for females.

After speaking to my father I then rang my mother and poured my heart out to her over the phone. She was worried about me and was concerned that neither Roger nor I had eaten since lunch. Half an hour later she came to the station with a dinner plate for both of us. It was much appreciated because otherwise we'd have missed out. We hurriedly ate at our desks, paperwork surrounding our plates. We continued to bang away on the old manual typewriters and it was 11.30 p.m. before everything was finalised.

Roger asked if I wanted to go to his place and have a drink but knowing my mother was at home waiting up for me, I declined. Mum and I sat up into the early hours talking about the death of the two boys. I felt guilty about turning down Roger's offer, perhaps I should have gone and had a drink? Roger lived alone and

I couldn't imagine how hard it would be going home to an empty house. The next day I regretted my decision even more when I saw him enter the station covered in scratches and bruises.

The night before, still wearing his bloodstained uniform, he had gone to the RSL club and asked the night manager for a bottle of scotch. After attempting to drown his sorrows, he found himself absolutely distraught, yelling and running through the bushes at the back of his house. I have never got over the guilt of letting him down. I should have gone with him and at least we could have had each other's shoulder to cry on. At the accident scene everything happened so fast, your adrenaline is pumping, it's not until you walk away that you realise what you have experienced. Twelve years later we had a conversation where we finally discussed how we felt. It was an enormous relief to find that I could finally express my profound pain. Roger confided that he had driven the same road over and over trying to reconstruct how the accident had occurred. I was shocked when he admitted this, but I could understand his torment.

Roger kept in touch with the family and attended the funeral of the boys. He asked me if I wanted to go with him but I couldn't face it; I knew I would break down and cry. On the morning of the funeral a beautiful arrangement of flowers was delivered to the station. Attached was a card with an emotional message of thanks from the family.

# 4 There's a whale in the bay

Roger and I often worked together in general duties and I developed the utmost respect for his ability as an excellent police officer. We became good friends and regularly socialised in the same circle. Whenever we worked together we always seemed to be called to unusual jobs and one Tuesday afternoon was no exception when we were called to the scene of a car accident. Upon arrival we were confronted with an injured cow that had initially caused the accident. The cow was now causing chaos as unsuspecting drivers were confronted with it darting back and forth across the busy roadway. It was clear from its injuries that it should be put down. We called for a vet to attend but how were we going to corner the cow so it could be given a lethal shot? We tried herding it into a paddock but it was so distressed that it careered straight through the fence and out onto the road again. It was obvious that if we didn't do something quickly there was going to be another accident. Roger drew his revolver, stood in the ready position and aimed, but as soon as the cow saw the gun it took off again. We decided to close the road as the whole scene was getting out of control. Roger eventually shot the cow but only managed to hit it in the nostril. That's when it really started to go berserk, charging anyone standing nearby. More shots rang out and finally the cow fell to the ground. By this time the vet had arrived and was able to put it out of its misery. We drove back to the station to fill out the reports outlining the circumstances surrounding the discharge of a service revolver.

'Just another day at the office,' I said.

During my first year in the job, I was rostered on as 'nighto' driver. This involved driving the district inspector to all the police stations in the area and checking records or anything else that needed to be inspected during the night shift. Probationary constables were often used for this duty and I did my share like everybody else. In those days the area covered by I District was much larger and also included other stations in the H and J Districts. We would set off at 11 p.m., the beginning of the shift, and spend the whole night driving from one station to the next. The order of call was a secret so the night inspector could spring himself on any station at any time. While the inspector was checking the prisoners, the station staff would get the driver aside and find out where we were going next. Once we had left, a phone call was made to the next station on the list.

'There's a whale in the bay,' were the words, after which the phone line went dead.

Then all hell would break loose as the staff scuttled about fixing everything up so that all would be correct when the nighto arrived. It was common practice to find staff having a quiet drink and bottles would quickly be disposed of in the appropriate receptacle (garbage bin)!

One particular night towards the end of my first year, we stopped off at Liverpool police station during our rounds. There weren't any policewomen working in the station that night so I asked one of the young fellows where the women's toilets were. He asked around the station in a rather loud voice if anyone knew whether they had a female toilet and the consensus was that the only one in the building was upstairs in a locked office. I was embarrassed as I didn't know any of the staff working in the station that night and suddenly everyone knew I needed to use the toilet. One of the more senior police called out at the top of his voice from behind the station counter that I could use the male dunnies and one of the guys could stand guard at the door. As this appeared to be my only option, I complied, although I really didn't want to see the inside of the men's loo and felt quite uncomfortable once inside.

As I came out I walked straight into the middle of a huge debate between the district inspector and the sergeant-in-charge of the station. The boss was absolutely furious that I had been told to use the men's toilets and demanded that the station sergeant find the key to the upstairs office and let me in. I explained to the boss that it was too late, I had already used the male toilets. This made him even angrier and he then berated *me*, saying that it was totally inappropriate for a female constable to use the male toilets and that in future if I wanted to use the toilet I was to let him know first. I was amazed at how an innocent request could turn into a huge drama but in those days policewomen were not particularly well accepted and female toilets were not available in the main area of the police station. I had no intention of discussing my personal needs with the inspector during our rounds, so after that I never used the toilet on the nighto run, I just held on until we got back to Campbelltown.

The amazing result of my request that night was that I became known to the police at Liverpool as a troublemaker who had got them all into strife!

Some of the stations we visited were small lock-ups, which were isolated from the larger stations. One night I visited Camden police station, a smaller station then, compared to today. When we arrived I saw the young detective whom I had worked with on the previous rape case. Ken was working the night shift with one of the other detectives from Campbelltown. They had come across to Camden to arrest an offender who had assaulted someone in a pub brawl. Entering the charge room, I saw the station sergeant listing the prisoner's property before he could be taken to the cells. The two detectives were standing either side of the offender, leaning up against the charge table. As the duty inspector entered the charge room to check the books, the station sergeant walked past the prisoner with the keys to the cells in his hand. Upon seeing the keys, the prisoner went berserk and king hit the sergeant right in the face. The two detectives jumped on the prisoner and wrestled him to the ground where they handcuffed him and dragged him out to the cells. The whole time the prisoner was screaming obscenities and abuse, as he struggled to get away. The sergeant's nose was broken and bleeding profusely.

It was the first time I'd seen such an act of violence and it taught me how quickly a situation can change from routine to violent and out of control. It was such a steep learning curve, but most importantly I was becoming aware that decisions had to be made in a split second or else there could be serious consequences.

Each night, while on our rounds, we drove to the new station being constructed at Macquarie Fields, which was in the far north-eastern end of the patrol. The station had been broken into several times during its construction so we would drive around the perimeter and check that it was intact. One of the sections to be housed in the new station was the scientific investigation section in which I was particularly interested; I was keen to pursue my career in the scientific field and to work there when the station was completed. Forensic work had always intrigued me and I was interested in doing complex behind-the-scenes work. The station was large enough to house the tactical response group, drug squad and the accident investigation section. It was rumoured at Campbelltown that a number of police were to be transferred to Macquarie Fields to fill the general duties section, and I'd heard that my name had been mentioned. Macquarie Fields had a large housing commission estate within the patrol, which was becoming a regular trouble spot, and Campbelltown police were constantly being called. There was a strong criminal element in the area and a lot of unemployment. We knew that the work at Macquarie Fields would be tough. As we sat in the car looking at the station we discussed how the building would provide many facets of policing and how it would be good for the division. It was almost as though I knew that I would be working there. I had a feeling that it was somewhere I belonged.

Towards the end of my first year in the job, I was rostered to work three days straight with Ron, one of the guys my buddy had warned me about during my buddy training. I was worried and went to my buddy to ask him about the roster. His advice was to keep my mouth shut and do as I was told and everything would work out fine.

As the day approached, I become more apprehensive because

I respected Ron as a very experienced policeman, although I wasn't sure what to expect. When I arrived at the station I was greeted by Ron leaning on the front counter.

'Seen the roster?'

'Yes,' I said. 'Everything all right by you?'

'Sure. Better get your gear on 'cause there's plenty of legacies left from the night shift,' he said in his usual gruff voice.

We walked out of the station together and headed towards the truck. In the car park he warned me that if I wasn't a good driver, he'd make me sit in the passenger seat and he'd do the driving. As we went about the various jobs I was impressed at how professional he was and I began to relax. We chatted about all sorts of stuff and I found him to be quite a nice bloke who shared my sense of humour. As a team we worked well together and I wondered what all the fuss was about. One thing I did learn was that this guy was not to be messed with; he was an old-style cop who was tough and got the job done no matter what.

When we worked on the afternoon shift together we were called to a break and enter at a house in one of the housing commission areas. Ron knocked on the door and a dirty, middle-aged woman greeted us. As soon as she opened the door, I could smell a foul stench. The woman began telling us how she had been away on holiday with her family and during their absence someone had broken in and graffitied the walls and carpet. My partner interrupted her to ask what the foul smell was.

'Come inside and see for yourself,' she said as she indicated that we should follow her down the hall.

We entered the doorway to a small lounge room with a kitchen running off to our left. As I walked down the hall the smell became so bad that I covered my nose with my hand. Standing in the doorway next to my partner I noticed that he too had covered his nose with his hand, although he had the added protection of a handkerchief. Directly across from where I was standing was an old lounge with four kids sitting on it eating their dinner. Sitting on top of the TV was an opened paper containing fish and chips. The woman said she had no idea who had broken in and put shit all over her house. Written on the wall in excrement behind where the children were sitting were the words 'Fuck' and 'Shit'. Also written in excrement was the word 'Fuck' on the lounge room floor, just in front of where the kids were enjoying their dinner. The whole scene was disgusting and I felt sick to the stomach to see the children eating in the room. The woman was talking when I saw the youngest child, a boy of about eighteen months, flop off the lounge onto the floor, crawl across the carpet and into the excrement with a piece of greasy fish in his hand. The mother, without batting an eyelid, allowed the child to pop the food into its mouth. Ron could take no more and gave the woman a serve.

'What kind of mother are you? How can you let these children eat in this pigsty? I should report you to DOCS and let them know what sort of environment you're living in! If you wish to further this complaint, you can talk to us outside, because I'm not prepared to stand in here.'

The woman looked surprised and I could see that she didn't have any problem with the state of the house or that her children were sitting in a room covered in shit. We moved out to the front porch where she continued with her complaint. Ron took down the necessary information and then insisted that she go straight inside and clean up the mess.

'I left it there because I wanted you to see it,' she said.

'How long have you been home?' Ron asked.

'Since eight o'clock this morning.'

Considering that it was now 5.30 p.m. I was amazed that this whole family had been waiting for the police to come and see the state of the house. The woman hadn't even reported the incident until 4 p.m.

Many of the burgled housing commission homes we visited had food splattered all over the walls, piles of filthy plates, dirty pots on the stove and kitchens full of empty cartons and food scraps. The residents didn't seem to notice the filthy environment or the smell of rotting food mixed with body odour. Sometimes we would be asked to take a seat and I would step from chair to chair trying to find somewhere to sit that looked at least partially clean. Usually I would remain standing as I worried about being bitten by fleas or attacked by cockroaches. Many times I would be interrupted by bouts of furious scratching whilst taking down reports in my notebook. Whether my mind was playing tricks on me or not, I still had the feeling of being attacked by invisible vermin while standing in living rooms listening to endless tales of misery. I was utterly shocked and repulsed that people could actually live like this.

After my three shifts had finished I felt quite comfortable working with Ron and afterwards always took the time to say hi and talk shop. It wasn't until some time later that internal affairs swooped on our station and I heard that three senior constables had hit the dock. To my surprise, my buddy was also implicated and I now realised why he had given me the cryptic warning about working with Ron. I was disturbed to think that my buddy was involved but it was hard times in the cops for many of the blokes and most struggled to support their families. The pay and conditions were not what they are today and it was forbidden to hold down a second job. To make ends meet, many cops did in fact have second jobs and did so at their own risk. If they were discovered working elsewhere it could mean dismissal so secondary employment was done on the quiet. It was this mentality that caused the downfall of many good cops as sooner or later they came to the notice of the hierarchy. My buddy, like many others, had been working on the side. With the other two men who were charged he had started a concreting business installing barbecues and pergolas. The allegations related to the stealing of reinforcing mesh from local building sites and then using it on the concreting jobs. The whole station was affected by the incident. My buddy avoided me after the allegations surfaced but I always wished that I could have talked to him. The three police were initially suspended without pay and later reinstated after the police association made representations to the commissioner on their behalf. Eventually they were all convicted and left the force. We felt the gap at the station after they left as all three were extremely competent police officers and were part of the backbone of the general duties team.

Night work in our patrol usually developed into an extremely busy shift, especially on weekends or a full moon. We often got ourselves into tricky situations where we required backup. One night we attended a domestic and got a shock when we knocked on the front door.

Through the door a woman yelled, 'Get down, he's got a

gun pointing straight at you.' My partner Andy and I immediately hit the deck and drew our guns, not knowing where the gunman was or whether we were in full view. Andy yelled for the woman to open the door and let us in and we crawled commando-style through the doorway and rolled over behind an old lounge chair where she had retreated. She told us her de facto husband was hiding behind a clump of bushes up near the road. He had watched us walk straight past him down the driveway and onto the front porch of the house, the whole time aiming a .44 magnum pistol at us. We discovered he was a hardened crook and was in fact wanted by the police for attempted murder. For a while there we were bailed up in the front room of the house as we waited for backup. Andy used a portable radio to call for help, though it was pure luck that we had it, as we often didn't bother to carry a portable with us. By the time backup arrived, the gunman had disappeared. This sparked a huge manhunt as we looked for the armed offender in the surrounding neighbourhood. Eventually he was found driving his clapped-out Holden wagon and the detectives brought him in.

Another night I was again working with Andy when we attended a noise complaint. We pulled up outside the house at about 2 a.m. and wandered around the back in the direction of the loud music. We hadn't bothered to carry our batons as it seemed a fairly routine job – that is until we discovered it was a full-on bikie party with about two hundred angry-looking bikies who were not prepared to take any shit from the police. We were videotaped as we were approached and surrounded by about thirty of them. Some pretty quick talking from my partner got us out of trouble as one wrong move could have been the end of us both. Andy made a joke of the situation, seeming to sympathise with the party goers. This did the trick and they let us go without causing any trouble. Later that night the party erupted into a war zone as some of the revellers began to fight. We went back to the scene, but this time with the support of the tactical response group who sorted it out. The TRG guys went in and arrested the troublemakers, bringing them out onto the street where we then threw them into the back of the van and took them to the station to be charged.

As time went on I started to develop a taste for alcohol, a part of policing which developed along with my progress and experience. The younger police often socialised down at the pub after work with the more experienced senior constables and occasionally with detectives, usually on afternoon shifts. On many occasions at the end of a heavy shift we would simply meet in the police station car park and stand around in a dirt paddock amongst the cars, drinking beer, bourbon and Coke or whatever was on offer. Sometimes staff on the next shift would drift out into our party and this was becoming a problem to the shift supervisor. These parties became a bit of a ritual until the station boss found out and banned us from meeting in the car park after work, so we simply went elsewhere. The Wednesday night cook-up was also a cause for celebration as it was the last night on night duty. In those days, a couple of drinks on duty was no big deal and mostly the bosses turned a blind eye to it unless someone got out of hand and caused themselves to be noticed. Every second Thursday we would meet at the local bowling club where we could have our cheques cashed.

During these drinking bouts we would talk about work and what had happened over the preceding week. In a sense it was a do-it-yourself debriefing session where anything could be said without fear of judgement or ridicule. Family or outside friends were never present, these sessions were purely for police, almost like a secret society that met once a week to discuss classified information. It was our main means of coping with the pressures of police work, and a tradition that was passed down from senior police to the new junior constables.

# 5 Secondary training, pogo men and evil spirits

At the end of my first year in the job I had to return to the police academy for secondary training. The training lasted six weeks and, at this point, most of the group were looking at the direction their careers might take. Many section leaders attended the academy to give talks on the various areas of policing we might be considering for our career paths. One afternoon we had a lecture scheduled by the scientific investigation section. I found the lecture extremely interesting as I was already leaning towards a career in this area. I was drawn to this field as I was more interested in behind-the-scenes work than in front-line policing. I had little knowledge of exactly what work this section did, but by the time the scientific officer had finished his lecture, which involved the most horrendous crimes of the past decade, I felt compelled to find out more. One part of the lecture involved a series of slides projected onto a large screen. The slides depicted various pictures of a man who had been hacked to death with a tomahawk. The slides drew progressively closer and closer to the man's wounds, showing an enlarged view of the side of the victim's head with the weapon held up to the wound for comparison purposes. The wound was directly behind the victim's ear and the last slide showed an enormous ear projected up on the screen.

The lecturer walked up to the ear and with his hands cupped over his mouth yelled, 'Halllooo' into the ear cavity.

The whole room exploded into laughter and this broke up the icy atmosphere that had descended. It was then that I decided scientific was going to be my chosen field.

After passing all the required exams I was sent back to Campbelltown police station where I continued to work in general duties. In early February 1986, I was rostered to perform station duties on the afternoon shift, just days after the kidnapping, brutal rape and murder of Sydney nurse Anita Cobby. The community was reeling from the shocking details of her murder and a state-wide manhunt for her killers was underway. Brothers who were known to the local police were implicated in the murder and police were making every effort to locate and apprehend them. While answering the police switch, I received an anonymous call from a female who rang in around 8 p.m.

'If you want to catch the Murphy boys,' she said, 'they're at 5 Tari Way, Glenfield.'

With that, the caller hung up in my ear. It took a few seconds before I comprehended what she had said, but I had routinely jotted down the address as she spoke. I suddenly realised this was important, tore the note from the pad and hurried to the supervisor's office. The senior sergeant was at his desk and I told him about the anonymous call.

He immediately jumped from his seat with excitement.

'That's the call we've been waiting for,' he said. 'Time to set up a command post.'

I was sent back to man the switch as well as the police radio, which was operated from the police console. As I worked I witnessed the night's events. Every available police officer was contacted and brought back on duty and soon, recalled police, detectives and members of the tactical response group arrived at the station for briefing. During the briefing a radio operator was put into place and each group was given a call sign. Once all police were deployed, they were assigned a section of either the inner or outer perimeter, and the house at Tari Way was surrounded. Helicopters were on standby, ready to arrive on the scene to coincide with the assault that was to take place.

The police radio became eerily quiet as each member answered their designated call sign when they were in position. Once the signal was given to converge on the premises, all hell broke loose over the radio. I was literally sitting on the edge of my seat as we all gathered around the radio listening to the raid in silence. The tension in the station reflected the seriousness of the operation. The Murphy boys were not going to give up without a fight and there was a real possibility one of our work mates would be caught in the crossfire. The TRG had entered the house and were reporting on the clearing of each room. Then came a breathless call as one of the members chased a man into the backyard and over the rear fence. I could hear the sound of the helicopter overhead as he called for lighting and a dog. In the next instant he called back to report a man in custody. Reports then came from inside the house where the other target had been located hiding in a wardrobe. The Murphy brothers were in custody and the operation had been an enormous success. Sydney let out a sigh of relief.

One afternoon, while on relieving duties at the newly opened Macquarie Fields police station, I received a message that I had been transferred to the Bureau of Crime Intelligence (BCI). This was disappointing as I was not interested in doing a desk job and felt that it was some kind of punishment. I was not the least bit interested in collating crime statistics and reporting figures back to the station commander. I telephoned the inspector in charge and inquired why I had received the transfer.

His reply was short and sweet: 'You will do what I say and I won't put up with insubordination!'

My simple inquiry had been taken as a mark of disrespect. It was obvious the decision had been made, so I decided to accept the transfer without making a fuss. A few weeks later I learned that I had been earmarked for a favourable transfer to an outlying station, which would have been closer to home. Instead, I had been caught up in an internal decision relating to another policewoman whom the station wanted to move because she had been the subject of rumours and the boss wanted to get rid of her. She was firstly sent to the BCI but kicked up such a fuss that the hierarchy decided to give her my cushy posting, and put me in her undesirable job because they expected I would accept the transfer without question – which is exactly what happened. I learned then that good work doesn't necessarily guarantee any rewards.

I accepted my desk job and duly attended to all the intelligence reports, filing and the occasional station newsletter. The inspector in charge of the station, whom I disliked, was constantly ringing me and demanding that I get his lunch, drive him somewhere or do any odd job he felt I was suitable for. I did what he asked but never spoke to him unless it was absolutely necessary because he would twist the conversation and take offence. It was like walking on eggshells whenever I was in his presence. I learnt to deal with him in time, but as most of the station staff disliked him immensely I would be grilled for any gossip I could pass on. Even though I was often in the inspector's office I never talked about anything I heard as I felt that it would immediately be traced back to me and I didn't want to be the object of his wrath. One day, when he saw me talking to one of the public service staff in the hall, he summoned me to his office and tore strips off me. I was a policewoman, he said and I was to stay away from the public service staff. In his view, they were not to be trusted. He warned me that if he caught me talking to her again, I would be paraded. I was horrified to think that I could be stood up in front of the District Commander and reprimanded; it was hard to believe. On a number of occasions he called me into his office where I would find one of the female constables standing to attention and he would make me demonstrate how I pulled my hair back in a bun so that the constable could learn how to tie her hair back correctly. He would also point out my finely pressed culottes, spit-polished shoes and the colour of my stockings, which in his mind was the correct attire. These episodes were embarrassing to both myself and the constable involved, and it wasn't long before I was teased around the station for my spotless presentation.

I was also on call to take sexual assault statements, and this broke up the monotony. I became desperately bored and was looking for any way out when I was approached by the sergeant in charge of the newly formed foot patrol. Lloyd assured me that if I agreed to go to the foot patrol, he could get me transferred out of the BCI and would also help me any way he could to get into the scientific section. I decided to take this option and found myself walking the beat. At times foot patrol was extremely boring and we would spend the afternoon shift endlessly walking around in circles looking for any sign of trouble. The occasional shoplifter was pounced upon because it made the shift go faster. At times we were called to assist security guards who had stumbled on someone doing a bust or stealing a handbag. If we were nearby, we would rush to the scene holding our hats in one hand with the other on our baton to stop it hitting our legs as we ran. We estimated that we walked approximately 10 kilometres per shift, so we were all fairly fit.

One night on patrol we received a call from the local bowling alley to assist regarding a stealing incident. When we arrived, we were met by a security guard who gave us the offender's description and told us he had run off down behind the bowling alley. We all split up to search for him. After searching for some time with the aid of torchlight, I decided to see whether the security guard had had any luck locating the thief. As I walked around the side of the building, I shone my torch along the wall and to my surprise found the security guard standing in the shadows with his pants down around his knees. He was masturbating in the darkness while the police were running around looking for the offender. Needless to say his pants came up swiftly and he ran off in the opposite direction. Neither the security guard nor the thief were ever seen again!

While working over the Christmas break I was summoned to the supervisor's room and told there was a job that needed to be dealt with in a delicate manner. I was required to attend the scene of a suicide where the estranged wife of the dead man had complained that the police should have acted sooner. She had rung the station asking if police could attend the family home, as she hadn't heard from her husband in a week and he wasn't answering the door. The locks had been changed so she couldn't gain entry, and she had concerns for his welfare. The request had not been attended to for some hours and when the police finally gained access, the man was found dead in his car, which was parked in the garage. The allegation was that the police could have prevented the tragedy had they acted upon her request sooner, but when I attended the scene I found the body to be in an advanced state of decomposition. He had been dead for approximately five to six days.

I explained to the woman that her husband had been dead for some time and that even if the police had arrived several hours earlier, it wouldn't have prevented his death. It appeared that he had killed himself within hours of her last seeing him and it was unfortunate that he had not been discovered earlier. She accepted this and, although extremely distraught, she now realised that the police were not responsible.

The scene in the garage was particularly gruesome. The body in the driver's seat was maggot infested and had literally melted in the extreme heat. There was a pool of body fluid under it and parts of the man's skin had swollen into fluid-filled sacks, which were at breaking point. The stench was disgusting and I could only spend short periods of time near the body before I had to move away to get some fresh air. When the officer from the scientific section arrived we stood back while he did his job, which involved photographing the scene and taking notes. He examined the method the man had used to gas himself. He had inserted a length of garden hose into the exhaust pipe then jammed it into the back window. The car's engine had been idling for so long that it had actually run out of petrol. When the car doors were opened a large swarm of blowflies flew out and we all took cover as they escaped, buzzing around our heads. The deceased was rather a large man and it was going to be difficult to remove him from the car without bursting his stretched and swollen skin. When the two body snatchers (government contractors) arrived to transport the body to the mortuary, they assessed the scene and decided to push the small hatchback into the rear yard through the rear roller door. This secluded but accessible position meant we could take the body straight from the car onto a stretcher. The deceased was so bloated one of the government contractors decided to burst the fluid-filled sacks of skin to avoid being sprayed should they explode when he was moved. He used a screwdriver and this was particularly distasteful to watch. As each sack was broken, the fluid burst out into the air filling the atmosphere with the foulest stench I had ever smelt. We all stood watching as the body was finally removed from the car and wrapped in green plastic sheets. Then we all took a corner and pushed the vehicle back into the garage where it could be secured.

Once the body was taken away I went back into the living room and told the widow that the body had been removed and was en route to the local mortuary. I also had the difficult task of telling her about the state of the family car and advised that it would not be a good idea for her to try to clean it herself. She asked me about finding a suitable cleaner and I called the station for advice on which local car detailer might be able to assist. After some time, the phone rang and it was a panel beater who had been contacted by the station staff and who worked in the local wrecking yard. He thought that the car was only worth fifty dollars, explaining that they would not be attempting to clean it. According to him, the smell could never be fully removed and the vehicle would only be good for parts. I took his details and relayed what he had said. The widow was shocked at his offer as the car was only two years old and probably worth something like eight thousand dollars. I left her with the decision and offered her further assistance should she require it.

Back at the station I filled out the appropriate forms and signed off the occurrence pad including the entry relating to her complaint. The boss called me into his office and thanked me for dealing with the situation. We had successfully avoided further complaint. A couple of days later, I received a call from the widow asking for further assistance concerning the car. She was of Aboriginal descent and had a large family, and she'd offered two nephews fifty dollars each to come and clean the car. But once the two men got wind of the car's foul stench they reckoned it was possessed by evil spirits and ran from the scene, leaving the car stranded in the back yard. The widow now faced the dilemma of what to do with the car. Her relatives were extremely distressed and she was too scared to look at it herself. After calming her down I explained that I could contact the local wrecker again and get him to tow the car away. As she now believed that the vehicle was filled with evil spirits, she was glad to accept the fifty dollars.

On the beat we were always welcomed when we ducked into a cafe for a coffee and something to eat; it also gave us some relief from the bitter cold in winter or the oppressive heat in summer. In winter I would wear two pairs of socks and my feet would still be frozen to the bone. In summer it was agony wearing the wool-blend culottes with stockings underneath along with all the paraphernalia that policing required, gun, baton, handcuffs, portable radio, notebook etc. My legs would get really itchy from the heat and any airconditioned shop would be better than sweating it out pounding the pavement under the hot summer sun. I became close friends with all the foot patrol team; we would talk as we walked, and spending eight hours chatting about almost anything that came to mind forged good friendships. We would often play jokes on each other. I received a Valentine's Day card in 1986 which was signed, 'The Pogo Men'. The vision of my male police counterparts jumping along the pavement on pogo sticks came to mind, and I had a chuckle. Overall, it was a happy time during my stint with the foot patrol; we were a close-knit section and all of us got on extremely well.

# 6 Relieve and assist

To his credit, my boss, Lloyd, did help me with my application for transfer to the scientific investigation section. There were limited positions and it was difficult to transfer because of the station commander's resistance to losing trained police. It was almost impossible for me to achieve this transfer without Lloyd's help. I was hoping he would sway the commander by giving me a favourable work appraisal and pointing out that I would still be working within the district so it would not be a total loss. The new suburban scientific section had only just opened at the Macquarie Fields police station and there were adjustments being made which included staffing and the acquisition of equipment. It was also a great opportunity for me to work close to home. Previously it was only possible to work at the scientific section in the city where all staff were trained. This new concept of training at a suburban level opened up opportunities for police like me who lived out of the metropolitan area and would find the travel to the city each day frustrating.

I discovered that my best chance of being chosen for a

position would be after performing 'relieve and assist duties'. This would give me an idea of the variety of work the section performed, and at the same time I could be assessed as to my suitability. Luck was on my side and my timing was good – the scientific section was grossly understaffed and needed any help they could get. Later on I learnt that the scientific section was perpetually understaffed. This worked very much to the detriment of its members, who were always desperately trying to keep the section running.

I was getting married the following month so it was decided that when I returned from annual leave, I would be temporarily transferred to Macquarie Fields to perform relieve and assist duties. At the time I was very focused on the wedding arrangements and was looking forward to our honeymoon on Dunk Island, before moving into our new home in Camden where Greg had grown up. We thought it was perfect that I was starting my new job the same time as we were starting our married life together. Greg supported the change and was happy about my move towards behind-the-scenes work rather than walking the streets on the beat.

The scientific section consisted of three staff: one sergeant and two constables. The sergeant, John, was extremely welcoming and went out of his way to help me learn the ropes. The two constables, Greg and Adam, were also great guys and spent many hours showing me various facets of the job.

My first week was spent poring over files and photo albums of the most horrendous crimes and incidents. One of the folders I was looking at contained photographs of a plane crash in which six people had perished. The plane had burst into flames on impact and the photos depicted bodies displayed with identification numbers pegged into the ground. The scientific officer in the photographs was wearing police overalls and gloves and was examining one of the burnt bodies. It wasn't until that moment that I realised that we had to physically handle bodies and at times examine them closely as part of our duties. The scientific man depicted in the photo was Greg, who was sitting across the desk from me as I flipped through the album. I asked him what he was doing in the photograph and he explained that he was performing 'Disaster Victim Identification' (DVI). He went on to tell me that DVI was a part of scientific work and that I would be required to learn and later perform this duty in the event of a multiple fatality or at a disaster scene. If I didn't think I was up to it, maybe scientific work was not for me.

'No, no,' I replied.

I felt that I could manage that part of the job, but it was a shock coming to terms with the reality that someone had to perform such distasteful tasks. The pictures didn't dampen my enthusiasm one bit but only served to heighten my will to learn.

It seemed during those first three months that the job would be extremely hard to master and I felt overwhelmed by the seriousness of the duties I would be performing. Not knowing anything about photography also felt like an enormous handicap as the antiquated manual camera equipment looked like something from outer space. We had a makeshift darkroom set up in the toilets located in the drug squad office and I spent hours in there with Greg or Adam learning the procedure. It was a time when the scientific section was considering transferring from black-and-white printing to colour, which would mean the laborious task of processing and developing each roll of film would no longer be necessary, and a central photographic section would develop all colour film. There was some opposition to the changeover to colour. Some thought photographs would be too graphic in full colour and that jurors couldn't cope with them. It would also restrict the formatting of the photographs, as the old system allowed the officer to decide the size of the enlargement. As each photo had to be individually processed, it limited the amount of photographs that were produced in court mainly due to the sheer workload. With the introduction of colour printing, the photographs could be churned out by machine which allowed for a larger volume.

But I was keen to see the introduction of colour film, as we were one of the first sections to be issued with the new Nikon cameras that were much easier to use. I still spent hours practising my photography and took every opportunity I could to pick the brains of one of the experienced staff for tips and ideas. Each camera kit was issued to a particular staff member and was one of the most important pieces of equipment at a scene. It was imperative that you didn't touch anyone's kit unless you had permission. Once, when I had been practising with Greg's kit, I forgot to put the bracket that holds the flash onto the camera body back into the camera case. Next morning Greg came into the office and gave me a serve because he had been called out during the night to a stabbing, and he had to photograph the whole scene trying to balance the camera and hold the flash at the same time. After this I never touched anyone's equipment, and as time went on and I was issued with my own equipment, I became extremely possessive about my kit.

It was an exciting time for me. I was intrigued by all facets of scientific work and there were many different types of jobs to attend. I thoroughly enjoyed going out on jobs with the guys. At that stage I wasn't a great deal of help at a scene but I could at least go and fetch equipment or make requests over the radio. It wasn't long before I was able to take the exhibit photographs, which was a pain in the neck for the scientific section. This task seemed trivial compared with the seriousness of most of the jobs we attended.

Each station in the district had an exhibit officer who kept all items catalogued and stored in a secure room at the back of the station. Each week, as new items were entered into the register, we would receive a list of what needed to be photographed. For instance, all items that had been the subject of a break and enter, drugs, or a weapon used during an assault would have to be recorded photographically so the officer in charge could produce the photograph in court or the item could be returned to its owner. At least it helped with my photography and if a photograph didn't turn out I could always go back and photograph it again. Luckily my photos were okay. They may have been a bit blurry, or not centred correctly in the early stages, but at least I would always have an image. It wasn't a huge contribution to the workload but it did relieve the already overworked staff of one extremely time-consuming duty.

Each station had to be visited at least once a week. The patrol was so large that just driving to the outlying stations could take up to forty minutes. At the time we covered Fairfield, Cabramatta, Liverpool, Macquarie Fields, Campbelltown, Camden and Picton. The patrol was eventually rezoned and we lost Fairfield and Cabramatta, which were transferred to the Parramatta patrol. The workload was so heavy that the scientific guys, while on recall to duty, sometimes in the middle of the night, would attend to the exhibits so that they wouldn't have to drive all the way back to the station the next day.

I noticed my new workmates always looked tired. Being awoken in the middle of the night and attending crime scenes took its toll on their health. It was a ritual in the scientific office to have a gourmet morning tea and it was the responsibility of the 'on call' person to pick up an elaborate cake on their way in to work. I was always disappointed when the on call person didn't make it into the office until after lunch and we would all whinge about missing out. I think the cakes actually helped to raise the spirits of the person on call because often they had endured a night of physical and emotional strain. The conversation usually touched upon horrific crime scenes, which would be dissected in minute detail.

One morning Greg came into the office and announced that I would be accompanying him to the scientific head office at the old hat factory. This was the name given to the old Criminal Investigation Bureau building, which housed the now-defunct CIB at Surry Hills. It was the hub of all major Sydney investigations and was the site where the various units within the scientific section were located. I had heard about the building but hadn't visited it before. When we got there I was amazed at the age and state of the building. It was very dilapidated and had a distinct air of seriousness about it. Greg took me around to the various offices and introduced me to the staff. We visited ballistics, photographic, photogrammetry, mapping, handwriting, motor vehicle and the crime scenes sections.

Greg also introduced me to Detective Inspector Henry Delaforce, who later became the section leader. After shaking hands we discussed my application for transfer into the scientific section and he informed me that there were in fact two positions being allocated to Macquarie Fields, and it was most likely that I would be selected for one. I was excited by this news – it was the first I had heard of a position I could apply for and I was keen to be earmarked for it. Inspector Delaforce then went to his filing cabinet where he selected a document and handed it to me. It was a copy of an entire brief of evidence which contained a statement he had written in relation to a murder that he had investigated at Wollongong, on Sydney's south coast, when he had been performing scientific duties there. He asked me to read it. In those days, information handed down by senior officers was used to assist the training of junior staff. I learnt an enormous amount purely by reading briefs of evidence that contained interesting or breakthrough scientific techniques. I was thankful to Henry Delaforce for giving me the opportunity to read his work as he was highly respected for his scientific expertise. I felt privileged that he had acknowledged my genuine desire to learn.

Superintendent Harry Blackburn was the section leader at the time and had he been available, I would have been introduced. However, he was not at his desk. Should my application for transfer be successful I would meet him later, at a formal interview. I was overawed by the experience of actually meeting the hierarchy but at the same time was keen to be accepted into the section.

It was time for Greg to attend the section meeting so I was left to my own devices. I headed for the crime scene unit where I wandered about looking at the various photographic displays on the walls. The photographs depicted dead bodies in all kinds of situations: there were stabbing and shooting victims, bombings, road accidents and a horrific picture of an infant's feet pointing upwards inside a toilet bowl. There were trace evidence charts where fibres had been crossmatched from a victim to an offender; plans of road accidents showing skid marks; and a variety of fire scenes depicting carnage. As I turned around I found myself standing in front of a large examination table in the centre of the room and I looked at the odd assortment of blood-stained clothing that had been put out to dry. There was no ventilation over the exhibits and the only distinction between the victims' and the offenders' clothing was that they were on two separate tables, which sat back to back. No one stopped to talk to me, everyone seemed to be in a hurry, scurrying in and out holding photographs and paper bags. Across the hall in the photographic section there was a constant stream of police entering and leaving a revolving door. I wandered through the revolving door and found myself in a large darkroom that was a hive of activity. Through the murky light I could distinguish silhouettes holding photographs up to the dim photo lights. Over in the handwriting section I peered at charts containing comparisons of handwriting and typefaces. I was intrigued by all the different equipment ranging from microscopes, copy stands and light boxes, to the more elaborate detection devices to enhance hidden writings. Ballistics contained hundreds of guns catalogued into various sections. They were hidden away in large drawers which were fitted into a gun cabinet. The photogrammetry section was completely new to me as I hadn't even heard the word before let alone entered the realms of scale plan drawing and plotting machines. Overall, I was totally overwhelmed by what I had seen and was struggling to take it all in. Scientific work was a mysterious part of policing that was not for the faint-hearted.

At the end of the section meeting, Greg came back to collect me and we set off to return to the office. But once we were in the car, Greg mentioned that he considered this a good time to show me the city mortuary, so we headed towards Glebe.

On the way Greg described the layout inside the morgue and it sounded a lot larger than any morgue I had visited. Yet even though Greg had tried to prepare me, when we arrived I was still taken aback by the sheer size of the place. Greg rang the buzzer and the morgue attendant welcomed us in. Once inside the foyer, Greg and the morgue attendant chatted as if they were old mates. I was to learn that you become quite friendly with the morgue staff, even socialising with them at Christmas parties and forensic functions. The association is forged during the many hours spent at the morgue attending post-mortem examinations.

We were given the all-clear to wander through the plastic doors and have a look around. Greg led me into the weighing room and showed me the procedure for weighing the bodies as they came in. Later, I sometimes weighed myself on the morgue scales to fill in time while waiting for a body to be brought out of the fridge. He showed me the 'dirty' necropsy room where the post-mortem examinations are carried out on filthy maggot-infested bodies. This is a separate room away from the main examination area so that the smell doesn't engulf the whole morgue. The room was set up for its next victim with knives, scalpels and scissors sparkling in the intense light overhead, all at the ready for cutting and slicing. In the corner was a dilapidated viewing platform. It had two steps leading up to its rickety landing and an old worn handrail with chipped paint. Greg told me how one of the scientific men had been standing on the platform, leaning over to photograph a body with its stomach cavity opened up, when the landing tipped up and sent him toppling into the open body, coming to rest with his face in the cadaver's stomach. He also pointed out that the landing was still in use and that it was pot luck as to whether it was likely to give way again, something to remember if I should need to use it in the future.

Next we wandered around the main examination area, which consisted of row upon row of stainless-steel tables all ready for the next post-mortem to take place. There were two post-mortems in progress and we stopped to see what was going on. Greg chatted with the pathologist as he dissected an organ on a stone cutting board, discussing the cause of death. It was all very interesting from a scientific point of view and I could see how looking at this working environment in a clinical way helped distance the fact that we were dealing with dead human beings. The science behind the task at hand completely took over and the staff seemed to be going about their work as one would in any occupation that required discipline.

As Greg wandered off I tagged along close behind, following him through another set of large doors which led into the controlled environment which was the main storage fridge. The cold air hit me immediately and the unusual ionising smell was unpleasant in an insipid way. It looked like something out of a horror movie. There were rows and rows of naked bodies lying on steel shelves three layers high. As we walked along Greg paused several times to examine a body of particular interest. He looked at the injuries or lack of, surmising the cause of death. A small blond-haired boy lay on one of the end shelves and Greg indicated to me to come and see. 'Poor little boy,' he said as I came closer. 'Looks like electrocution, or maybe he drowned.'

We paused in silence, our heads bowed as if in prayer. As we continued on I noticed wads of shredded colourful towelling packed into the opaque plastic sheeting covering some of the bodies. I thought how strange it appeared, the brightly coloured material in such a place devoid of any colour whatsoever. Greg turned to me and asked if I'd seen enough and I nodded. He stopped to chat to one of the morgue attendants on our way out, inquiring about the little boy. The attendant shook his head. Yes, indeed it was a sad case, he said, a six-year-old boy had drowned.

As we made our way back to the foyer Greg pointed out the viewing room where relatives came to identify their loved ones through a glass window. This small room, its window suspended high on the wall, looked dark from my perspective, inside the morgue looking out. Out in the foyer we said our goodbyes and stepped out onto the street.

Back in the unmarked scientific car we decided to take time out to eat lunch. My sandwich tasted like cardboard as I tried to deal with what I had just seen. Greg, on the other hand, was famished and ate heartily, chatting away about the morgue. Lunch completed, we set off for home but we only got a couple of kilometres down the road before we drove across a serious accident. Lying in the middle of the roadway I saw an unconscious and bleeding young man. A short distance away was his crumpled motorbike and a sedan with damage to the front section. We immediately went to the aid of the injured man and I could see he was in a bad way. Greg made sure his airway was clear while I took over traffic duties and directed vehicles around the crash scene. Shortly after, the ambulance arrived and the roadway became a hive of activity as the ambos went to work. An inflatable suit was placed on the injured man and plastic syringe wrappers littered the roadway as they prepared him for transportation to hospital.

Once he had been taken away, Greg and I were left to contemplate the scene. It appeared that the driver of the car had lost control on the sweeping bend in the roadway and crossed onto the wrong side of the road, which culminated in a head-on collision with the motorcyclist. From the obviously serious nature of the young man's injuries, it was likely that charges would be laid. The accident wasn't in our area but it was a good opportunity for Greg to show me how to examine a culpable drive scene, so he went to work. I watched him photograph all aspects of the roadway, taking particular note of the skid, gouge and debris marks left on the roadway. He established and recorded the point of impact along with the damage to the motorbike and the car. The entire scene was then recorded with a measuring wheel, and a plan was drawn up to record measurements and marks on the roadway and the position of the vehicles.

The whole process took at least an hour to complete. During this time, the local general duties truck had set up a detour and traffic was diverted so that the road could remain closed. It was now getting late in the afternoon and we were unlikely to get back to the office before the end of our shift. The day had been an enormous eye-opener for me as I began to realise the diversity of duties performed by the scientific section. As I drove in the peak-hour traffic, Greg became quiet and I realised he had fallen asleep. This was to become a normal part of the day when we were out in the car. The long hours worked during the night on recall took its toll and an hour in the car was a good opportunity to catch up on some much needed sleep.

A couple of weeks later Superintendent Blackburn asked me to come to his office for an interview. My application for transfer had finally been processed and this was the last stage before selection. The morning of the interview I made my way into the new Sydney Police Centre by train. I walked through the tiny back streets of Surry Hills, past the old hat factory, until I looked up and saw it – the new Sydney Police Centre. It was just as it had been described to me, a massive concrete monstrosity perched on the side of a steep incline, shadows looming along one side. It was as if it had fallen from outer space and landed in no-man's-land among the old terrace houses. The scientific section had just taken up residency in this high-tech building which contained purpose-built offices for each section. The new building was state of the art for its time, and with such modern equipment and facilities the NSW Police Scientific Investigation Section planned to take the lead in forensic investigation. As I walked onto the forecourt I heard the clatter of flags overhead.

Once inside, I was directed to the third level where the scientific administration office was located. I was right on time as I stood at Superintendent Blackburn's office and tapped on the side of the open door. He looked up through his glasses and after I identified myself he beckoned me in. He was a gruff man and had a reputation for being tough. He didn't suffer fools gladly and I had been told to treat him with the utmost respect. I found his manner to be direct as he asked me a battery of questions relating to my service history. I had taken my most recent work performance appraisal with me and he sat back in his chair as he thoroughly read the document. When he'd finished he looked up through his glasses with a smirk and asked if my uncle had written it. I wasn't sure what he meant at first and replied that it was written by my immediate supervisor. He then went on to say with a laugh that he had never seen an appraisal describing the recipient in such glowing terms.

I was in the superintendent's office for just over an hour.

The interview concluded with a friendly handshake and he expressed his positive attitude towards my inclusion in the scientific investigation section. As I left I gave a sigh of relief and hurried back to the station to tell the others how it had gone. When I stepped back into the office the first thing I was asked was, 'Where have you been?'

I explained that I had been in the super's office for over an hour and everyone was surprised. The general consensus was that he must have liked me as he normally kept his interviews short.

About a week later I received a call from Detective Inspector Delaforce. He informed me that there was both good and bad news. The good news was that two positions had been assigned to Macquarie Fields scientific section; the bad news was that I was to get the second position. The first position was to go to a constable being transferred from the ballistics section. As he was already within the section, it was more important to move him quickly. The second position could not be filled until the following April, which meant that in the meantime I would continue relieve and assist duties – as long as the district commander didn't want to use me elsewhere. I was disappointed but accepted the decision, although it meant that I was at the mercy of the district commander. If he wanted to move me out of the scientific section, he had the power to do it at any time. And, in fact, this was exactly what happened.

After my first three months working at the scientific section, at Macquarie Fields, I was returned to duties at the foot patrol office at Campbelltown. It became a waiting game until again I was seconded back to scientific work. I was hoping that this time I would be able to stay in the position until my vacancy became available, but it was not to be. One afternoon the local district commander made a surprise visit to our office and was annoyed to see me working within the section. Even though the other staff supported me, he was determined to have me transferred immediately. Later I found out that he did not approve of women working in the scientific section. Apparently the commander had had dealings with a female scientific officer in a country area and had not been impressed with her performance. His opinion was that all women would share the same lack of commitment and therefore he would not allow a woman to work in that area within his command.

At 4 p.m. that afternoon the commander rang and informed me he was not happy that I had been working in the scientific office without his knowledge. I was to be transferred to Macquarie Fields general duties immediately and I should attend at 11 p.m. that night to start night work.

I was now back into monthly rotating shifts, where we worked seven nights straight then four days off, followed by a variety of day and afternoon shifts. It had been almost a year since I'd worked nightshift so it was a physical shock to be thrown back into it without notice. After being up all night I usually slept well during the day, but I found it difficult to assimilate back into normal daylight hours at the end of the seven-day period. It also meant I missed family get-togethers or invitations to go out with friends, depending on my rostered shift. I was always cancelling arrangements at the last minute because of a change to the roster. Greg often sat home alone on Saturday nights and I often sat home alone during the week. It was an unconventional start to our married life but we both accepted it – work came first.

# 7 Macquarie Fields

With the stroke of a pen I had been transferred out of foot patrol and back into general duties. I now found myself attached to a particularly busy patrol. I knew the work would be tough but I was ready for the challenge. The good part was that now I was at the same station as the scientific section, I could still assist with smaller jobs when I had the time. The first shift I worked at the new station was very busy, and as time went on I found myself as senior member of the car crew most of the time. I was still relatively junior and should have been rostered with a senior constable, but that was a luxury we didn't have at Macquarie Fields. I now took on the responsibility of my junior partner and the burden of making all the decisions. Most shifts were rough and unpredictable and the people we dealt with were desperate and violent. It certainly wasn't boring. We spent most of the shift in and out of the local housing commission estate. It didn't take me long to get to know the locals. Domestic disputes were played out most shifts and I was constantly being called around to the same houses to break up fights or mediate neighbourly disputes. Drugs were a big problem; combined with unemployment and boredom they fuelled violence and hostility in the estate. Funnily enough, many of the homes here had the same filthy stench as the ones I had visited in the housing commission estates in the Campbelltown area. I never got used to the smell but it was part and parcel of the job.

One afternoon shift I received a call to attend a reported break and enter at an address I knew well. It was the home of a local drug-addicted prostitute. When we got there, we had to talk to her through the flyscreen door. She said she couldn't find the key so wasn't able to let us in. More likely, she didn't want us snooping around. I wasn't too keen to go inside anyway. We knew she was suffering from hepatitis B and she was an unstable person, likely to spit at us or attack us with her long fingernails. In her drug-induced stupor she struggled to list her stolen possessions. Eventually, we gave up and asked her to make a written list of the items and ring the station when she had completed it. Later that shift we received the call to go back and collect the list, which she passed to us under the still-locked door. Back at the station, my partner and I tried to decipher the list which included the following items: one garden hoss [sic], one foot poof [sic], two dog balls, one hamer [sic], one jewlereg [sic] box of most expensif [sic] and heredick [sic] jewlereg [sic] priceless, one dog leach [sic] and one wiper sniper [sic.]

Whether the poor girl really did lose her most prized possessions, or whether it was all a figment of her imagination I'll never know, but the list certainly was unusual. I'm still not sure what the thief was going to do with the two dog balls, but it must have been quite a stash!

About 7.30 one morning, I was driving home from work

after night shift when I saw what appeared to be a body lying on the side of the road. Close by was a huddled group of people. I pulled over and an elderly man approached, saw my uniform and asked me to help. He explained that he had been cycling with his lifelong friend and there had been an accident. He believed his mate was dead and, sadly, he was right. After checking for a pulse and seeing the man's obvious head injuries, I confirmed that he was dead. As he was lying by the road in full view of the passing motorists, I went back to my car and got an old blanket, which I used to cover his body. Shortly after, another car pulled over and I recognised the parents of an old school friend. They had a car phone and I asked them to contact Camden police. I went back to the elderly man who was now shaking and tried to comfort him, but there was also a young man who was close to tears and needed support. He was the driver of the car that had hit the cyclist. Both men were in shock and wanted to explain what had happened.

The older man described to me how he and his friend were both in their seventies and had been cycling together for more than twenty years. They had a regular route that they followed which meant that after entering busy Camden Valley Way they would ride north along the dirt verge of the road until the traffic was clear and then do a U-turn to travel south. This particular day, the cyclist closest to the roadway had turned into the traffic without looking. He was hit by the small sedan travelling north and thrown into the air, landing on the roadway heavily. He explained to me that the dead man's wife would be at home preparing lunch as she did every Sunday. He was extremely distressed at the thought of informing her about the accident.

'I've lost me old mate,' he said.

I put my arm around his shoulders. I didn't say anything,

I just listened. I could see that he needed to sit down as he was becoming unsteady on his feet so I suggested that he wait in my car until the Camden police arrived and gently steered him in the right direction. After three years in the police I was now accustomed to dealing with the grief of others. At first I had been uncomfortable in such situations, but now it was just another part of the job. I treated people the way I hoped I would be treated if I ever found myself in a tragic situation, it was just a matter of showing sympathy and understanding. The younger man who had been driving was becoming more upset. He thought he might end up in jail and was distressed over the prospect of being considered at fault. He explained that he was driving north along the road at the speed limit when the cyclist turned into the road in front of him, leaving him no time to avoid the collision. He didn't even have time to hit the brakes, he said. I reassured him that it appeared to be the cyclist's misjudgment. From all accounts, it looked like the bike rider had simply forgotten to check if the roadway was clear before he did his U-turn.

Shortly afterwards, the Camden police attended and I went and asked the elderly gentleman to come and sit in the police truck so he could give his version of events to the investigating officer. A highway patrol car also attended to look after the traffic situation, and an ambulance arrived but, because the cyclist was dead, the ambos refused to transport him to hospital. This meant that the government contractors would have to be called. I felt this was a callous decision as the man had now been lying beside the roadway for nearly half an hour. Although he was covered, it would have been obvious to anyone driving by that there had been a fatality. When the highway patrol officer heard that the ambos were refusing to take the body he became angry and yelled at the top of his voice, 'We need to get the body off the road. Why can't you guys move the body?'

This was insensitive as the dead man's friend could hear what was going on and was upset at the description of his mate now being referred to as 'the body'. I approached the highway patrol man and asked him to have a little respect and to keep his voice down. But by then the damage was done and I was embarrassed at how insensitive my colleague had been. It was obvious his main concern was to clear the roadway and get the traffic moving, which was his job, but it struck me then how detached he had become in his highway patrol world. I apologised to the elderly man and tried to explain why the ambos wouldn't take his friend to the hospital.

Once all the statements were taken and arrangements made to take the cyclist home I again set off to go home and have a sleep. It was 11 a.m. and I had been up since 12 noon the day before.

About two months later I was driving my little red panel van to work when I pulled up at a set of lights in Macquarie Fields. Sitting on his bike beside me was the man I had helped at the scene of the accident. He recognised my car and we waved to each other with a smile. It was good to see him out riding again doing what he truly loved. But sad to see him riding alone.

A most unusual incident occurred on a hot summer afternoon in February 1988. I was called to Macquarie Fields railway station where a baby had reportedly been hit by a goods train. When I arrived, two ambulance officers were attending to a small child. I went to the stationmaster's office and spoke to the station assistant. He said that he had not actually witnessed the accident, although he had called an ambulance after being approached by the child's mother for help. She was now standing at the rear of the ambulance looking extremely distressed, but after calming her somewhat, she tried to explain what had happened, though her English was limited.

'My baby hit the train, I sit near pram and train went past, pram rolling, I couldn't stop, it hit train. My baby hit fence, I pick her up and her eyes rolling back, she asleep, not talking, I yell, help, someone help, my baby not waking, she got blood on her head!'

With her was a small boy of about three. My partner took the mother and the child to the police car while I spoke to the stationmaster who described what he had heard.

'I was told that a goods train had been passing through the station travelling in a northerly direction when a pram containing an eighteen month old baby girl had been sucked into the train by a wind tunnel effect and subsequently hit the side of the train causing the baby to be thrown out onto the platform.'

The stationmaster showed me where the incident occurred. At first I thought that perhaps the pram had rolled towards the train along the slope of the platform, but the platform was relatively level. After taking down the necessary notes, my partner and I headed for Liverpool Hospital. We guided the mother and her son to a waiting room where the mother went straight to the corner and crouched down on the floor, rocking back and forth. As she wailed and cried, rocking to and fro, the little boy stood beside her all alone. He looked scared and confused so I went to him and asked if he was all right but he didn't answer me, he just stared into space in a trance. I tried to communicate with the mother but she didn't seem to speak or understand a great deal of English. Hysterically she kept repeating the name

'Emma, Emma' over and over and I realised Emma was the name of her baby girl.

Finally I was able to get through to her that I needed to know her husband's work address. She wrote down his phone number on a piece of paper but I was unable to find out his name. I rang the number and located the father of the child, who attended the hospital. His English was broken but good enough to communicate, so he interpreted for his wife. She said that she was seated on a railway bench on the station platform waiting for a train to Liverpool with her little boy sitting beside her and the pram positioned by her right leg. The little boy wanted a drink and as she looked in her carry bag she heard the goods train passing through the station. She was adamant that the train was travelling very fast and that she felt the suction of the wind as it passed through. The next thing she remembered was that she saw the pram rolling towards the train and was unable to stop it before it hit the side of a carriage which dragged it along the platform and threw Emma out of the pram. The mother saw the baby flung into the air and then hit a fence before she fell to the platform, where she managed to pick her up. When she cradled the baby in her arms she saw that her eyes had rolled back into her head and she was not conscious. She called out for help and the stationmaster called the ambulance. She was sure that the train had sucked the pram into the side of the carriage and she repeated this several times.

At the conclusion of her account I watched as the couple had a heated debate. Although I couldn't understand what they were saying, I could see that it was an aggressive exchange. The husband did not appear satisfied with his wife's explanation and he questioned her for some time. After, he turned to me and asked how this could happen? He wanted a full investigation to establish exactly what had occurred. Meanwhile, the baby had been examined and had been transferred to Westmead Hospital. She had received a serious head injury that might prove fatal. She was in a coma and the examining doctor said that if she was lucky enough to come out of it, she would probably have permanent brain damage. The news was not good and I felt that the baby would probably not survive. It was heartbreaking to be told her prognosis but I spoke at length to the father and assured him everything possible was being done for his daughter.

The parents left for Westmead and I returned to the station and attempted to write the job off on the occurrence pad. But it was difficult to accurately pinpoint exactly what *had* occurred, so I contacted the detectives and explained the circumstances of the incident. The next day I attended the scene with the scientific man, who took photographs and measurements. We discussed the mother's version and agreed it really was an unusual sequence of events. There wasn't anything at the scene that would point to the pram rolling towards the railway tracks of its own accord and her story of the wind sucking the pram into the train was difficult to believe.

As time went on I routinely rang Westmead Hospital to inquire after Emma's progress. She was in a coma for quite some time before awakening from unconsciousness. As predicted, she had suffered severe brain damage and would never progress beyond her eighteen months. She would require full-time care and would rely on her parents for the rest of her life. Eventually Emma was allowed to go home and I contacted the parents to find out how things were progressing. I arranged to visit them to take a statement so I could write off the occurrence pad.

When I arrived the father took me to their lounge room

which had been converted into a mini hospital to care for the baby. She was lying in a cot, her features were swollen and distorted and she appeared to be retarded. The mother started to cry and I asked the father if I could talk to him in another room. When we were alone he said he felt that the incident had not been fully investigated and he wanted to know what further inquiries had taken place. I told him I had spoken to the detectives and that crime-scene officers had examined the scene but unfortunately there was no physical evidence to support his view that his wife was not telling the truth. The lack of witnesses also made it difficult to prove that there could have been foul play involved. He was animated and aggressive and wanted to know what he could do to find the truth. Unfortunately, there really wasn't anything more I could do other than leaving the investigation to the detectives.

After this meeting I received several more telephone calls from the father during which he demanded to have the incident investigated further. I tried to calm him and reassure him that everything possible had been done to investigate the incident.

Finally, twelve months later, baby Emma died of pneumonia. An inquest was held before the Coroner, as it was deemed an unusual death. By the time Emma died I had been transferred to the scientific section and now worked alongside the constable who had attended the crime scene the day after Emma's incident. It was Barry, the former ballistics man, who had been transferred into the first available crime scene position that I had hoped for. The Coroner requested a re-enactment of the incident to ascertain whether it was possible for the pram to be sucked into the side of the passing train. This was difficult to arrange as we had to obtain a copy of the train records to accurately recreate the time and speed of the train as it passed through the station. Further, we had to recreate the contents and position of the pram on the station platform, and set it up exactly as it had been on the day of the incident. In the video taping of the re-enactment, I played the part of the mother sitting on the station bench.

A lightweight rope was attached to the handle of the pram to pull it back in case it rolled towards the train as the mother had described. Using the same train travelling at the exact same speed, on a day of similar weather conditions, we set the pram up on the platform with a sand bag inside to simulate the weight of the child. As the train approached, the video unit began to film. I sat beside the pram and watched as the train passed through the station. The pram remained steadfastly parked on the platform. It did not move a single inch. The wind tunnel the mother had described did not occur and I felt only a slight breeze as the train passed by. After documenting all angles of the re-enactment, a report was prepared for the Coroner.

On the day of the inquest I met Emma's father outside the Coroner's Court. He was interested to know the results of the re-enactment but I thought it better if he heard it from the court. I was first to give evidence during which I described the scene and my conversations with both the mother and father. I also described the scene as I had observed it on the day of the incident, and the steps I had taken to report my findings to the detectives. Next the detectives entered the witness box and reported their findings, and finally the crime scene detective gave his evidence, which included the results of the re-enactment. The video tape was played to the court and afterwards the Coroner asked a barrage of questions relating to the research and setting up of the re-enactment. He wasn't satisfied that the video accurately depicted the events that took place and therefore placed little importance in the findings of the experiment. Many years later, when I studied physics for the diploma of applied science in forensic investigation, I realised how inadequate our re-enactment had been. With no formal training in setting up a scientific experiment of this type, it was a wonder we were able to produce any credible evidence at all.

At the conclusion of the evidence the Coroner found that Emma's death was attributed to accidental causes which were unexplainable. He found that there was no evidence to establish any person or persons were involved in the death and therefore could not recommend any further investigation of the matter. Emma's father was not satisfied with the findings of the court. But in some ways, the court's conclusion made no difference: it was still a tragedy that the life of a little girl had been lost. The unusual circumstances of Emma's death would always cast a shadow of doubt over her mother's actions that day.

Night work was particularly busy at Macquarie Fields as we only had one car crew and a single constable to man the station. I was always rostered out on the truck with the most senior member on the shift looking after the station. It became necessary for him to lock the station doors as the locals soon discovered they could enter the station, intending to overpower him and get to the prisoners being held in the cells. At any time there could be a number of offenders who were refused bail and waiting to attend court or transfer to prison the next day. We complained to the police association about this obvious threat to workers' safety, but our complaint fell on deaf ears. There was no funding for extra station staff on night shift and we had to do the best we could with the limited manpower we had. Compared to

Campbelltown we were the poor cousins, grossly understaffed considering the large patrol we had to cover. We were basically left to run our own race. Luckily we had a good team of honest cops working there as there wasn't any supervision after dark.

Having the tactical response group attached to our station was a bonus because if there was any real trouble, I could call on them for assistance, and on the rare occasions that they were in the station they would be on the scene in minutes. The TRG were across the hall from the scientific office upstairs and I got to know a lot of them personally. They were always on call and attending jobs all over Sydney, so it was a general rule that they weren't to be called unless it was absolutely necessary. One particular shift I was working the night roster when we were called to a domestic in the nearby housing commission estate. My partner and I drove straight there and were met by a frail looking couple on the front lawn. Their nineteen-year-old son had gone berserk inside the house. I could hear the sound of walls being smashed in, so without hesitation my partner and I went towards the back door. The father grabbed my arm and begged me not to go in. He said his son was armed with a hammer and capable of killing. My partner and I insisted that we would enter and try to subdue the man, but the father was adamant that his son was dangerous. I'd never considered calling the TRG before, but it appeared we had a maniac on our hands and might well find ourselves out of our depth. My partner agreed that perhaps we should wait for backup before attempting to make the arrest. So the decision was made and I requested the TRG to attend.

Within minutes the truck arrived and the troops came bounding out of the vehicle ready for action. I explained the situation, as did the father, who reiterated his belief that his son was in a deranged state of mind and armed with a hammer. In these situations the TRG take over so it was decided that the TRG would storm the house and my partner and I would act as secondary backup going in after them. With guns at the ready, they stormed the premises and within seconds had the offender down on the ground. As I entered the house I could hear laughter – the offender only had one leg! The TRG were in fits at having been called to storm the house and arrest a one-legged man. It took a few minutes to control myself so I could tell the father that his son had been restrained. I asked him why he hadn't mentioned that his son only had one leg and he said that he hadn't thought it was important.

One of the crew got straight on the radio and announced to anyone who was listening that the one-legged man had been caught on the hop and no further assistance was required. The story did the rounds of the station and it was a long time before I heard the end of it. Luckily I didn't require the assistance of the TRG again – after this incident they probably wouldn't have come.

The nature of our work at Macquarie Fields was volatile and I was often concerned about getting hurt. I had been called several times to back up other car crews when they were trying to make an arrest, and on almost every shift I ended up struggling with a violent offender. One night I was working with a fairly inexperienced young probationary constable when we found ourselves in the middle of a family dispute on their front lawn. I saw an abusive female kick another member of the group and as I approached her, I was abused by a man and turned to deal with him. All of a sudden the woman leapt onto my back and began to punch me around the head and shoulders. I managed to throw her off, pushing her down to the ground. I reached for my handcuffs but she pulled away and we ended up in a swinging match during which she punched me in the ribs and managed to rip my shirt open. To my amazement, my partner literally froze and stood there like a statue. I yelled at him to help me cuff her but he didn't respond. I had heard about police being bashed and receiving no assistance from their partners but this was the first time I had experienced it first-hand.

Meanwhile the rest of the group were surrounding me and I thought I was in deep trouble. While yelling at the group to get back, I managed to restrain one of the woman's arms behind her back and get one handcuff on. This was a dangerous situation because if she broke free before both hands were cuffed together, she could swing the handcuffs around as a weapon. I was desperate for my partner's assistance. Still he just stood and watched as I struggled. Eventually I was able to get both cuffs on the woman and pushed her down the front lawn towards the police car. We were working out of a sedan, which was a further problem as I couldn't leave her and go back to the crowd to sort out the disturbance. I slammed her into the back seat and yelled at my partner to get in the bloody car and watch her. The rest of the group headed towards the police car, yelling abuse and demanding that the prisoner be released. I grabbed my baton and held it up in the air.

'Get back, get back,' I yelled as I swung the baton in the air. 'Come any closer and I'll use it.'

At that the group retreated, and I managed to disperse the attackers. With my shirt in tatters and feeling the worse for wear I returned to the police station with the prisoner. The detectives were brought in and she was charged with 'Resist Arrest' and 'Assault Police'.

I went straight to the supervisor and reported my partner's cowardice. I wondered whether he was suitable to be confirmed as a constable. To stand by and not assist your partner when their life is in danger is one of the worst acts of cowardice – it could not be tolerated. I had serious doubts whether this constable was suitable for police work; I thought he did not have what it takes to be a cop. The constable was counselled about his behaviour but could not offer an explanation for his actions. The following day, my local doctor referred me to Camden Hospital casualty department for X-rays. I had suffered trauma to the left cheek bone as well as tissue trauma to the ribs.

The stress was mounting. I have never been a smoker but on occasion when out socialising I would now puff on a couple of cigarettes. I started to keep a packet in the glovebox of my car, and to calm my nerves I got in the habit of having a cigarette in the car on the way home from work. I don't really know why, I certainly didn't enjoy the taste. One night while driving home I went to throw the cigarette out the window – the thought of causing a fire hadn't entered my mind – but unbeknownst to me it ended up in the back of my panel van and there it simmered away, burning a hole in the vinyl floor mat. When I realised the car was about to catch fire I almost had an accident as I screeched to a halt and jumped into the back to put the cigarette out. I thought then that I needed to find other ways to relieve the stress but the service didn't offer any type of help. Drinking was the only outlet we had. A bourbon and Coke became my routine when I got home from work, no matter what time it was. One drink seemed to be enough to clear my head and for a long time I was happy to drink just that one. Arriving home alone on most occasions meant I had no one to talk to and I found it hard to relax. I was dealing with a build-up of emotions that I couldn't quite put my finger on. It was as though I was becoming detached from my old world and was sinking into a violent, aggressive and tough world that was new to me. Even my language had started to deteriorate: I was swearing and talking in a way I never had before. When I caught myself speaking like this I was disgusted, but I felt powerless to stop it. I was definitely at the stage where I wanted to get out of front-line policing. I could see the dangers and I'd had enough of general duties. I was marking time, waiting for the phone call to let me know when I could start scientific work. Eventually it came and I was permanently transferred on 17 April 1988.

# 8 Scientific

To describe my initial experiences with scientific work as being thrown into the deep end would be an understatement. Staffing was inadequate, job numbers were high and there simply wasn't time to learn in an academic sense. I was needed to attend crime scenes straight away and the time I had spent doing relieve and assist was all the training I was going to get. With a camera in hand I was out on the job and started doing basic work such as the exhibit run. Whenever a major incident, such as a suspicious death, serious car accident or arson, came in, I would attend the scene with one of the more experienced staff and assist with collecting evidence, taking photographs or making notes. Most of the scenes were large and complicated and required painstaking investigation.

Within the first couple of weeks a new boss arrived. He had his own methods and felt the best way to learn was to get stuck in and do the job. I found myself working alongside Barry, the other new scientific man, and together we didn't have much experience. Sometimes we would be on afternoon shift together and hope that nothing too serious occurred. Within eight weeks I had started attending serious crime scenes on my own. Without experience or training I found myself in a difficult position, but that was the way it was. If I was unsure I would always seek out assistance, even if it meant getting my boss out of bed in the middle of the night to give me his opinion. I stumbled through each job, taking photographs with my limited knowledge, collecting evidence and taking notes, hoping that I had covered every last detail adequately. Sometimes the more experienced investigators would give me a hand and guide me in the right direction. From the outset I felt a sense of agitation – there was so much to do with so little time.

Working on call was my next progression, which meant that I would cover the entire district, from Liverpool to Picton, for twenty-four hours, seven days in a row. We worked one-out (alone), so jobs would be attended from home if scientific investigation was required during the night. Armed with only three months' experience, a pager and a car fitted out with camera equipment, shovels, picks, measuring wheel, crime scene tape, tape measures, glass jars, containers, plastic and paper bags, arson bags and tins, tweezers, swabs, distilled water, box cutters, gloves, plaster casting equipment, overalls, boots, hard hat and a plano box (the box used to carry forensic equipment), I entered the world of availability.

For seven days I was at the ready to attend scenes any time of the day or night. It was quite a transition from general duties to working alone in an entirely different field. I became jumpy at the sound of the telephone – it brought bad news – and I became accustomed to my body's reaction when it rang. Sometimes I would flinch or jump out of my chair. When it rang during the night I would sit bolt upright from a deep sleep and try to catch my breath. Death was becoming more a part of my life as many jobs involved at least one, if not several fatalities. Greg was working afternoon shift in the coalmines and it wasn't easy going home to an empty house. It was difficult to forget the scene I had just attended and I had trouble getting back off to sleep. Sometimes I would lie awake for hours going over and over the gory details, wondering if I had missed something.

Fortunately, my first call period was relatively quiet: I attended a fatal motor vehicle collision and a couple of suicides, all of which occurred during daylight hours. Although I struggled through each scene I managed to cover all the necessary aspects of the scientific examination. It was a relief not to be called out during the night, because night scenes were far more complex without adequate lighting. I didn't feel confident about taking photographs in the darkness. At this stage I felt I needed to do a photographic course of some description, but there was no outlet or time allocated for training. I battled on, trying to learn as much as I could from the more experienced officers in our section but it was difficult to find the time to show me the ropes. Sometimes I had to perform certain tasks with nothing more than a 'you'll be right' attitude.

The job description was long and varied, covering a wide range of scientific disciplines. With no formal training, I had to be a Jack of all scientific trades and was expected to provide forensic support for criminal, coronial and incident investigations. I was to attend crime or incident scenes with the purpose of searching for, locating, recording, examining, identifying and collecting relevant physical evidence. I was then required to perform the subsequent examination of collected material and, if necessary, to forward exhibits to the approved laboratory, organisation or other agency for specialised examination. I was required to attend suspicious deaths, suicides, murders, industrial accidents, fires and explosion scenes, vehicle collisions where death or serious injury had occurred, hit and run scenes, drug plantations and clandestine laboratories, suspected stolen motor vehicles and property with obliterated numbers, exhumations, plane crashes, train accidents involving derailed carriages or deaths, post-mortem examinations, impression examinations of tool marks, footprints and tyre marks, among others, and internal affairs inquiries. I was also expected to photograph and record the injuries of assault victims, perform facial identification using Penry or photo fit and disaster victim identification at major disaster scenes, plus prepare detailed briefs of evidence, including scale plans, sketches, comparison charts and models for presentation, for various courts, inquiries and commissions.

It was very daunting but I was keen to learn and get the job done as efficiently as I could. I began to build a rapport with the many detectives I worked with and this helped to open communication channels. In the initial stages I would often confide that I had not actually examined a scene like the one in question before and was open to guidance or advice. I think my honesty was appreciated as it was better to discuss all avenues of investigation at the scene rather than realise after the event that a point of evidence had been overlooked.

Arson and stolen motor vehicles were a large part of our work and I attended as many arson scenes as I could to gain some basic knowledge about cause and origin. I understood that arson investigation was a complete science in its own right and found it interesting from a forensic point of view. I liked poking around in fire scenes. It was not unusual to spend hours at the scene digging for evidence. Arson investigations also involved the attendance of an investigator from the fire brigade, so I always had a second opinion, or at least someone to discuss ideas or possible scenarios with. This made an investigation so much easier and more enjoyable. The work was dirty, back-breaking, and often involved exposure to toxic chemicals and unstable buildings. But I didn't mind getting dirty, I actually felt comfortable wearing the police overalls and boots.

To examine the scene I had to start at one end and systematically clear all debris away until the floor could be examined. The evidence located on the flooring was an integral part of the investigation, and at times enormous amounts of debris would have to be cleared before the investigation could begin. Burn patterns in wood called 'alligatoring' are an indicator of the intensity and origin of the blaze and these helped with determining the best place to collect a sample for forensic testing. Arson tins or plastic bags were used to collect evidence and usually the next day I would drive to the Department of Analytical Laboratories to deliver the samples for analysis. It was at least a year before I received any formal training in investigating arson, so for the time being I had to do my best and hope that I didn't miss anything.

Stolen motor vehicles and cars sent in to have their identity checked from the roads and traffic authority were a weekly occurrence and from the outset I enjoyed these investigations. The main objective was to verify the true identity of the vehicle by examining the engine and chassis numbers. Sometimes this would involve chemically etching the surface that contained the vehicle identification numbers in an attempt to reveal the ground off original number. I would throw on a dustcoat or overalls and stick my head under the bonnet and get my hands dirty. I was given a crash course on how to mix chemicals for the etching process, and a brief overview of what information was required to be checked, and off I went. I have always had a love of cars, new or old, and a real appreciation of all makes and models. This fascination for all things mechanical seemed to be part of my make-up. After leaving school my brother Peter became a motor mechanic leading me to believe that my interest in cars was a genetic trait.

Vehicle investigations were not favoured by most of the staff but for me it was a welcome break from the more frequent incidents involving death. It was almost therapeutic being able to shrug off the emotional load I carried when attending fatalities. The only drawback was the potential health risk and I now fear the consequences of my frequent exposure to chemicals and paint strippers. At the time I didn't consider the possible health hazards and wasn't given any warnings about getting chemicals on my skin or inhaling their fumes. I would sit cross-legged on the lino floor in the station's basement with Shane, one of the new scientific constables, and we would laugh about playing 'Milton the Monster' as we mixed the chemicals. We didn't wear gloves or face masks and we would splash the chemicals into the beakers from the test tubes, decanting them into small glass jars and depositing them into a wooden carry box known as the 'etching kit'. The floor where we mixed the chemicals was stained and the lino had started to rot in clustered spots. Likewise, the sleeves of my dustcoat were spotted with holes where the chemicals had eaten through the material. I recall a stinging sensation, usually on my lower arms and hands, whenever I accidentally leaned on an area where chemicals had been spilt. I developed small patches of stained yellow skin but never really thought anything of it. The job was a dirty one and I accepted that working with chemicals was part of the process.

The rebirthing of stolen vehicles involved stealing a car and grinding off its identification numbers. Engine and chassis numbers, along with compliance and identification plates, usually obtained from a wreck of similar make and model, would then be stamped over the original numbers and the plates attached in place of the originals. Many of the cars I examined required the exposure of their original engine and chassis numbers. We did this by cleaning the area with acetone until the number was visible. Then we would photograph the identification numbers and, if necessary, begin the etching process to restore any obliterated numbers. It could take a couple of hours before the obliterated number was restored. Often, though, the etching process would not produce a significant view and only a partial ghosting of a number would be restored.

After photographing the evidence, I performed a computer search which ran until the program was complete and a result obtained. This procedure could take hours or even a whole day, as the computer searched all possibilities to obtain a match with the year, make, model and colour of the car in question. I thought the computer system was state-of-the-art, although compared to today's standards it was fairly basic and slow.

I gained a real satisfaction from the identification of a stolen car and I felt the task of returning it to its rightful owner was an important one. I always searched to find the true identity of any car I examined no matter what its monetary value; a car was a major asset and to be deprived of that asset was a serious crime. Although I wasn't aware of it at the time, I was becoming quite experienced at vehicle examinations and it wasn't long before the word got out that I was happy to help detectives whenever they were investigating this type of theft. Around this time I suggested that an etching kit should be part of the equipment stored in the call vehicle. I discussed this change with the boss and I was disappointed when it was decided that it would be too dangerous to include an etching kit as part of the standard equipment because of the potential for the chemicals to become unstable when exposed to heat. Shortly afterwards I went to the scientific store in the Sydney Police Centre and requested an etching kit. When I got back to the station I made up my own supply of chemicals, wrote my name on the lid and from then on carried my own personal supply. This way I wasn't risking an explosion by leaving the kit in the car but could always take my kit with me when I went out on a job, just in case a vehicle examination was required.

Changes were afoot in our office and one of the more experienced guys had decided to leave. Greg had been a great mentor to me when I first started at the section and I was disappointed to see him go. The stress and strain of scientific work had finally caught up with him and his health was deteriorating. I didn't really understand this at the time. It all seemed new and exciting to me and I planned to spend the rest of my service in the scientific field. I couldn't imagine why someone would want to leave after mastering the science of forensic investigation. It seemed such a waste. In later years, I realised that Greg had to get out of scientific work before it killed him. I began to understand how the constant exposure to dangerous and horrific crime scenes changes you both physically and mentally. But for now, I was blissfully unaware of any future impact of scientific work. There was no support in those days and any talk of the dangerous working conditions was met with suspicion. Any concerns we might have had were quickly swept under the carpet. I was beginning to see a pattern with the experienced scientific officers – they were leaving in droves. It was a cycle that repeated itself every five to seven years and constantly drained the section of experienced investigators.

With Greg's departure I felt the burden of losing someone who had a wealth of experience, putting more pressure on my limited knowledge to carry the load. I was told I would have to perform more on-call duties, possibly covering the seven-day on-call period every second week, and that this would be the case until such time as we were assigned more staff. The roster was drawn up and the next few months passed in a blur.

# 9 Six bodies in seven days

My second call period was busy and I found myself working day and night. My first evening at home was interrupted by a shooting suicide. When I got to the scene I discovered a young man who had apparently taken his own life by shooting himself through the mouth with a .410 gauge shotgun. He had been suffering anxiety and depression, had recently been admitted to a clinic, and had been released in the care of his parents. He was twenty-one. He had been left alone in the house during the morning and it appeared that this was when he had committed suicide as his parents had not heard any gunshots while they were in the house. Around 7 p.m. that night they had become worried when their son didn't answer their knocks at his bedroom door. When they tried to open the door they discovered it was jammed from the inside. They finally broke into the room through the window and they found their son lying in a pool of blood on the bedroom floor. His lifeless body was cold and blue.

This was the first incident I had investigated that involved a firearm. I had a poor knowledge of ballistics and didn't feel confident about examining the scene on my own. Adding to my concerns was the fact that I found that the gun had been discharged a number of times. As I examined the scene I found a single entry and exit hole through the pillow on the bed. There were powder burns around the hole, which indicated that the muzzle of the firearm had been placed in contact with the pillow. I also found shot marks in the bedhead, and behind this a hole in the cupboard where the projectile had travelled. This bothered me as I was uncertain how the holes had got there, and after searching for some time I couldn't find the spent cartridge.

The dead man was lying on his back beside the bed with the gun at his feet. Rigor mortis had set in. Rigor starts around six hours after death and can take anywhere up to twelve hours to subside so it appeared that he had been dead for quite some time which confirmed his parents' belief that he had shot himself when they were out.

I decided to phone my boss, Dave, and ask him for assistance. The general duties police on the scene managed to guide the parents into the kitchen so I could make the call without them overhearing. I filled Dave in on the scene details. As always, he was very laid-back and unconcerned, explaining that it was common for someone intending to commit suicide to test-fire the gun first. That would explain the hole in the pillow, as the young man had probably used the pillow to muffle the sound of the gun going off. It also explained the powder burns. Dave asked me if I had found the spent cartridge case as the young man could not possibly have shot himself through the pillow and ended up on the floor in the position I had found him in. The gun had been fired at least twice, with the second cartridge still in the chamber of the gun. I explained that I could not find the cartridge and that this worried me. We decided that I should go back to the room and make a thorough search for the spent cartridge. Dave advised that sometimes the would-be suicide will hide it before they shoot themselves. At that point they are unsure if they will actually go through with it and if they change their mind they would not want anyone finding the spent cartridge. I went back to the room and searched every inch of the scene, but I could not find the missing cartridge case.

I again rang Dave and at this point asked him to attend the scene. He was reluctant as he felt I had the job under control, but I wasn't convinced and preferred to have his opinion. When he arrived he went over the scene and checked my notes, the gun was rendered safe and the spent cartridge was removed. He was satisfied that the young man had test-fired the gun into the pillow first, having folded the pillow over for added padding. We also examined the shot marks in the bedhead and a hole in the cupboard where the projectile had entered. Dave examined the body and was satisfied that the young man had, in fact, committed suicide and that there were no suspicious circumstances.

I collected the gun and cartridge for testing and completed my notes. I was now confident that the job had been investigated fully and that all evidence had been collected. The knowledge and experience Dave had gained over his many years as a crime scene investigator were the key to a thorough examination and this gave me the conviction I needed to complete the job.

The following day, I was on my way home from work when I received a call to attend a fatal motor vehicle collision. A motorbike had collided with a semitrailer on the Hume Highway at Casula. Witnesses stated that the motorcyclist was travelling at high speed. As he tried to avoid colliding with the rear of a sedan that had slowed down to enter a service station, he clipped the car and was speared off into the right-hand lane and under the rear wheels of a petrol tanker. The motorcyclist sustained massive injuries and died at the scene.

Peak-hour traffic was beginning to build and I was under pressure to complete my investigations as quickly as possible. I wanted to get the photographs taken before sunset so I completed this part of the investigation first. I examined the sedan, petrol tanker and the motorbike, making notes and taking measurements of the roadway in case I was required to draw a scale plan for court. The body was removed before the vehicles and debris could be cleared from the road, allowing the traffic again to flow. I chatted briefly to the general duties police at the site and they mentioned that the dead man had been on his way home from his job in the army when the accident occurred. They were about to visit the young man's family and inform them of the death. As I drove away, my thoughts lingered with those parents. I conjured up a picture of their red-brick, three-bedroom home, and I imagined their reaction. It was dusk and the end of another day.

A couple of nights later I was called out to attend a suicide hanging. A twenty-three-year-old man had come home drunk and argued with his parents. The police were told that the parents left the house to give their son time to calm down, but when they returned they found him hanging from a rope in the pergola. The father untied his son and tried, unsuccessfully, to resuscitate him. When I arrived, the body was lying on the paving under the pergola, with an aluminium stepladder nearby. I examined the body, paying special attention to the neck area where he had sustained abrasions from the rope.

There was a large pool of vomit beside the body and I struggled with the sight and smell of it. To examine the body I had to lean over the vomit and it was difficult not to dry retch. The pergola was dark and I had to look closely at each part of the scene to examine it fully. Finally I was satisfied with the examination and found there to be no suspicious circumstances. But as this was the first scene of this type I had examined, I mulled over the details for some time when I got home. It was well into the early hours of the morning before I drifted off to sleep.

The next night I was called to attend yet another suicide. It had been an extremely busy shift and I was having a late meal when I responded to the call. The incident had occurred in a local caravan park that housed mostly full-time residents. It was a modest residential establishment and most of the caravans were old and decrepit. I made my way to an old brown and white caravan looming in the darkness. Two uniformed men were standing at the base of the aluminium steps leading up to the van.

Pointing inside, one of them said, 'He's in there on the floor.'

I walked up the stairs with the uniformed constables behind me and as we stepped inside I could feel the van swaying on its unsteady legs. In the darkness I saw the figure of a man lying across the floor on his back and was immediately struck by the strong odour of gas. One of the constables was holding a torch and I asked him to shine it on the body. He pointed the torch at the man's face, revealing his contorted facial features. His mouth was wide open and his eyes were staring up towards the ceiling, a hideous sight. I had moved closer to the dead man to get a better look and the only way all three of us could stand in the confines of the van was for me to stand with one leg either side of his torso. I asked why there was no lighting in the van and was told the park operated on a user-pay system, with the caravan's occupant inserting coins in a metered box to access the power. Obviously the deceased had been lying there long enough for the money to run out. I asked the constables to go to the site office and ask the management to connect the power so I could conduct my examination. I was amazed that they hadn't done this already and my impatience was obvious.

Heeding my request, both constables turned and stepped outside the van, slamming the door shut as they left. I stood there frozen to the spot, all alone in the dark, at my feet the contorted figure of the decaying corpse. The dim filtered light along the rows of vans crept through the front window and I could barely make out my surroundings. A cold chill immobilised me and I was unable to lift my leg back over the body. I realised I was locked inside and powerless to leave the darkened tomb until the constables returned. My heart began to pound heavily in my chest. I focused on the light and encouraged myself to stay calm, don't panic, be still.

In the distance I heard footsteps and then, closer, the sound of someone opening a box with a key. The lights finally came on; my nightmare was over. I rushed to the door, nearly falling in my haste as I called out to the constables to open it. As the door flung back they were confronted by my ghostlike appearance; I was white as a sheet.

'What the hell do you think you were doing? You locked me in the van!'

'Sorry, mate, didn't realise. You'll be right. You're used to dead bodies, anyway.'

I gritted my teeth and pushed past to collect my camera and equipment from the car. I opened the tailgate of the station wagon and sat beneath the opened door. I needed some fresh air.

It suddenly struck me that I was considered emotionless by both the constables. My position as the scientific investigator put me into a unique category and I was now regarded as a hardened character who would not be affected in any way by death or tragedy. I was supposed to be used to it, after all, that was the major part of my job, investigating suspicious, unusual and unnatural deaths. I wasn't comfortable with this attitude. The dead man was someone's loved one and he deserved respect and compassion no matter what the circumstances of his death. He wasn't just a piece of meat to be poked and prodded.

Grudgingly I went back to the van and stepped inside. I examined the array of medication strewn about the kitchen table. There were numerous types of antidepressants and sleeping tablets along with empty beer bottles. I found three separate suicide notes, all relating to the man's depression after the break-up of his marriage. After a thorough search I made a number of notes and took photographs. I found the oven gas jet was on, which explained the smell of gas inside the van. I turned my attention back to the dead man and after taking a number of photographs, I began my examination. His lifeless body showed the effects of gas poisoning – redness to his lips, inside his mouth and the back of his throat. The position of the body suggested he had fallen back from the oven after inhaling the gas that, mixed with the drug and alcohol cocktail, had done its work.

After getting home and snatching four hours' sleep, I was recalled to attend a serious car crash where a young women had allegedly jumped from the cabin of a moving truck. It was a cold and wet night, not the best conditions for standing out on the roadway and collecting evidence. I waited some time for the lighting truck to arrive to illuminate the scene, so I could take photographs and measurements of the roadway. The young woman was in a critical condition with internal injuries and numerous broken bones. She had jumped from the moving truck, become trapped under the rear wheels and was dragged for approximately three metres. She was not expected to live. The truck driver could not explain why the young woman had jumped from the cabin. The detectives had been called to the scene and after a short conversation they decided to take the driver back to the station to make further inquiries.

By the time I got home the sun was coming up so it seemed pointless to climb into bed. After a shower and a change of clothes I headed back to the office. I barely had time to fill out the job book with the previous night's events when the phone rang. I was required to attend another fatality. I couldn't believe it. When I got to the scene I spoke to the general duties constables standing beside the road. An elderly man dressed in jogging gear had been discovered lying face down in the ditch by a passing motorist. An examination of the body failed to reveal any suspicious circumstances. There were no signs of injury, although he displayed blueness to the face and hands indicating he had possibly suffered a heart attack while out for his morning run. I was concerned because the dead man did not have any form of identification on him and at that moment the local police were conducting a doorknock to try to find his family. I certainly didn't want to be at the scene when a distraught relative arrived. Every time a car drove along the road I looked up to see if it was going to stop. Thankfully, I finished my examinations before the relatives were found, and was spared the ordeal of coping with the emotional side of such a sudden death.

My second call-out period was nearly over and I was exhausted, both physically and emotionally. Nevertheless, the job had been completed and I was satisfied with my examinations of all the scenes I had attended. The bodies were part of my work, but there was still the paperwork and associated matters to deal with. Post-mortem examinations had to be attended and photographs sorted and put away. The minor jobs, such as exhibits, stolen cars, assault victims, drawing plans and writing statements, were peppered throughout the seven days and each job had to be attended to as quickly as possible. I wondered if this pace would continue. Others in the office weren't surprised by the number of dead bodies I had investigated during the week; we just did the best we could with the limited staff we had. Little did I know that equivalent sections in the city had the luxury of working in pairs and were not permitted to start call-out duties until they had completed one year in the section. My working conditions were very different to that of my city counterparts but I was oblivious to this and dealt with the situation as I found it, which was to get stuck in and get the job done.

During this initial stage of my forensic work, I had a strong feeling of impatience. There was too much to do in too little time. At many of the jobs I found myself standing around waiting for the arrival of other people necessary to assist with the scene. I found this waiting intolerable and it added to my frustration. I quickly came to realise that time was everything, and if I didn't get the job done expeditely I would be held up at the end of the day. There were tasks that couldn't be completed quickly and I felt the frustration of having left loose ends. I kept saying to myself, 'Get the job done, let's get this over with so I can get out of here and onto the next one.'

My agitated state was what kept me going even if I was tired or distressed. The sense of urgency kept me focused. It was a constant adrenaline rush.

I also learnt that a meal was often out of the question. I was thin and had a tendency to skip meals when I was stressed. I lost weight easily and couldn't afford to lose any more. I realised it was necessary to have food in the car so I could at least grab something quick if I had missed a meal. Muesli bars were my solution on many occasions when I hadn't eaten for hours. The Salvation Army was always a welcome sight at road scenes and, in particular, a man I affectionately knew as Deputy Dog. He provided hot coffee and sausage rolls which I appreciated greatly, especially in the middle of the night. The Salvos do a great job, not only supporting the emergency services but also victims and their families. It was always a great relief when the Salvos turned up and took over the job of assisting distraught relatives and friends.

It was hand-over time. I unloaded my equipment from the car, handed the keys and pager over and set about wading through the unfinished paperwork I had accumulated over the past week. I now had three days to write off my jobs and handle the mundane incidents that came in during the day. This usually involved assault victims who needed to be photographed in the studio, or roads and traffic authority examinations where cars had to be checked to verify their identity. Occasionally I would go out on a job with the on-call person, either to give them a hand or to learn how to examine a complex incident or scene.

At the end of ten straight working days, I headed off for four days' rest, back to my daily life and away from the human tragedy that had completely absorbed me at work.

Life had become deadly serious and it was hard to disassociate myself from the world of catastrophe and crime. There was no demarcation line as work and home had merged, become one, linked by a phone call or the sound of a pager. I was continually waiting for that call. I began to gauge my life on how bad the on-call period had been. At the time I didn't realise how the dark side of life was slowly pulling me down. Most of my conversations revolved around the tragedies I investigated, and secretly I worried about my inexperience when investigating these scenes.

Around this time Greg and I had sold our house and bought ten acres of land. We were now renting an old farmhouse which was on part of the subdivision until we could afford to build a new home. I named the house 'The Dump'; it was a decrepit old fibro dwelling on fifty acres retained by the developer. It had been previously rented by a group of bikies who had left it in a filthy state. The owners made a half-hearted effort to clean and fix it up. They tacked on a makeshift bathroom out the back and we rented it for fifty dollars a week. At first I was worried about the state of the place, but once we settled in we managed to make it comfortable. The biggest problem I faced was the terrible smell that emanated from an old fireplace in the kitchen. It was a filthy, rotting, dead smell and it made me feel sick to the stomach. The real estate agent had tried everything but had been unable to locate what was causing it. The smell reminded me of decomposing bodies and I found it difficult to ignore its association with work. On occasions, I sat down to eat the evening meal and was unable to ignore the smell lingering around my plate, so I would throw the meal in the bin and go without. After some time the smell decreased, although every now and then it would again engulf the room.

On the rare occasions that Greg and I were home together, we would sit on the old verandah drinking coffee and dreaming about the house we were going to build on our land at the end of the road. We were surrounded by open green pasture, which gave me a sense of tranquillity and freedom from work. I had a couple of horses on the property and riding was my outlet from the stresses of crime-scene work. But I spent most of my time at home alone. Greg left for work in the mines about the time that I was getting home. And if I'd been called out before 2 a.m., the time Greg got home from his shift, I'd return to an empty house. We could go a whole week without actually seeing one another long enough to talk. We would often miss each other by minutes. This was long before the invention of mobile phones so I couldn't call him if I was out on a job and he had no access to phones once he had gone underground.

On weekends we would try and catch up on the week's events, but even then it could be just for a fleeting moment as Greg loved to play golf every opportunity he got. Saturdays were usually taken up with squash in the morning and golf in the afternoon, followed by more golf on Sunday. It was difficult coming home from work to an empty house and I often found myself staring at the television. Sometimes I talked to friends on the phone, and this helped, but I kept many late-night anxieties bottled up inside. Whenever we did talk about my work Greg always listened intently and would sympathise or make a little joke to lighten things up, but we only scraped the surface, we never discussed anything in depth.

I urgently needed training but there was no one available to give me the necessary information. My biggest concern was not knowing how to identify the cause of death. I needed to know about forensic medicine. Right from the beginning I searched for information on this subject and I eventually did a forensic medicine course at Sydney Uni. I learned an enormous amount during the course, which was run by a forensic pathologist. He showed slide after slide of post-mortem examinations he had performed, pointing out the particular injury of interest and giving his determination of the cause of death. I can't explain how much more confident I felt when called out to fatalities of any kind after I had completed this course. For now, though, life went on, day after day, repetitive scenes of blood and guts.

# 10 Cut by a knife, hung by a noose

Over the next couple of months, as I settled in, my confidence slowly grew, and I became accustomed to the unpredictable nature of my work. It was only a matter of time before I found myself involved in the investigation of my first murder case. The call-out roster began with a triple recall to duty on the first night. After finishing afternoon shift I was recalled to attend a fatal car crash, followed by the suicide gassing of a young man in his car. Having been up most of the night I was not required back at the office until after an eight hour break, but at 2 p.m. that afternoon I was woken by the pager. I was in a deep sleep to which I promptly returned, only to be woken again by the telephone ringing. It was the duty operations inspector asking me to attend the murder scene of a teenage girl.

The murder had occurred in a housing-commission estate called Airds, on the outskirts of Campbelltown. It was a two-storeyed town-house at the end of a row of identical houses fronting onto the corner of the street. The close proximity of the houses, together with the community areas in front of each home, created a ghetto. The narrow lanes and access paths harboured criminal activity.

When I arrived I saw my old academy classmate Sharan on the grassed footpath beside the town house. She was involved in a scuffle with an hysterical woman who was screaming, crying and lashing out with both arms and legs.

I ran to help just as they both hit the ground, and with the help of a general duties constable we managed to restrain the woman, who was the dead girl's mother. She was desperately trying to enter the house to see her daughter. After learning that her daughter had been murdered, the woman went berserk, launching into a frenzied attack. Through tears and screams she yelled at Sharan that she had already lost two daughters, and this was the third to have been killed in two years.

The blue uniform had been the target of her grief and disbelief. Sharan had experienced this type of assault before and accepted it as part of the job; she had amazing resilience. I considered her to be a great policewoman. She got the job done, went straight to the next one and never considered herself first. In her eyes the job came first, and that was the way she had always been.

I was distressed to see someone in so much pain. The mother had to be restrained, for her own safety more than anything. Her agonising screams becoming shallower and her breathing laboured as she collapsed on the ground, sobbing uncontrollably. Her first daughter had been killed in a car accident, her second daughter run over on a pedestrian crossing, and now her third and last daughter had been murdered. None of the girls had reached their twenty-first birthday. We called the Salvation Army chaplain, and the ambulance officers in attendance monitored the woman until the chaplain arrived. The Salvos were always available in times of crises, just a phone call away.

The detectives came out and filled me in on the location of the body. The government medical officer, who attends scenes of suspicious, unnatural or violent deaths when required and later reports his findings to the Coroner, had been called. We decided to wait until his arrival before I commenced my investigation, but in the meantime I walked through the rear door to make a cursory examination. I entered a lounge room with a fairly steep staircase leading to the second level on the right. At my feet I saw a clump of hair and an amount of blood. I followed the detectives towards the upstairs bedrooms and the first things that struck me were the splash marks of blood and clumps of hair sticking to the stairwell wall. Continuing up the staircase I saw more blood spatter and clumps of hair and there was also blood smeared along the stairs. It was obvious there had been a violent struggle. At the top of the landing on the left was a child's bedroom where the murder had taken place and, in the hallway between this room and the rear bedroom, I saw a bloodstained stay-sharp knife with a yellow handle.

I carefully stepped over a number of bloodstains on the carpet at the entrance to the bedroom and stood in the doorway to get an overall view of the scene. I was immediately hit with the pungent odour of drying blood. I had never seen so much in a crime scene before and it was obvious from the splash patterns on the walls and ceiling that this had been a frenzied attack. The young woman lying on the floor had been slashed to death with a large machete, the resuscitation tube in the victim's mouth evidence that the ambulance team had tried in vain to save her. The weapon, covered in the victim's hair and blood, was lying at her feet. It had a large curved blade that was spotted with rust, the handle was wooden and worn as if it had been left out in the weather.

The brutality was overwhelming. As I stood in the doorway absorbing the horror, the detectives filled me in on the circumstances of the killing. A number of witnesses had given their version of events and at that stage it was apparent that the nineteen-year-old had been involved with a young man of the same age. The two had been in a relationship which had soured and the victim had ended their affair a couple of days before the killing. It was known that the young man was violent and he had struck the young woman a number of times in the past. The victim had confided to her mother that she was terrified of her ex-boyfriend who had threatened her with violence constantly since the relationship had ended.

The young woman had been visiting a friend who lived a couple of houses away from her ex-boyfriend. Word had spread that she was seeing a new man and this incensed her former partner. He had burst through the front door of the house she was visiting, grabbed the girl by the hair and literally dragged her along the street back to his house. Once inside a violent argument took place during which he accused her of seeing someone else. Realising that he was about to attack her, the young woman started to cry, repeating that she loved him but he dragged her by the hair up the stairs during which he hit her several times in the face. In his bedroom he reached to the top of his wardrobe where he had a large machete. There was a scuffle and the young woman broke free and fled, the ex-boyfriend in pursuit. He cornered her in the adjacent bedroom and hacked at her with the machete in a frenzied attack.

He struck her over and over again until she could no longer fend him off, and she collapsed on the floor, bleeding profusely.

Her hands were covered in defensive wounds. He had literally hacked her to death with repeated blows to various parts of her body, and her face was obliterated by the attack.

As I stood discussing the events with the detectives, I heard a helicopter flying overhead. One of the detectives had a portable radio, so we paused to listen to the hunt for the killer. He had been sighted and tracked to local bushland by air, and now the ground crew were closing in. After a short chase he was captured and placed under arrest. This was a welcome relief. The detectives were needed back at the station and, excited at the thought of interviewing the suspect, they made a hasty exit.

The government medical officer arrived and I watched as he walked up the stairs, greeting him at the top. He cautiously stepped over the machete, the pools of blood and the clumps of hair on the carpet. He stood over the body, his hand resting on his chin and uttered in a broad Irish accent, 'Vicious attack, vicious attack.'

He examined the young woman's body closely, rattling off in medical terms the type and size of injury, laceration here, laceration there, two and half inch, three inch by one inch, horizontal, rear head laceration, shoulder, posterior and on and on, there were too many to list. He finally stood back and declared he would leave the rest for the post-mortem. Before he left he bent down and gently drew his hand over her eyes. I was glad. She had been staring wide-eyed, the terror of her impending death frozen in time, and I was thankful that I didn't have to look at her like that as I worked.

The doctor left and I was all alone with the dead girl. The house was ghostly quiet, the urgency had faded. It was unnerving being alone in the room with so much blood, I could taste it in the back of my throat. The humidity in the air mixed with the blood gave it a decaying smell and I compared it with the smell of menstrual blood. I wondered whether I was up to examining a scene such as this and I decided I could do with a little help. A young policewoman, rostered to do work-experience with the scientific that day, had been patiently waiting for me in the office and had heard of the murder over the radio. She asked whether she should attend. At least I would have another set of hands to help with the recording of the scene.

I tried to contact my boss, Dave, though I knew he had travelled to the Sydney Police Centre that day to attend a course. The only other member of staff from my office was also at the course in the city and both he and Dave declined to take the trip out to the suburbs. I decided to ring Parramatta crime scene office and finally found someone there with experience who was prepared to come out to the scene and guide me a little. Basically, I knew what I had to do, but my lack of experience made me anxious that I might overlook something. With the offender in custody there would be a murder trial and everything at the scene needed to be checked and examined. I wanted to be sure that every ounce of evidence present was discovered. Next I contacted our photogrammetry section requesting a scale plan, achieved by taking a three-dimensional photograph using specially designed equipment. The photogrammetrist was also at the course in the city and he alerted the superintendent in charge of the state wide scientific investigation section that I was alone at the murder scene. The superintendent promptly hauled my colleague out of the course and directed him to give me a hand. The fellow from Parramatta, Mark, was called off and two hours later help arrived. Years later I was to work with Mark, who I always felt was a great support. He was the only one prepared to put himself out on that day and lend me a hand when I really needed it.

I examined the dead girl closely, taking notes of her injuries and clothing that would be later transcribed onto a running sheet. She was dressed in a pink and aqua leotard with a black skirt around her waist, all of which were soaked in blood. Scattered around the floor I discovered jewellery – her watch, earrings, a broken bracelet – that had been hacked from her body. On closer examination I saw that she had been cut to the bone and sliced from head to toe. Both wrists had been cut exposing the bone, the hands hanging only by a thread of skin. This injury could not have been caused by the large blade of the machete, the knife in the hallway was the more likely weapon. But why? The injuries caused by the machete alone were fatal. The perpetrator of such brutality knew exactly what he was doing and clearly he had meant to kill. He had hacked so furiously that he had struck the walls with the machete as he drew the weapon back to strike, slicing through the gyprock and spraying blood and hair about the room. Every part of the room – the soft toys, bed linen and clothing – was covered in the dead girl's blood. I wondered how it could be cleaned. It seemed it would be impossible to eradicate the gruesome mess from the room, violated beyond repair.

Every so often I was overcome by my gruesome task and I would stop to collect my thoughts and decide what to do next. The only place I could look without seeing blood was through the window, which was draped in sheer pink lace. Outside the shiny green leaves of a rubber tree swayed slightly in the breeze. I watched, hypnotised by the gentle movement, concentrating on the world outside as some kind of relief from the ghastly task I was trying to complete. Just a few moments of the beauty of that rubber tree gave me the sense of another reality and I used this to stabilise my thoughts, keep focused and get on with the job. Whenever I needed a break, I'd go to the window and gain some relief.

I painstakingly documented everything and as time went on the smell became stronger and stronger until I felt sick to the stomach. Finally the young policewoman on work experience arrived and at least I had someone to discuss the scene with. She was obviously horrified and asked me why I was working alone. We discussed the fact that scientific work in the suburbs is often done this way and working one-out was part of the job. She then asked how I felt working alone in such close confines with a mutilated body. I felt a twinge of annoyance. There was nothing I could do about working alone. It wasn't the ideal working conditions but it was how things were done.

It was a welcome relief when my colleague, Adam, arrived with the photogrammetry expert. But Adam didn't seem too impressed at having been told to assist me, and he wandered around the scene with a casual air. He told me I didn't need assistance and I shouldn't have asked for it. He played the whole scene down, refusing to help, answering my questions with a curt, 'Treat it like an assault, the only difference is the person has died. No big deal, just take your photos and collect all the exhibits. It's your job, just do it.'

I was pleased that he thought I'd adequately examined the scene but, on the other hand, a little encouragement would have gone a long way. I was tired, I'd been up all night and this was the biggest scene I'd examined so far. Later, I understood that Adam had his own workload to carry and I can't blame him for not wanting to do more than his share, especially as it was his week off-call. He no doubt felt he had enough on his plate without getting involved in one of my jobs. At that time, I didn't understand the varying ways we dealt with stress.

Everyone had their own mechanisms for survival. But I was inexperienced and I needed encouragement.

I assisted with the photogrammetry survey placing the numbered cones in their carefully measured positions so a three-dimensional photograph could be taken. The equipment is heavy and cumbersome and requires at least two people to operate it. I helped as we dismantled it from its tripod and reassembled it again in each new position. I then waited as the operator slid glass plates into the machine each time he took a photograph of the cones so he could later draw a scale plan for presentation at court. Shortly after finishing the survey the fingerprint experts arrived and I gave them a run down of the scene. I had found a bloodied fingerprint on the rear gate and I pointed this out to the two men.

I began to collect and label the exhibits that would later be examined and tested as part of the evidence. I placed bags over the victim's hands to protect evidence that might be hidden under her fingernails and collected hair and took blood swabs from the gate and inside the house in numerous locations. The murder weapons were carefully placed in paper bags, including the stay-sharp knife, sheath and bloodstained machete. I collected the broken jewellery and noticed that the girl's watch had stopped at precisely seven minutes to two, the time of her death.

It wasn't long before I was working in the dark and finally getting to the point where the body could be removed by the body snatchers. The two forlorn figures had been standing at the rear gate for hours, like vultures waiting for their prey. So, too, had a contingent of cameramen and reporters trying to get a glimpse of the activity inside. They finally got their footage when I took the blood swab from the rear gate – I was blinded by the lights and flashes of the photographers' cameras. They hung around until the body came out on the stretcher, zipped up in a large black plastic bag, amid a flurry of cameras clicking and flashes going off. It was 9 p.m. and I had spent a total of six and a half hours at the scene, but my job was far from over. There was still the offender to examine and a meeting with the detectives back at the station.

I packed up the wagon with my array of exhibits and drove the short distance to Campbelltown police station where I went straight to the detectives' office. I found the two investigators sitting at their desks banging away on typewriters. Like me, they hadn't had a break since early afternoon and were working towards getting the job finished. The investigation was headed by Detective Sergeant Allan Taylor and we discussed the scene while I described the evidence in minute detail, mentioning at length the horrendous injuries the girl had suffered. I had brought a number of exhibits into the office to present to the offender so that the detectives could confirm details of how he had used them during the killing. I was told that the offender had made a full confession. The detectives gave a chilling account of the offender's ferocious indifference to the girl's murder.

I was eager to read his record of interview and began to view the formal account of the facts before the prisoner was brought out from the cells to be shown the murder weapons. I sat at one of the desks and read the lengthy statement, in which he admitted his anger at the break-up of his relationship with the dead woman. He described the attack as it occurred from the time he burst into the neighbour's house where his ex-girlfriend was visiting. He grabbed her by the hair, yanking her along the road as she cried and begged him to leave her alone. As he thrust her through the doorway of his house he punched her in the face and threw her up against the stairwell wall. Bleeding and frightened, she declared her love for him. He recounted how she had sworn over and over that she loved him and that she wanted to resume their relationship. It was her deceptive words of love that caused his mind to snap, he said, he didn't believe her and the thought that she was lying to him further added to his insecurities.

In that split second of fury, his judgment marred by his rage, he dragged her to the top of the stairs and into his bedroom where she desperately struggled with him as he reached for the machete stored on top of his wardrobe. As he reached for the weapon, she momentarily slipped from his grip. Why she didn't run down the stairs is a mystery, as she may have escaped, but instead she ran blindly into the adjoining bedroom where he cornered her. He struck her over and over with the enormous blade, slicing her into oblivion, hacking at her hands and arms as she held them up to defend herself. He wanted to shut her up, he said, wanted to stop her lies and false confessions of love.

When she finally collapsed he bent over her prone body on the floor, peering into her staring eyes, wanting her to die. He said he could hear a gurgling sound as if she were choking. To make sure she was dead, he used a stay-sharp knife to cut her wrists deeply, almost severing them. There was to be no possible chance of survival. The gurgling sound faded and finally stopped. He made sure she was dead then ran down the stairs and out into the street, crossing the main road, heading into the bush, ripping his jeans and scratching himself as he fled through rough terrain. Then police closed in and he was cornered, handcuffed and arrested.

I handed the papers back to the detectives and began to lay the exhibits out. I placed large sheets of brown paper out on the desk and carefully removed the murder weapons from the exhibit bags with a gloved hand. The smell of blood filled the room as I laid the blood-coated machete out. Handcuffed, and with a detective on either arm, the offender shuffled into the room. His head was bowed and long, brown, scruffy hair hid his face. The sight of him disgusted me, he seemed such a puny, insignificant figure with an air of imbecility. His ugliness absorbed the putrid smell he had created. With his head still bowed he looked up through his matted hair, swiping at it with his handcuffed hands. I saw his eyes staring glassily at the bloodied machete laid out before him. He seemed almost monkey-like to me, his face covered in bum fluff, as if he had only just reached puberty.

The detectives read him his rights before continuing with the interview. He was questioned about the murder weapons and I photographed him as he indicated the weaponry before him confirming that he had used these to kill his ex-girlfriend. I then photographed the offender and noted the scratches on his stomach, chest and arms where he had been injured while fleeing from the murder scene. He was asked to identify a pair of blue denim jeans, socks, white singlet, underpants and running shoes and he confirmed that he had worn each item of clothing at the time of the murder. There was a bloodied hand print on the right leg of the denim jeans and bloodstains around the ankle area of the socks. There were also bloodstains on the singlet and the running shoes. His clothing and shoes were itemised and placed in paper bags which were labelled individually for later examination. The prisoner looked on impassively as we followed protocol, officially documenting each item as it was handed over to me. Once all the exhibits were accounted for, the interview was concluded and at 11 p.m. the prisoner was led away and taken back to the cells. The next time we were to meet would be under very different circumstances.

The next day I spent a lot of time examining the array of exhibits I had collected from the murder scene. Again I was struck by the stale smell of blood as I removed the items from their paper bags. Each item was photographed and categorised according to where it was required to be sent for further examination or stored in the exhibit room. Most of the bloodstained items needed to be sent to the Division of Forensic Medicine at Glebe for blood grouping, but until the post-mortem had been completed, were locked in the office fridge, likewise a number of hair samples were stored in the freezer compartment. I spent most of the day filling out forms and attending to matters concerning the murder. Photographic film was sent off, job books completed and loose ends tidied up.

During the day, I spoke to one of the detectives over the phone. He had been asked by the dead girl's mother to release the jewellery I had collected at the scene. I described the condition of the items, each piece broken and stained with the girl's blood. I feared it would further traumatise the mother if she saw them. We talked about it for some time, discussing the possible impact on the mother's mental state. Eventually we concluded that the items were exhibits and could not be released until after the court proceedings had been finalised. This was the decision the mother was to be given and we hoped it would put the matter to rest. A short time later the detective rang back and told me that the mother did not accept this explanation and was insisting that the jewellery be handed over to her immediately. She intimated that perhaps we had stolen the items as some of the jewellery contained precious stones. I gave the detective an itemised list of the jewellery hoping that would alleviate the mother's fears. Sadly, the jewellery wasn't worth anything to anyone apart from its evidentiary value or sentimental value to the girl's mother. It was so damaged that the stones needed removal and resetting, or more simply, to be left as they were, mementos of the dead girl.

Early the following morning I attended the Campbelltown mortuary where I met Detective Harding. In the autopsy room, we were met by Doctor O'Dowd who was preparing to perform the post-mortem on the dead girl. She was lying on the steel trolley just as I had last seen her, dressed in her leotard and little black skirt, her skin smeared with dried blood and her hair stickily matted. Her clothing was removed and the doctor commenced his examination while I took photographs and Detective Harding filled out the anatomical chart. His job was difficult because of the numerous large incisions made by the machete blade. Each one had to be examined, measured, drawn, photographed and described. There were over fifty of these lacerations, of varying length and depth, each one cleaned by the morgue attendant to reveal the ferocity of the attack. He hosed each one, simultaneously wiping the wound clean with a sponge as the doctor bent down to peer at the evidence and remark on the varying points of interest.

It was a distasteful task, but my youth and keen interest in forensic medicine allowed me to dissociate myself from the ugliness of the injuries. Throughout the examination, the strong odour of decaying blood overpowered the usual morgue smell. It was a constant reminder of the horrific sight I was faced with when I attended the murder scene. I pushed the smell aside, absorbing myself in my duties as a crime-scene examiner and concentrating on my responsibility to document every minute detail to ensure that the court would later have a clear and concise record of every aspect that contributed to the death of the young woman.

As is the usual procedure, the body cavity was cut open and a number of organs and samples removed and measured. Some were replaced, while others were secured in plastic bottles for later transportation to the Department of Analytical Laboratories. I listed each as they were examined: liver, bile, stomach contents, blood and so on. The bags I had placed over her hands at the scene were still in place and fingernail clippings were removed and secured in bags for inclusion with the other specimens. Lastly the head was opened with a circular saw and I turned away as the doctor cut into the thick skull bone. After the brain was examined the doctor concluded his examination and the morgue attendant took over. He had the task of sewing the body back up and washing her down in preparation for her burial. I set off with a car load of exhibits, heading first for the Department of Analytical Laboratories at Lidcombe, to deliver a blood sample for alcohol analysis. Next I went to the Division of Forensic Medicine at Glebe where I handed over a number of exhibits for blood grouping. The job was now complete – until the laboratory results were finalised and the photographs came back from being processed.

Back at the office I set about completing the running sheet, which gives a chronological account of events as they occurred. Each part of the investigation is set to a time and date with every exhibit collected detailed: when and where it was collected, what examinations were performed and where it was sent. The running sheet has to be completed as soon as possible and handed to the detectives so they can include it in the brief of evidence. A statement would be prepared at a later date after the photographs had been sorted and labelled.

On the last night of my seven-day call period, I was again woken by the phone ringing. It was 2.30 a.m.

'There's been a hanging in the cells,' was the message. I couldn't believe it.

As if it wasn't enough to deal with the murder a couple of days before, I now had to attend the hanging death of the perpetrator of that murder. A death in custody is a serious matter and is usually scrutinised by all and sundry. It is also dealt with by internal affairs, and all police involved in the incident can expect to be thoroughly interrogated.

When I arrived at the station I could feel the concern of all present. Obviously the officer-in-charge of the prisoners was nervous. He was responsible for carrying out the correct checking procedure of prisoners housed in the cell complex that night. After hearing the circumstances of the hanging, I prepared to attend to the scene in the male cells. It was the first time I had come across someone in death that I had briefly known in life. I felt anger at the dead man. He had already caused me a lot of work over the past week. Now, again, he was holding centre stage.

I followed the station sergeant down the long concrete corridor that led to the male cells and into the area just outside the four identical lockups. The young man lying motionless on his back on the cold concrete floor looked even uglier in death than he had in life. His puny frame was dressed in a pair of blue shorts, his hollow chest revealed with its clumps of brown spindly hair. His head, with its big mop of dark fuzzy hair, was turned to one side, his long skinny neck unable now to hold his head up. His eyes stared right into mine, his mouth frozen open in a contorted shape as if he had something dumb to say. I had no pity for him. I felt nothing but contempt. To me, he was disgusting, gutless, unable to face his crime. Rather than take responsibility for his actions, he had escaped by ending his life. He left four suicide notes expressing his remorse for killing his girlfriend.

'If I can't have her no one else will,' he wrote.

He justified his suicide by admitting he wasn't any good to anyone now and he would rather go and be with the one he loved. 'I loved her so much,' he added.

Those words made my stomach turn. In that moment I thought him to be a worthless piece of dirt, expressing undying love for the one he murdered so cruelly in cold blood.

Once again I found myself in a situation over my head, having no training in investigating deaths in custody. With no one to seek advice from, it was up to me to get on with the job. I examined the plaited piece of ripped blanket he had used to make a noose and found where he had attached it to the upper cell bars in the left-hand corner of cell number four. The remainder of the noose, cut off by the constable on duty who had brought the body down, lay beside the dead man. I found where the two pieces of blanket matched and the remainder of the grey blanket from which it had been cut. When I searched the cell I also found an area concealed by two cell mattresses where the concrete wall had been chipped away. Exposed and slightly protruding from the wall was steel reinforcing; most likely this was how the prisoner had cut up the blanket, laboriously cutting it into thin strips, then plaiting them into a length long enough to make a noose.

I photographed the scene, took measurements, drew a plan and made notes. Once again I returned my attention to the dead man, making a full examination of his body, checking the ligature marks around his neck, comparing the marks to the discarded noose. I rolled him over and checked for any sign of further injury but found nothing of interest. He had lividity on his back and legs where the blood had deposited itself in the lowest part of his body, firstly while he was hanging and secondly, when he'd been cut down and laid out on the concrete floor. I photographed his body and laid out the four suicide notes to be recorded and photographed. Just as I was concluding my examination a detective inspector from internal affairs entered the cell complex and I filled him in on the circumstances as well as the findings of my examination. He wanted a full report as to the crime scene examination and questioned me intensely as we stood beside the body of the dead man. We walked into the cell where the hanging had taken place and I pointed out the remnants of the noose hanging on the upper bars as well as the exposed reinforcing protruding from the cell wall. Satisfied, he turned and walked away, leaving me on my own to finish my examination and pack up my equipment.

I walked up the cell complex corridor and into the charge room where I passed the inspector now standing at the counter going through the prisoner's logbook with the charge sergeant. He was inspecting the interval times that the prisoners had been checked the previous night. The regulation time is every fifteen minutes and each time a notation has to be placed in the log book and signed by the appropriate personnel. This particular point was later severely scrutinised at the coronial inquest, with much questioning and discussion about the actual times the prisoners were checked. My job at the station was finished and it was time to call the government contractors to take the body away. After a quick chat with the inspector, I was excused and headed home for a few hours' sleep.

The next morning I went into the office and dealt with the

paperwork relating to the death in custody. I sent photographic film off for processing, wrote off the job book in relation to the incident and prepared a brief folder. Now that the girl's murderer was dead, there would no longer need to be a murder trial, only an inquest. Over the next couple of weeks I prepared two briefs of evidence for the Coroner and eventually gave evidence at the Westmead Coroner's Court. I was not required to give evidence at the inquest into the death of the teenage girl, my evidence was handed up and accepted in my absence.

Day after day my life was consumed by killings, distress and gruesome sights. Each one added another piece to an ever-growing mosaic that seemed to be made up of bloodied disposable gloves, plastic bags and human waste. My mind became filled with these remnants, storing them for later, when a trigger would jolt them back into my memory.

# 11 Bill and Ben

Changes were afoot in the office; out with the old and in with the new. My boss Dave had accepted a transfer to the crime scene unit in Penrith, which was closer to home, and we were getting a new boss called Pieter, who had recently been promoted to the rank of sergeant. Although he had many years' experience as a crime-scene examiner, this was his first post as a supervisor.

I struck up a good working relationship with Pieter, who gave me the support and encouragement that had been lacking and I felt he had the staff's best interests at heart. He immediately took me off the call-out roster and expressed concern about me working alone with less than a year's experience. He was not happy with how the office had been running on a skeleton crew. I wasn't sure why he didn't want me to work one-out but he reassured me I hadn't done anything wrong. He felt that I had been thrown in the deep end and this could be a recipe for disaster. Now I could take a step back and learn without the pressure of investigating major crime on my own. Initially,

Pieter and I worked as a pair attending crime scenes together so I could learn how to do each job properly. It wasn't long before my confidence was such that he felt I was ready to go back on the call-out roster. I was now much better prepared and was on the list to do the crime-scene examiners course that would give me the technical knowledge I required. We were completely overworked and Pieter was also struggling with the hierarchy to get more staff. We needed at least two more people to cope with the workload effectively.

One of Pieter's main concerns was our welfare and he constantly checked on us. Right from the start he touched on the subject of stress, saying that at some stage we might all suffer varying degrees of stress, and even to be prepared for a possible nervous breakdown. It was his experience, he said, that after working in the scientific field for two to three years, all sorts of symptoms such as sleeping difficulties, stomach upsets and avoidance of the workplace might occur. It was almost as if Pieter was suggesting it was par for the course and at the time I was surprised at his frankness – this was a subject that was never discussed. It was part of the police culture that emotional problems were kept quiet, because any indication that you weren't coping could mean a transfer and a notation on your service register excluding you from future promotion. This was why stress was usually resolved by a visit to the pub. It was the first I had heard about this 'stress' problem and I listened intently as Pieter described the symptoms he had suffered several years before and how it had affected him personally. He also recounted similar episodes that had affected other members of the scientific investigation section, including members who had gone on to become senior officers. Even though I listened to what Pieter said, I felt that stress was something that wouldn't concern me, it wasn't in my game plan and I really had no time for it. I was young and enthusiastic and still had no concept of the long-term effects of exposure to trauma. It seemed to me that even if I *were* to succumb to this annoyance, it would not affect my long-term goals in the police force. Surely, it would put me in a category of dedicated people who had suffered and soldiered on. Pieter assured me that it was the normal procedure to simply go off sick for a while; a couple of weeks away from work would do the trick. That way no one needed to know that anyone was suffering from burnout and we could return to work without our service records being tarnished with the word 'stress'. I filed this information in the back of my head where I thought it would remain. I believed I certainly wasn't the type to lose the plot. This might happen to others doing scientific work but I was pretty sure it would not happen to me. Later I discovered that there were far more sinister side effects to working in the scientific field than I could ever have imagined. In 1988 I had never heard the term 'post-traumatic stress disorder' and I doubt that any of my colleagues had either.

Although Barry and I accepted Pieter's supervisory style, Adam was not too impressed and felt that we were being watched a little too closely. Adam came from an era where once you were qualified you worked out on your own and, having worked like this for many years, he felt overpowered by Pieter's supervision. It wasn't long before they were clashing. Pieter used to say there was only room for one prima donna in the office, and that was going to be him. Adam decided to leave to pursue a career in the police prosecuting branch where he was well suited with his quick wit and eye for detail.

For a little while it was only Pieter, Barry and me in the office and we started doing call every third week unless one of us was on leave, when we would do it every second week. As the work flowed so too did the piles of statements that were required for court. At one stage I had a backlog of thirteen statements, which were usually around ten to fifteen pages long. By the time I had completed them I had typed nearly two hundred pages of information. These were the days of the manual typewriter so we were all relieved when Pieter managed to get a second-hand electric typewriter for our office. After campaigning long and hard we were finally given a personal assistant. This meant there would be someone in the scientific office to man the phones, book jobs in and type our statements.

Anne, the government support officer, did a great job and we all relied on her for her organisational skills and dedication to her work. Once we had her in our office there was a lot of sour grapes from other sections within the station, who constantly tried to undermine us and take her away. This led us to believe that our divisional leader did not acknowledge our enormous workload. Pieter was required to attend the divisional office every Monday morning to brief the commander on what was happening in the scientific area and after their meeting he would stay for morning tea. I accompanied him one particular morning and casually discussed our concerns with the commander over a cup of tea. It wasn't long before the information started to flow and it gave Pieter and me an opportunity to unofficially voice our concerns. Our morning tea became a regular thing and as a consequence we were treated much more fairly. The first improvement was to get permission for two additional staff members.

Shane joined the team and, shortly after, Whayne was transferred to our section. I had worked with Shane before at Campbelltown police station. We were both young and shared a similar sense of humour. While working at Campbelltown we both had to have wounds stitched and were required to be examined by the police medical officer prior to resuming full duties. Like two country bumpkins we drove the police divvy van to the city and got hopelessly lost in the maze of Surry Hills' one-way streets. Every time I looked up from the street directory we were back in Riley Street. We both became hysterical with laughter at the ridiculous sight of two cops driving around in circles unable to find police headquarters. From that day we enjoyed a good joke and that was the essence of our friendship.

I hadn't met Whayne before and it wasn't until his transfer from the rescue squad at Green Valley police station into the scientific section that I got to know him. Like Shane, he was tall, slim and fair. At times I would confuse the two, especially when looking at them from behind. Although Whayne and Shane had very different personalities they shared a good sense of humour and right from the start played jokes on each other constantly. The three of us were all in our early twenties.

Barry was older, having joined the police later in life. He had the unfortunate habit of getting his wires crossed and I was often amused at the stories he told. I worked with Barry at the scene of a sexual assault and after finishing at the scene we went to Campbelltown police station to check on the victim, who was being interviewed by a policewoman. While giving her statement, the victim asked to use the toilet so the policewoman asked Barry if this would be okay as the victim had not yet been examined by a doctor. Barry handed the victim a paper bag, instructing her to put all used toilet paper into it so as to preserve any possible evidence. After a short time the policewoman came out of her office, very exasperated, to inform us that the victim had misunderstood Barry's direction. She had done as she thought she had been instructed, which was to urinate in the paper bag, but halfway through the bag had collapsed, covering the toilet floor with urine that the policewoman then had to clean.

With the additional staff we had to rearrange the office. Whayne and Shane sat opposite each other in the second office, and Pieter, Barry and I sat in the main office with Anne. The separation of Whayne and Shane from the rest of the staff created a 'them and us' situation. They could be debating one minute and then helping each other out the next. They became almost inseparable and would often go out on jobs together to give each other a hand.

One morning, after one of their fierce debates, they left together to do a job. While they were away Pieter made up a sign for their office door which read 'Bill and Ben the Flowerpot Men'. He drew a comical sketch of the two flowerpot characters with a weed in the middle. The names stuck, the plaque remained and somehow I fitted into the picture, just like the weed in the show. We all became extremely protective of each other, especially looking after the person who was on call. Just being able to talk about the previous night's events could be a great relief if you had been up all night attending a grotesque crime scene. The three of us were able to express ourselves without fear of judgement or ridicule and we knew that anything we said would stay between us. Also, a second opinion was often helpful as we were all fairly new to the world of forensic science.

Each day at the office brought many events both happy and sad, and the pressure of never having enough time to get everything done. The sense of working on overdrive became the norm and every job felt urgent. Shane seemed to feel the effects of the workload in a similar way to me and we often talked about it. It became almost a competition between the three of us to be the one who had attended the worst crime scene.

'You won't believe the job I got last night,' one of us would start.

We were all steadfast in our working relationships, all pitching in at one hundred miles an hour. Even though our job was dark and depressing at times, there was always the funny side of things to keep our spirits up. Shane returned from a job where a man had died of a 'ferocious liver', according to his relatives. I was called to the banks of the Georges River to investigate the discovery of human bones, only to waste hours excavating the remains of a dead fox. Another time I discovered what I thought was a human leg among the charred remains of a burnt house, only to discover after taking a closer look that it was a prosthesis caught up in leather bondage equipment. There was the regular appearance of my bum in the local newspaper. The paper's photographer would wait until I bent over to examine a piece of evidence at a crime scene and then click away to show my backside in the best possible position in the local weekly paper. There was also a constant array of gory, weird or unusual photographs cropping up on the office noticeboard, with captions to match. This competition developed into a display of personal ingenuity that would greet you first thing in the morning. At least this way we started the day with a smile, even if we ended the day in quite a different mood.

At times I would work alone all weekend and this was usually the job of the on-call person. It was up to me to stay motivated and self-reliant and it became my custom to drop around at my mother's house for breakfast on Sundays when I was on call.

This had a two-fold effect: the food was good, and she provided a sympathetic ear. Many a Sunday morning I'd turn up still wearing my work clothes, having been up all night doing a job. There were no mobile phones in the late 1980s so I'd just turn up whenever I could. If I didn't show, Mum would know that I'd been held up at work and wouldn't think anything of it.

One cold Sunday, I was called out at 4.30 a.m. to attend a drug overdose at the housing commission estate of Rosemeadow, on the outskirts of Campbelltown. I greeted the detectives huddled together at the front of the house and we spoke in the shadowy darkness by the front steps as the sun had not yet risen. The house, eerily quiet, stood out in the darkness lit up like a Christmas tree. The story unfolded as a complex series of events starting at a pub in Mount Druitt the night before. Two mates in their late twenties had driven together to the pub primarily to score heroin. At Mount Druitt they drank in the pub for a few hours before they managed to score. Then they drove along the back road towards home, stopping in a driveway to a horse stud. There, they injected each other with heroin and discarded the used syringes in the grassy paddock beside the road. One of them became groggy and semi-conscious in the car during the return journey, and by the time they reached Rosemeadow, he was slumped in his seat. With the help of others inside the house the driver managed to drag his mate to the front steps and prop him up against the house. The victim then apparently fell to the side, hitting his head on the edge of the front steps. After this he vomited and passed out. It was midnight when the victim was carried inside and taken to a child's bedroom where he was put into a single bed and left to sleep it off. In the early hours of the next morning, the victim was discovered dead in the bed. The fact that the friend had admitted to police he had injected his mate with the drug that appeared to have contributed to his death meant he would be charged with manslaughter.

The detectives were eager to get back to the station and interview the offender so I was left at the scene alone to perform my examination. I entered the house and went straight to the bedroom where the dead man was lying. Once again I found myself working alone with a dead body in a child's bedroom. Did the child know someone had died in her room among her possessions? What was the dead man doing in the child's bed anyway? These seemingly trivial details annoyed me.

It was obvious the man had been dead for many hours due to rigor mortis. He was stiff as a board and the lividity present was consistent with the body lying on its side, legs bent at the knees. I photographed the scene, took notes and drew a sketch of the layout of the house as well as the position of the dead man. I examined the body and located a fresh needle puncture wound on the inside of his right elbow. It was difficult to photograph the wound as his arm, due to rigor mortis, had become bent at the elbow and it was necessary to pull it straight to get a good photograph. I struggled with his arm for quite some time trying to get it into the right position. As quickly as I would straighten his arm by pulling his hand down it would resume the bent position, concealing the puncture wound and making it impossible to photograph. I could definitely have done with an extra set of hands. I cursed the fact that I had to work alone. Eventually I got my photograph, albeit haphazardly, and I hoped it would be in focus. To do my job properly, I had to remove clothing and examine the body for any possible injuries. To add to the unpleasant nature of my work, the man had soiled his pants and the smell of excrement was suffocating.

It was around this time, the late 1980s, that HIV AIDS became a matter of concern. I was worried about the victim's HIV and hepatitis status and although I wore gloves I didn't feel that this was adequate protection. Occupational health and safety was really understated for crime-scene personnel and the 'She'll be right' attitude prevailed. I had not received any formal training on the protection or control of HIV and it was before the Grim Reaper advertisements that at least gave the public an idea on how the disease was spread. So I carried on and examined the body with my inadequate protection. This type of exposure would never be tolerated today. Forensic police now wear a full AIDS suit – a lightweight, disposable paper space suit that covers the examiner from head to toe with additional surgical mask and goggles for eye protection – as a mandatory measure whenever investigating a scene of this nature.

Finally I took the external photographs of the house and front steps, waiting until the sun had risen for better lighting. By mid-morning I was finished and allowed the body snatchers to transport the body to the morgue.

I pulled the front door closed and headed off to the detectives' office to discuss the scene and work out where to go next. As it turned out, the offender had given a detailed statement mapping out the exact sequence of events and places he had visited the night before with his dead mate. It was decided to take him in the detectives' car and I would follow so we could retrace the steps of the two men and record any possible evidence.

First, we visited the hotel where the heroin had been purchased and I photographed the building and surrounding car park. Next we drove back along the same road and attempted to find the driveway where the two mates had pulled over and injected each other with heroin. We pulled into numerous driveways only to get out of our cars and stand around listening as the offender dithered about, unsure as to whether this was the correct place. Finally we pulled off the road into a dirt track surrounded by whitewashed post-and-rail fencing, the driveway to a horse stud and possibly the place we were looking for. After following the detectives halfway down the dirt driveway we pulled over and got out of our cars. This was definitely where they had stopped to inject the drugs, said the offender. He looked around and pointed out a couple of possible areas where the used syringes might be. My heart sank. The paddocks beside the road were covered in dense grass.

We spent the next hour combing through the grass in a desperate search to find the two syringes and we were lucky to find both of them a short distance away from each other, still suspended on the soft green grass where they had landed after being thrown from the car the night before. I photographed the offender pointing to the spot where the syringes were found and after photographing them both I carefully sealed them in a labelled sharps container.

It was 4 p.m. when I arrived at the office to finalise the day's notes and write off the job book. I was thinking about calling it a day and looking forward to going home when the phone rang. With a sigh I picked up the handset.

'Crime Scene Unit, Constable First Class Mckay speaking.'

'What are you doing?' The cheery, unmistakable voice of Detective Sergeant Berthally was on the other end.

'What are *you* doing?' I countered. It was our usual greeting and always preceded bad news. 'I've been up since dawn on a manslaughter and I was just about to go home,' I said.

'I've got a job for you,' he said with a chuckle. 'It's a good'un. A man's been shot. We think it's an attempted suicide but you better come and check. He's had half his face shot off, then he's jumped into the pool and tried to drown himself. He's been taken to hospital but he might not make it. He definitely won't be eating steak again!'

'I guess I'm not going home then,' I said.

'Nope, sorry.'

'Better give me the address,' I said. 'And I'll meet you there in about half an hour.'

He rattled off an address at the back of Liverpool and I hung the phone up with a clunk.

At the scene I sat in my car until the detectives arrived, pulling up in their sedan beside me and winding down the window. Bob stuck his head out the passenger side.

'What are you doing?' he yelled.

'Waiting to find out what *you're* doing,' I replied. I got out of the car and met the two detectives on the footpath outside the house. 'I'm gonna kill you, Bob,' I said. 'I've had a shit of a day and I'm absolutely stuffed.'

'You'll be right,' he said. 'When you've finished the job come and have a drink back at the station, it'll cheer you up.'

I followed him into the house and out through the back door where he led me into a detached fibro garage. The district inspector was standing at the door, waiting for my arrival. It was a warm afternoon and the first thing I noticed was the mass of blowflies swarming in and out of the open door. It was hot and stuffy inside the old building and directly in front of me I saw an old grey blanket laid out on the concrete floor and a large military-style rifle lying at one end. Pieces of human flesh, and teeth and bone fragments littered with droplets of blood, peppered the room. Gingerly, I stepped inside, warning Bob not to step on the remnants of the victim's face, which were being attacked by hungry blowflies.

Apparently the man had decided to end his life by placing a rifle in his mouth and shooting himself. He had laid a blanket on the floor to avoid making a mess and, lying down on the blanket, he had pulled the trigger, jerking the barrel out of his mouth as the gun went off. The bullet tore his mouth off in its path, taking with it the front part of his face and forehead. Although severe, the injuries were not sufficient to kill him and in desperation to finish himself off the man had run bleeding out into the rear yard and jumped into an in-ground pool to drown himself. His two young children, who had been playing inside the house, ran out and rescued him from the pool and called an ambulance. When the police arrived they found one of the children so traumatised he was hiding in a wardrobe. The police had great trouble coaxing him out.

After recording the scene photographically, my main concern was to render the weapon safe. The rifle appeared to be primed with a round ready to fire and I needed to find someone with knowledge of this type of weapon to talk me through the procedure. I was about to go and ring ballistics when an ambulance officer came rushing to the garage to tell us that the victim was about to go into surgery for facial reconstruction and the medical staff had requested that as much of the man's face that could be saved be collected in paper bags and sent urgently to the hospital. With a brown paper bag and gloves I started collecting pieces of flesh, some with the victim's moustache still attached. I swatted furiously at the flies before picking up each bloodied specimen. The inspector dutifully stepped around the room pointing to large pieces he thought were worth collecting. As I retrieved a number of teeth I looked up to see another piece of flesh and before I could finish saying, 'There's a bit,' the inspector stepped back in his size twelve police boots and squashed it. With a sigh I cut short the rest of my sentence and decided not to mention the squashed morsel under his boot as it was obviously useless now and not worth collecting. I carried on and promptly forgot all about it. With all visible remnants of the man's face finally collected the ambulance officer rushed away and I got on with the job.

Inside the house I found a telephone and rang the ballistics section. I was lucky to actually find someone in the office on a weekend and was given step-by-step instructions on how to disarm the weapon. This was tricky for me as I had limited knowledge of guns and wasn't conversant with the many types of rifles. I had been given absolutely no instruction on ballistics so how I was expected to be able to render safe any type of firearm was a mystery. Nevertheless, I felt responsible for the weapon as part of my duties and basically improvised the best way I could. I followed the ballistician's instructions and managed to make the rifle safe to transport back to the station as an exhibit.

By this time I was hot, sweaty, tired and in desperate need of a shower and a change of clothes, but I also felt that the offer of a glass of wine would be a good chance to wind down before I went home to an empty house. My husband had started doing pre-shifts on a Sunday afternoon which meant he went into work early, starting several hours before his rostered duty. I knew by the time I got home he would have left for work, whereas at least back at the station I would have someone to talk to and could have a joke and try to release some of the tension that had built up over the past thirteen hours. I hadn't even had time to have a meal throughout the day and I felt I deserved a break. So off I went back to the station and, true to his word, Bob was waiting with a cold plastic cup of cask wine.

He had been down to the hospital to take a statement from the man who had shot himself, and when he described the horrific facial injuries the man had suffered, we all agreed we'd rather be dead than go through the agony of the surgery and slow recovery he had to endure.

I was enjoying my wine when something made me look down and I noticed something a little odd on the floor beside my chair. I pushed my seat back and bent down to take a better look and was so shocked I flew out of my chair, knocking it sideways. I stood up, pointing to the floor and I cried, 'Look! There! It's a lip with a moustache from the crime scene! Someone's brought it into the meal room on their boots!'

Everyone in the room jumped out of their seats and peered over the table at the piece of flesh deposited right beside me.

'Bloody hell, who's got ripple-soled shoes on?' Bob asked.

I knew exactly how the piece of flesh had got there and it wasn't from *my* ripple-soled shoes. I quickly recounted the incident where the station inspector had trodden on the piece of lip at the scene. He vehemently denied it and now I wished I'd mentioned it at the time but it was too late. Everyone in the room immediately blamed me because I had spent so much time in the crime scene and had been responsible for collecting the pieces of flesh.

To this day I cannot convince Bob that I did not bring that piece of lip into the meal room on my ripple-soled shoes. Even though I wasn't responsible for it being there, I was still held accountable for it. There was not one person in the room who was prepared to pick up the lip and dispose of it, so I dutifully went out to the car and got a pair of gloves and a paper bag. It was amazing how all the police present had taken off at a hundred miles an hour. It was almost as if a bomb had been discovered in the meal room and it was not safe to re-enter the room until it had been disarmed.

With the meal room declared safe for habitation again, the station staff filed back in and resumed their positions at the table. For the next hour we threw jokes back and forth about the lip and moustache until my stomach hurt from laughing. By 7.30 p.m. I was exhausted and decided to head home. Fifteen hours had elapsed since the call out that morning and I'd had enough.

The next morning I headed off to the city morgue to attend the post-mortem examination of the dead drug addict. After donning a white laboratory coat I walked through the plastic doors into the main waiting area where I met the pathologist who would perform the autopsy. After a few pleasantries she indicated that because the deceased was a drug addict, and a moderate health risk was involved, the post-mortem was scheduled to take place in the dirty necropsy room. She walked off to prepare for the post-mortem leaving me standing alone, and I saw a steel trolley being wheeled out of the main refrigerated storage room. I immediately recognised the body on the trolley as the man I had examined in the child's bedroom the day before. On a bright yellow card attached to the foot of the trolley I saw the words 'HIV POSITIVE' in bold red ink. I was shocked.I had used very little protection at the crime scene and to say I was absolutely terrified would be an understatement. My heart began to pound and I felt faint; my hands trembled. Following closely behind the morgue attendant as he wheeled the trolley into the dirty necropsy room I found it difficult to stay steady on my feet. Once inside I approached the attendant.

'Is he really HIV positive?' I asked.

The attendant looked at me with a startled expression and

walked around to the foot of the trolley to confirm the diagnosis. Peering at the clipboard attached to the trolley frame he began to smile and exclaimed, 'Oh no, no, no, that was the previous dead'un on the trolley.'

And with that he ripped the HIV card off and threw it in the bin.

I wondered what the hell I was doing putting myself at risk. HIV was relatively new and I had no knowledge about it or how it was spread. The risks involved had not been canvassed at all and I was angry that I had no way of finding out what I should do. It was almost as if HIV didn't exist and as long as we ignored it, it would go away. Even the fact that the trolley used for the previous body hadn't even been cleaned down was a significant worry, especially with the amount of blood produced during post-mortem examinations. Was the blood from an infected person simply being washed down the drain? I didn't know the answers and neither did the so-called experts at the time. Was the disease air-borne and therefore were we at risk during the cutting of the skull? I was not even advised to wear a face mask and neither the pathologist nor the morgue attendant wore one. I wondered what the implications were and I felt very concerned. There was far too much still unknown.

I was jolted out of my daydream by the sound of the body hitting the autopsy table as it was transferred from the trolley. Next the plastic doors were flung open and the pathologist entered the room, ready to tackle the examination. I photographed each point of interest and was shocked to see the doctor point to a particularly riveting item in the body cavity with her pen and then stand back in reflection and chew on the end of it. I could only stand silent, feeling revulsion for the complacent atmosphere I found myself in. What was going on?

No one present seemed to realise the risks to which we were all being exposed. I felt very much alone and disconnected from the outside world.

During the opening of the skull we discovered a subdural haematoma, which presented itself as a soft, closed-head injury. This meant that the dead man had suffered a blow to the head and as a result had bled between the skull and the lining of the brain. This was significant as it could have been the cause of death, or contributed to the death in conjunction with the drug overdose. We would not know the results of the drug analysis for a couple of weeks so until the doctor could assess the amount of drugs in the dead man's system, it would be hard to say what exactly caused his death. The dead man's friend had mentioned that his mate had fallen to the side and hit his head on the front steps of the house after being propped up against a wall. Was it possible that he could have survived had he been taken to hospital rather than being tucked into bed? The discovery of the head injury opened up a whole new line of inquiry and as soon as the post-mortem was completed I telephoned the detectives to inform them of our findings.

There was another risk lurking in the dirty necropsy room that day. Twenty-four hours later I came down with gastro-enteritis. Not surprisingly, the pathologist had also come down with gastro and had reported in sick. I rang her at home to talk to her about the autopsy and it was during this call that I described my symptoms and she agreed that we had both been infected by the drug addict. I had one day left before going on three week's leave and could not afford to go off sick as I had mountains of paperwork that could not wait. Thus, I dutifully struggled into work the next day to complete a number of statements that were due for court during my absence, although

I had been up most of the night vomiting and felt like death. Between bouts of vomiting and diarrhoea I sat typing until I had finished every single statement and tidied up every piece of paperwork that needed my attention.

After work I went straight to my doctor who was both shocked and angry that I had gone to work when I was so sick. She gave me two lots of prescriptions for the gastro-enteritis and warned me not to go away up north on my holiday immediately but to stay home for at least a couple of days until I was feeling a bit better. My husband was not happy about delaying our trip and insisted we leave as planned. We were staying with his parents, who lived at Laurieton on the far north coast, but I continued to deteriorate and obviously required further treatment. I visited my in-laws' family doctor, who happened to be an ex-police medical officer from Queensland. He was appalled at the state I was in. Since becoming ill, I had lost quite a bit of weight and my already small frame was looking decidedly gaunt. I told him about the drug addict and the post-mortem and he immediately responded by insisting that my illness was a result of Hurt On Duty and that I should inform the police force immediately, and reclaim any annual leave that I had taken while ill. He gave me a certificate setting out his diagnosis and told me he would be happy to talk to the police force about my illness if required.

He wrote out a script for Bactrim antibiotics. After going back to my in-laws' house I took the medication and immediately felt violently ill. My tongue began to swell, my whole body was engulfed by a hot, itchy red rash and I began to vomit violently. No matter which side I lay on, or whether I stood up or sat down, the lowest part of my body felt as if I was being burnt with a red hot poker. I honestly thought I was going to die as my tongue was beginning to completely block my mouth. My ears were itchy and ringing so I couldn't hear properly and I could only think to scream for an ambulance. My husband and his parents were panic-stricken. They rang the doctor who said I was probably allergic to the sulfur in the antibiotic and should take an antihistamine urgently. Luckily my in-laws had a packet of antihistamines in the house and within a couple of minutes of swallowing the tablet, I felt the reaction subside.

As soon as I was able to travel, my husband took me back to the doctor's surgery where he saw me straight away and did a complete check-up. He was extremely concerned with the ferocity of the reaction I had suffered and questioned me vigorously about whether I had had a similar reaction previously. I recalled that I had been prescribed a similar antibiotic some months before that had caused an itchy rash, but nothing to the degree I had suffered earlier that day. He told me about the cumulative effect of this type of allergic reaction and explained that each time the patient is exposed to sulfur the reaction will be more severe than the previous episode. Based on the reaction I had suffered, he felt that should I inadvertently take any medication containing sulfur again, it could be fatal.

I wondered how much worse I could get. The doctor assured me I would recover, but that it would take at least a couple of weeks. He advised me to eat whatever I felt like as I had lost so much weight. He also asked me about my psychological state because I appeared to him to be quite subdued. I hadn't noticed that I had sunk to such a low ebb, although when he asked I realised I was not my usual happy self. We discussed my work and he suggested I should seek counselling through the police welfare if I felt that things were getting on top of me. But I believed that once I was well again I would be fine. Only the fact that I was feeling so ill made me appear to be down. On top of this, I found my husband to be very unsympathetic. Whenever I was sick he treated it more like a hindrance than anything else. He had complained to me that I was 'wrecking his break' and he seemed to think I was making the whole illness up. It wasn't until I had the reaction to the sulfur and the doctor explained to him that I was extremely ill with gastroenteritis that he showed any sign of concern.

In all it took seventeen days for me to recover and that happened to be the time I was due to return to work. My annual leave had been a total right-off. On my return I submitted forms to have my annual leave recredited due to being hurt on duty. I had followed the correct procedure by informing my supervisor immediately the doctor had diagnosed the illness and because of the medical report I submitted I thought I would be recredited my leave without question. Instead, I was hauled up before the district superintendent to explain why I had taken so much time off sick. I was appalled to realise I was being paraded and had a notation on my service register to say that I had taken far too much sick leave and in future was not to be trusted unless I presented a doctor's certificate. Needless to say, my hurt on duty application was denied.

I was astounded to learn that the hierarchy now regarded me not as a dedicated member of the service, but as someone who was unwilling to work. Naively, I had thought it was obvious and evident to the powers that be that I was one hundred per cent dedicated to policing and that my work came first, above and beyond anything else in my life. I was starting to realise that good work and dedication were not necessarily recognised.

The whole situation was made more unbelievable by the fact that my boss Pieter knew full well that I had been infected during the post-mortem. But even *his* word carried no weight. The decision had been made. I was now branded a hypochondriac, or worse still, a liar and careless about my job. This hurt me deeply. Anyone who knew me knew I was passionate about police work. Now I was going to be disadvantaged for the rest of my career. That one notation on my file would crop up whenever the time came for promotion or consideration to be included in special duties, all because I did my job without complaint and contracted gastro-enteritis from a dirty, dead drug addict. If this was any indication of how the police force looked after its workers I hoped to God I didn't get sick ever again. I wondered how I would have been treated if I had in fact contracted HIV or hepatitis.

I made a decision not to take any more sick leave, to prove I was not rorting the system, and in this way I hoped to repair some of the damage done to my reputation. I dreaded the possibility that I could be dragged out of the area of policing I loved and sent back to general duties. I was determined to continue forensic work, especially since I'd struggled through without training to get to the stage where I felt confident to do the work. I understood better now what Pieter had meant when he suggested keeping any stress between ourselves. The hierarchy was not to be trusted. Any inkling of 'weakness' amongst the scientific staff and out you went.

# 12 Losing the plot

In 1989, Shane and I were both sent to do the crime scene examiners course at the Sydney Police Centre and it was at this course that we realised how inadequate our training had been. We also realised that we were working under very different circumstances to our counterparts in the city office, who were given much more training, supervision and time to adjust to forensic work before being sent out on the job.

At the end of the course, Shane and I had several lengthy assignments to complete in a relatively short time. This added extra pressure to our already hectic schedule. In between attending crime scenes and working overtime we tried to help each other finish our assignments. I felt I was almost at breaking point when I had one day left to finalise my submission. Both of us had worked the day shift and we decided to stay back and finish our assignments. At around 6.45 p.m. I was called to a fatal car accident, which meant I would almost certainly be working through to midnight to finish my assignment after I returned. I was swearing and cursing all the way to the scene, leaving Shane at the office to get his finished.

When I got there, I found that the road had been blocked off with witches' hats to stop traffic passing through. I drove up to the young constable, who was leaning against the police truck, and blew the horn thinking he would move the cones to let me pass. He lazily turned the other way as if to say, 'Move them yourself.' I flew out of the car and, grabbing each cone one by one, hurled them at him in a fit of anger, yelling abuse and finally telling him to put the fucking things back himself. Then I jumped back into the car, slammed the door and drove off like a maniac. A couple of hundred metres down the road I parked the car and walked over to the accident location. I wasn't impressed with what I saw. The scene consisted of a sedan in the middle of the bridge running over Dead Man's Creek, a car trailer with a station wagon dangling precariously over the side and a lone motorbike some distance away, smashed to smithereens. This was the carnage left after the sedan, which was towing the trailer with an illegally heavy load, had come hurtling down the curved incline leading onto the bridge. The driver had lost control and the trailer, swinging from side to side, had snapped the bolt coupling it to the car. The trailer then broke free shooting along on the wrong side of the road, overtaking the sedan and eventually colliding head-on with the oncoming motorbike. The accident had occurred in the centre of the bridge, giving the motorbike rider absolutely no chance. The runaway trailer speared him several metres over the guard rail and into the bush. The young man died on impact.

My main objective was to get the job completed as quickly as possible so I could get back to finishing my assignment. The first thing I noticed was a yellow chalk mark on the roadway where something had been removed. Turning around, I yelled at the top of my voice, 'Who drew this mark on the roadway?'

A young constable approached me and began to explain why he had moved vital evidence. I was in no mood for stupidity and interrupted, tearing strips off him for tampering with the crime scene. After my over-the-top display of foul language and abuse, the poor fellow calmly explained that the ambulance drove into the scene and would have run over the bolt that was sitting on the roadway. Because he presumed this was vital evidence, he had removed it so it wouldn't get damaged. I promptly apologised, realising I'd been out of order. As he walked away, I stood in the roadway and told myself to calm down, utterly shocked at my lack of control. One minute I was sympathetic at a scene, the next I was angry. Once I'd been able to take things in my stride. Now, fine cracks in my psyche were starting to appear.

As the sun set over the roadway, the tall trees threw shadows over the road, giving me no more than ten minutes to get my photographs done. If I failed to finish before the sun disappeared, it would mean calling the lighting truck and further delays in completing the scene. I hurried around the roadway taking photographs with the camera on the tripod to take advantage of the best timing exposures for the lighting conditions. Once I had finished the photographs, I took measurements of the roadway by torchlight and finally finished my notes by the interior light of the police car. I made my way back to the station, picking up a meal for Shane and myself on the way. It was 9 p.m. by the time I reached the office and we gulped our food down quickly so we could get back to work on our assignment. At 10.30 p.m. we had all but finished, so we called it a day. I was on call for the night so there was still the possibility of more work to be done. I was utterly exhausted and grateful that it turned out to be a quiet night.

Over the next couple of months I found myself becoming more and more affected by the steady stream of depressing jobs I was attending. I became quite jumpy and Shane said he was feeling the same way. The fight or flight response was a constant reminder of my deteriorating sense of well-being. I would jump when the telephone rang, or at the slightest noise. I even noticed that my hands would tremble after hearing a loud noise or when left alone with a dead body. My nerves were primed and I could be spooked by the simplest of things, like a paper bag blowing in the wind or a small branch falling from a tree. It was like my body was prepared for the worst and I lived in a constant, adrenaline-fuelled state of red alert.

I also noticed a change in Barry. We sat opposite each other in the office and would often talk about our work. Barry started to talk about how he felt when he was faced with death, and his way of coping involved a minute's silence and saying a prayer over each dead body before he left the scene. He also made reference to his conversations with God during which he would describe how God would talk to him and he, in turn, would talk to God. I wasn't sure whether Barry was actually hearing voices, or whether it was a matter of having a conversation with God in his mind. But I would listen intently, mindful not to make judgement as we all found our own special way of dealing with death. I must admit that after Barry had told me about his prayer method, I used it myself a couple of times, saying a short verse to myself when I thought it was appropriate. In some small way I did feel a little calmer after leaving the scene when I had said a prayer but I was unsure whether it made it right in the case of suicide. I began to struggle with this particular fact because although I believed suicide was wrong, I could see in some cases why the person had ended their life. This was a struggle, a battle of my conscience and something I couldn't speak about to anyone, not even to Barry.

One night around 10 p.m. I was called out to a dead'un, who had been washed up on a small sandy beach in an isolated area along the banks of the Georges River. From information gathered by the general duties officers at the scene, it appeared the man had been in the water for a number of days. When I arrived I was greeted by two police constables standing beside the police truck. With a torch they indicated the body of the dead man some distance away down an embankment. They had obviously decided not to stand too close to the corpse. I immediately realised how dark it was and asked if the paddy wagon headlights could be turned on and pointed towards the dead man. I also started up the scientific vehicle and shone its headlights in the direction of the sandy beach.

Walking down the embankment alone, with only the light from the cars above and a small torch, I headed toward the dead man. Neither constable was interested in accompanying me; instead, they stood with their backs turned, chatting. I placed my camera bag down beside the body and bent down to take a better look. Staring straight into my eyes was the contorted face of a man who had been nibbled on by passing fish as he floated around the river. His chest was bloated and he looked like the Michelin Man. One eye was missing and the other one protruded, grotesquely swollen, like a figure from a horror movie. I struggled to breath, overcome by the stench of his rotting body.

After taking photographs, I began to examine the man for

any signs of injury. After putting on rubber gloves I bent down beside his body and picked up his right hand. I was looking for defensive wounds, which may have been evidence that the man had been involved in a struggle. As I held his hand in mine I felt it pull away and, shocked, I threw the arm back onto the sand, hearing it hit the ground with a thud. I jumped up and took a couple of quick steps back, holding my heart as it thumped in my chest. For one awful instant I thought he was alive, and this gave me the fright of my life. Looking up the embankment I checked to see if either of the constables had noticed but luckily they were still engrossed in conversation. Once I had it in my head that the man had moved I was completely spooked. I just wanted to get out of there fast. Trouble was, I still had a job to complete and I resentfully resigned myself to the fact that I had no choice but to finish the examination. In the dark I proceeded to remove items of clothing, roll the corpse over and check every square inch of his body for signs of trauma. Unsure as to the exact cause of death, I requested the attendance of the government medical officer, who would have been of great assistance. I was disappointed when he sent a message back declining to be disturbed at 11 p.m. at night, preferring to view the body at the morgue the next day.

I completed my examination as best I could under the conditions but I was disturbed to think that I had considered for a moment that a dead body could come alive. My reaction was ridiculous considering that the man was in an advanced state of decomposition and had obviously been dead for several days. My mind was starting to play tricks on me and I no longer seemed to have control over my startled reaction. I was relieved that no one had seen my irrational response as I was quite embarrassed by it.

Shane was also displaying startled responses and gave me and others present a hell of a fright when he was attempting to gain access to a suicide victim inside a locked stationwagon. A number of police were standing around the rear tailgate when Shane climbed into the back seat and tried to unlock the driver's side door from behind the dead man's head. All of a sudden he came backwards at a hundred miles an hour and jumped clear of the car, sending everyone around him scuttling in all directions. After gasping a few swear words he explained that he thought he had felt the dead man moving and he had involuntarily run for his life. I knew from experience about being trapped in a confined space with a dead body. It had given me the heebie-jeebies and a panicky desire to escape. I understood Shane's reaction but the others at the scene all thought it was funny.

After doing crime scene work for fifteen months, I had overcome my initial concerns about my lack of training, and was able to examine crime scenes adequately. I started to wonder about how or why these desperate or unfortunate victims had found themselves in these situations. I became more aware of the extended family and the impact these deaths had on them. It almost seemed like I crossed the line from being a detached professional doing a job to a young woman overwhelmed by the unbearable pain of others. My emotions began to swing from one extreme to the other and this was something I had not experienced before. I was normally in control of my emotions but now I found this was no longer the case. I became extremely distressed at the death of my two cats, who were run over outside The Dump one Saturday night. After crying on and off for twenty-four hours, I slipped into a deep sadness that lasted two weeks. I felt I couldn't get over the death of the two cats. Even though I knew my reaction was out of proportion, I couldn't snap out of it. After this I felt a numbness take over and it was as if I had no emotions left. I was completely drained.

Up until this point I had only had one experience of seeing someone in death after I had known them in life. Usually the people who died at crime scenes were unknown to me. But when the duty operations inspector gave me the job over the phone, I immediately identified the familiar address. A young woman had overdosed and I was required to attend and examine the scene. Picking up on my reaction, the inspector asked if I knew the occupants of the premises and I confirmed that I did; it was the prostitute and heroin addict I had met many times before while working at Macquarie Fields police station. The last time I had seen her was when she'd reported a break-in. She had refused to let us in, but had pushed a handwritten note listing all the things that had been stolen underneath the flyscreen door.

I wasn't looking forward to attending the scene. It was 4.30 a.m. and the area was notorious for housing heavy crooks who wouldn't hesitate to attack police. Also, the dead woman suffered from hepatitis B and possibly HIV.

When I arrived I found a lone general duties constable standing on guard at the door. He was keen to get back to the station and left shortly after I arrived, leaving me alone at the scene. The air was heavy with the stench of body odour and rotting food and I covered my nose as I stood surveying the scene. Inside was utter chaos. The dead woman was lying face down on a filthy mattress pushed up against the lounge room wall. Soiled bedding littered the floor along with empty food wrappers, cartons and rubbish. The carpet was completely covered in stains and debris. So this was the end of the road for one of our regular customers, I thought, as I looked at her lifeless body, pale and stiff among all her worldly possessions.

I went about my usual routine, taking notes, drawing diagrams and photographing the mayhem before me. When it came to examining the body, I put on two pairs of gloves, just in case. I grabbed the woman by the shoulders in an attempt to roll her over but she was stiff as a board. Obviously, she had been lying there for some time. As I turned her over onto her back I was met by her staring eyes, wide open and glazed, still looking out of it on drugs. I grimaced and turned away.

It took some time to get under the multiple layers of clothing to inspect her skin. Under her sleeves I managed to find the needle tracks I was looking for. She was an absolute mess, she had abused her body with sex and drugs and was covered in bruises in varying stages from purple to yellow, giving her an almost colourful hue. It was strange being alone with her in silence. In life she had been such an abusive woman, loud and obnoxious, with disjointed, rambling speech. I had never known her to be quiet when in the presence of police; now she had no choice but to lie still and silent while I processed her in accordance with the law. After completing the job, I watched the body snatchers place her in a black plastic bag, just like garbage waiting to be collected and taken to the tip.

By mid-1989 I found I was starting to identify with aspects of jobs I attended. This became clear to me when I attended the death of a seven-year-old girl. She had been riding on a tractor driven by a seventeen-year-old boy while he was slashing grass on a property. She was killed when she jumped from the moving tractor and fell under the slasher blades. When I got to the scene, I was told that the mother of the child had gone to the toilet at the time of the accident. Now that I have children of my own, I have great difficulty leaving them unsupervised. Over and over my mind has replayed the death of the little girl while her mother was in the toilet. It continues to haunt me that a child could be allowed to ride on a tractor pulling a slasher, as if it was an amusement ride.

Feelings of anger and frustration engulfed me as I worked at the scene. When I got to the morgue later that day to examine the girl, I was distressed to see her lying on the steel trolley dressed in a little pair of jodhpurs and boots just like the ones I'd always worn as a child. The tears welled up and I felt this horrible ache in my heart. I could see myself lying there wearing those jodhpurs, I could almost feel the snug fit of the material against my legs. I looked around the morgue. I hated the godforsaken place, it was cold and ugly and I just wanted to obliterate the whole day from my mind.

The morgue attendant jolted me back to reality by pointing out the little girl's injuries. He pulled back her beautiful hair to reveal a horrendous gash in the side of her head. I pointed my camera at it and glassily looked through the viewfinder to get the best angle. The injury to her leg was just as bad as the head wound, and I photographed it too, as required. I was so absorbed in the little girl that I hadn't noticed the body of an old lady lying on a trolley against the far wall. The sound of the morgue buzzer rang out and the morgue attendant scuttled over to the old lady, laughing as he went. 'Shit, that's the old girl's rels here to do an ID,' I heard him mutter under his breath. I was appalled to see a copy of *Playboy* sitting open on the dead woman's chest. He hurriedly pulled a white sheet up over the body up to her chin concealing the magazine underneath, then scuttled over to the side door and spoke to a uniformed police officer standing on the other side. I was horrified to see the morgue attendant wheel the trolley over to the viewing window and position the old lady in front of the curtain. With a wide sweep he drew the curtain back and I could see an elderly gentleman standing with a young woman behind the glass partition. Unable to hear what was said, I could only watch as the old man nodded his head in agreement. With that, the constable indicated that they were finished and the curtain was drawn back over the glass window.

I could hardly believe what I had just witnessed. It was utterly repulsive to me to think that the dead woman had just been identified by her loved ones with a *Playboy* magazine concealed under the sheet that covered her body. I stood glued to the spot, watching the morgue attendant with contempt as he hastily buzzed around the cold room, avoiding eye contact as he shuttled the trolleys back into place before thrusting them into their refrigerated compartments. This was a matter I intended to take up with my supervisor first thing on Monday morning. As I turned and walked toward the loading dock I almost felt I had betrayed the little girl by leaving her in the care of that man.

Outside in the dark I stood beside the police car arguing with myself as to whether I should go back into the morgue and confront the attendant. Reason told me it was the wrong course of action, but I still felt guilty driving away and leaving him in charge. That night I lay awake staring at the ceiling well into the early hours until I finally drifted into a fitful sleep. Torturous images of the little girl's pale and flawless face gave me no peace.

I felt particularly down when I dragged myself out of bed at 6.30 a.m. It was a typical Monday morning at the office, phones ringing, messages piled up on desks and staff waiting at the doorway with urgent inquiries. I didn't have time to see Pieter about the events at the morgue and by mid-morning I was still wading through piles of paperwork and answering the incessantly ringing telephone.

I was interrupted by the arrival of a good-looking young probationary constable, uniform sparkling and standing at attention at the office door. Pieter introduced him as Richard and asked if I'd spend a little time showing him what type of duties the scientific section performed as part of his induction training. It was important to me that he be given a comprehensive knowledge of procedures to be followed whenever attending a scene that required scientific examination.

I grabbed a chair and pulled it up beside me at my desk, gesturing for him to take a seat. We sat side by side chatting about his experiences so far and how he was coping with his first week in the job. I asked him if he'd been to the morgue yet and he nodded in agreement.

'How was it?' I asked.

'All right, I suppose,' he replied with a shrug of his shoulders.

I asked him if it was the first time he had seen a dead body and again he nodded.

'My first visit to the morgue was really bad,' I said. 'The morgue attendant brought out a stillborn baby and that was my first dead'un.'

'Yeah, I saw a little girl this morning who'd been killed by a slasher and that was pretty bad,' he said.

'That was my job from the weekend,' I said, turning to look at him. 'I was pretty upset about it. She was so beautiful.'

He nodded. 'What happened?'

I explained the events involving the death of the little girl while he listened in silence. After a short pause he looked at me.

'There's something I'm a bit worried about,' he said. 'It happened to the little girl at the morgue. I'm not sure if I should say anything.'

'What's that?' I asked.

'There were three of us pros with the induction sergeant at the morgue and we were all a bit upset seeing the little girl but no one said anything. We just stood there and looked at her while the morgue attendant pointed out her injuries. As we walked away to leave he called out, 'Bye bye' and when we turned to look at him, he had the little girl's hand in his and was using it to wave at us. Don't say anything, I don't want to get anyone into trouble, but I was pretty upset about it.'

That was exactly what I was worried about when I left the little girl at the morgue in the care of that man the night before. I felt completely defeated and convinced I had not only let the little girl down but her mother too. Richard could see I was distressed and asked if I knew the morgue attendant he had referred to.

'I most certainly do, and I intend to have him investigated.'

Richard was alarmed at my outburst. He was concerned about revealing the incident as he was new in the job and didn't want to be involved in any sensitive issues. I reassured him his name wouldn't be mentioned. Then I explained why I needed to have the incident investigated. I called Pieter over and asked to speak to him in private. After hearing the allegations Pieter agreed the matter needed to be investigated. I typed a report outlining the sequence of events and handed it to Pieter, who also made comments and forwarded it on to the district superintendent. Unfortunately the report seemed to fall on deaf ears and was most likely put into the 'too hard basket'. I was never informed of the result of any investigation.

Shortly after this incident, I was summoned to the morgue yet again. This time I was greeted at the door by a pathologist who appeared to be quite anxious. She asked me to accompany her to the area of the morgue where she had been performing a post-mortem examination on a young female. As she began to explain her observations we were interrupted by the morgue attendant, who had obviously been sent away by the doctor so she could talk to me in confidence. With his usual abrupt manner he asked me why I was there and, sensing there was a problem, I asked him to butt out. The doctor turned her head away and whispered quietly that we should adjourn to the pathologist's office where we could talk privately.

Once we were inside the office I could see the little man hovering outside with his ear attuned to our conversation. Three times throughout our talk I had to open the door and ask him to leave the area. The pathologist told me she'd attended the morgue to perform a post-mortem on a young woman who had donated her body to research after dying of a terminal disease. Although there had been a doctor's certificate issued, there was still a post-mortem examination carried out by a specialist working in that particular area of research.

As the doctor began her examination she had noted a strong smell of semen and was initially concerned about this. Then, as she continued her examinations, she came to the opening of the throat and chest cavity. Stuck down inside the throat she found a one dollar coin, and again noticed the strong odour of semen. The dead woman had been a member of the Baha'i faith and it is customary to wrap up the body in a floral shroud and place a coin on the deceased's tongue for good fortune. The doctor explained that there was no possible way the coin could have made its way down the dead woman's throat without being physically pushed or forced down by something. She was highly critical of the actions of the morgue attendant and had found him intimidating when she started the post-mortem. As there had been a death certificate issued, the morgue attendant would not have anticipated an autopsy, he would have presumed the young woman would be buried without any further examinations taking place.

I immediately contacted the area chief pathologist and asked for guidance as to the appropriate action to take under the circumstances, seeing as the only person trained and available to handle the bodies at this particular morgue was the very attendant under suspicion. I also mentioned the intimidating behaviour of the attendant towards the doctor. My instructions were to supervise the attendant while he sealed up all orifices of the body, packing them with cotton wool so as to preserve any evidence that may be present. The body was then to be wrapped and transported to Westmead as soon as possible where a further post-mortem examination would be carried out to see if blood grouping could be ascertained from swabs taken from the body.

The whole time I supervised the morgue attendant he bombarded me with questions, asking me over and over why he had to seal the orifices and where the body was going. It was a battle of wits trying to keep a close eye on his every move while he constantly tried to undermine my authority. He even went as far as to complain about the pathologist who had carried out the autopsy, demanding to know why she had called police and generally criticising her professionalism.

My attitude towards the man before me was difficult to hide, though I was aware of the very slight possibility that he may not be the perpetrator and that I should keep an open mind.

But it was difficult to speak to him or even be in his presence, and I couldn't forget the two previous incidents. I was in no mood for his antics. I tolerated him because I had no choice and needed his expertise in the morgue. I am sure that if a similar incident occurred today, it would be handled differently. I'm sure that I would not have had to rely on the one and only person trained in the morgue to attend to the body's transportation, the person under suspicion. It would have been far better if I had expelled the morgue attendant from the room and simply packed the body myself, but things were different back then and many of the protocols that are now in place did not exist in the old hospital systems.

I felt frustrated and ill-equipped to act as I would have wished, which was to take control of the incident, follow through with the body to Westmead and present myself as witness to the taking of samples and their subsequent examination. But my relatively low rank prevented me from making the necessary decisions, and the hospital system was outside my jurisdiction. My hands were tied and I could only do as I was told.

I was not surprised to learn several months later, after many phone calls to Westmead mortuary and the Division of Forensic Medicine, that no evidence or traceable blood grouping had been found.

Not speaking out about these incidents created in me a turbulent state of mind. I felt I had done all that I could to try to have the morgue attendant investigated, but unfortunately it was not to be. Was it the case that a blind eye was turned because of the difficulty of finding a replacement for him? After all, how many people want to work alone in a morgue? I believe that this was the main reason for the hospital's denial of what really went on. They simply didn't want to know. Many years later that morgue attendant was present when his own son was brought in after being killed in a motorbike accident. Did the reality of seeing his own flesh and blood in death spark a change of attitude in him? I heard he was unable to perform his duties and left the morgue, never to return.

Greg and I had moved out of The Dump and were now living in a shed on our ten-acre property. We had decked the shed out like a mini-house, with kitchen, bathroom, bedroom and a separate living area. We were quite comfortable living this way but we didn't seem to be progressing towards moving into our new home. We had discussed plans to build but could not agree on the timing, the style of house or the amount we would spend. We were drifting apart both physically and emotionally. Our opposite shifts and my endless recalls to duty meant that we spent very little time together. I was always preoccupied with the latest crime scene I had attended and had become almost unable to talk about anything else. Greg and I didn't seem to have anything in common any more and I found it increasingly uncomfortable to be in his company. I was struggling to find anything to say. I began to feel isolated both at home and at work, spending many hours on my own with no one to talk to.

I found myself constantly mulling over aspects of crime scenes that were complex and morbid. As I went about my day-to-day routine, I associated mundane occurrences with deadly consequences. A tractor being driven along the side of the road immediately reminded me of the little girl killed by the slasher and my mind would flash back to the scene. Our neighbour would cut his grass with a ride-on lawnmower and prop his three-year-old son on the seat in front. I was incensed at the sight and thought it my business to warn him of the dangers. When he continued to allow his son on the mower I was preoccupied with fears that the child would fall off and be cut by the blades. I became obsessed, thinking that an accident was just waiting to happen. I mentioned this repeatedly to Greg, who would insist it was okay. I also began to avoid certain foods. I was no longer able to eat pizza. The cheese reminded me of a suicide I had attended where the dead man lay on his back, mouth wide open displaying a yellow froth inside. The sight of pizza made me sick. I began to brood about life in general and I didn't find the typical police culture of laughing at death funny any more. It was far too serious to be funny.

Mental and physical exhaustion, combined with a relationship devoid of any emotion, finally led to the breakdown of my marriage. It didn't feel like a difficult time, we simply parted and went our separate ways. During and after the separation I felt numb. It was as if our relationship had never existed and I simply didn't have the energy to be bothered to think about it. I found a house on three hundred acres a couple of streets away owned by a friend, who generously offered to let me stay there for six months until I got on my feet again. It was important to find a house with some land as I still had Ben, my ageing galloway, and was keen to take him with me. With my horse, dog and several cats I prepared to move on.

The day I planned to move I was recalled to attend the Grafton bus crash in which twenty people lost their lives and a further twenty-two people were injured. The accident occurred at Cowper, twenty-six kilometres north of Grafton, in the early hours of Friday 20 October 1989, when a Brisbane-bound tourist coach collided head-on with a fully laden semitrailer. The collision was described as Australia's worst road accident and sparked intensive public debate about the appalling condition of the nation's roads. The bodies were to be transported to the city morgue in Sydney in a refrigerated semitrailer so scientific police could perform disaster victim identification duties. DVI is a laborious and unpleasant task: each and every body must be painstakingly examined and photographed to ascertain correct identification. Information such as dental features, fingerprints, tattoos, scars and clothing worn are recorded and then correlated with details obtained from relatives to reach a positive identification within the Coroner's guidelines. Because there were so many bodies to be identified, as many trained scientific personnel as possible were called. This stretched to the limit those police left at the stations to continue daily scientific duties. Staff were snatched from various stations with members covering other areas as well as their own to make up the shortfall. Everyone was exhausted and much-needed annual leave had to be cancelled just to keep the section running. At times there were police working up to thirty days straight.

Moving house was no excuse, so I rang my mother and asked if we could make other arrangements. She insisted the move should go ahead regardless, whether I was there or not, promising to move all my possessions with the help of family and friends while I was on duty. At the last minute I was excused from attending the bus crash as the already depleted staff at Macquarie Fields would not have been able to cover our workload.

Two months later, on 22 December at 3.35 a.m., there was a second bus crash, this time at Clybucca, north of Kempsey. Thirty-three passengers and two drivers were killed. This time I was a couple of days into my annual leave when the phone rang and I was informed of a possible recall to duty to cover the section while Whayne attended the morgue to perform

DVI. A recall of this type would incur considerable expense to the department, so it was the last resort. I was available to return to duty but was pissed off at the prospect of spending the Christmas break working when it was finally my turn to take the holiday break. Typically, the police were able to find some other poor, overworked person to cover the area and I was spared the recall over Christmas.

It was a shitty time for Whayne, who had worked close to thirty days straight and was now required to spend Boxing Day and Christmas Day at the morgue assisting with the identification of thirty-five bodies and their parts. He spent two days at the morgue, firstly issuing each body bag with a morgue admission number as it was removed from the refrigerated truck and placed in the morgue. Once inside, he had to open each bag and write a description of its contents in the morgue admission book. This entailed opening thirty-five bags containing human remains along with three further bags that were full of body parts. After completing this duty he volunteered to continue assisting in the morgue and was assigned the job of removing the jewellery, personal effects, cash and papers from every dead body, cataloguing these for possible identification by the deceased relatives. It was a foul job. I had planned to spend Christmas night with Whayne and his wife Connie, but when I arrived Whayne had still not returned home from work and we sat for hours waiting for him. Finally he came home, still wearing his filthy overalls. Over Christmas dinner Whayne described what was involved in removing the jewellery from severed limbs or mangled pieces of flesh. After listening to Whayne I was very glad I had been spared such work.

Kempsey was the second bus crash in NSW in as many weeks, culminating in many fatalities. The scientific-investigation section was stretched to the limit but as usual got the job done owing to the tremendous efforts of its members. As luck had it, we had undergone training in DVI procedures a couple of months before, so were well prepared for a disaster of the magnitude of the bus crashes at Grafton and Kempsey. Unfortunately for the people of Newcastle, more bad luck came in the form of a third disaster, when at 10.35 a.m. on 28 December 1989, an earthquake hit the heart of the city.

# 13 Newcastle earthquake

The morning of 18 December 1989 started out hot for two fourteen-year-old boys living in the far south-western outskirts of Sydney. Making the most of the school holidays, they planned to spend their day swimming and exploring the dense bushland surrounding a popular swimming hole known as the Potholes on the Bargo River, near Tahmoor. By late afternoon they were missing, sparking a full-scale search of the area until nightfall. The evening news featured pictures of the boys, identifying them as Jaymie Egner and Matthew Kelly. Standing in my living room as the news item flashed across the screen I listened intently to the details. An overwhelming feeling of foreboding engulfed me, and even though I was alone, I silently stood to attention in respect for the dead. I was sure my intuition was right and I somehow knew the boys were dead, but why was I thinking this way? I felt disturbed and unsettled.

Each day passed with the evening news broadcasting the same headlines – the mysterious disappearance of the teenage boys. Day after day, a little more information was released, giving the public an insight into the lives of the distraught families desperately searching for their children. They were from different backgrounds and had different views on why the boys had disappeared. I believe the Kellys thought there was a chance the boys could have run away, while the Egner family never believed that to be true. As Christmas crept closer the search intensified and still no clues surfaced; Jaymie and Matthew had simply vanished without a trace. The parents made an impassioned plea for any information to be brought forward, but it was becoming apparent that the boys would never receive their Christmas presents, wrapped and waiting under their respective Christmas trees since before their disappearance.

Sydney watched and waited while police and emergency services searched the bushland in sweltering heat between Thirlmere Lakes, Tahmoor and Pheasants Nest day after day.

Although I was enjoying my annual leave and my new-found freedom from married life, I was constantly in contact with Whayne at the office and he kept me informed of the police efforts in relation to the disappearance of the two boys. Gossip was running rife and theories of paedophile rings and drug barons were starting to circulate in the local area. I voiced my concern that the boys would be found dead when I returned to duty and that I would be responsible for the scientific investigation. This was dismissed as being our usual negative talk. Then the Kempsey bus crash momentarily took over the news headlines until Christmas and beyond. Sydney was still reeling after the devastating loss of so many lives when disaster struck again.

Mid-morning on 28 December 1989, I was at home talking on the phone to a girlfriend who lived at Wollongong. Jane was a policewoman with whom I had become close friends while working in general duties at Campbelltown, and she was now engaged to Roger, my old colleague. We were discussing the usual police issues when all of a sudden I felt a shudder and the phone line crackled for a couple of seconds.

'What was that?' I asked.

'I don't know, but did you feel something?'

It felt like the whole house had moved and it was a strange sensation. I couldn't decide if it was real or if I'd imagined it. We continued our conversation, dismissing the strange interference, and finally hung up. Soon after a radio news broadcast reported that there had been an earthquake, the epicentre of which was in Newcastle, two hours north of Sydney in New South Wales. I listened intently throughout the day as the devastating news of the destruction of many buildings, including the Workers' Club in the heart of the city, filtered through. Emergency workers rushed to the scene and were desperately trying to find survivors buried under the rubble of the collapsed buildings.

Shortly after the second bus crash, all members of the scientific investigation section had been issued with a directive memorandum instructing them to telephone their respective offices in the wake of any further disasters and make themselves available for disaster victim identification duties. I immediately rang Pieter, who was also on annual leave. He told me that a disaster plan had already been put into place and I would be recalled to duty to attend the Newcastle disaster scene. Teams of three were prepared and I was nominated to attend the scene as part of the last DVI group to process the forensic identification of bodies and their remains as required by the State Coroner.

I was directed to travel to Newcastle with Pieter on 30 December to relieve the preceding DVI team, who had almost completed their forty-eight-hour shift. By this stage several people were listed as missing and two men in particular were known to be trapped in the underground car park of the Newcastle Workers' Club. One was believed to be the workers' club handyman, the other, a friend who would often attend the club and talk to his mate while he performed odd jobs. The evening news swung into action telling the general public about the disaster scene. Footage of rescue workers gallantly trying to rescue survivors filled the screen. Human chains were used to pass out rubble in an effort to uncover survivors and at no time did anyone consider that they were putting their lives at risk by entering the unstable remains of the collapsed building. It was estimated that there were thirteen dead, with the possibility of more casualties trapped in their cars in the underground car park. I had been planning a New Year's Eve party and had invited thirty people but now I wasn't sure if I was going to be home in time to greet the guests, let alone prepare food. Once again I rang my mother, who agreed to let the partygoers in should I be held up in Newcastle. With the impending job hanging over my head, I wasn't in the mood for partying and was annoyed that I'd have to let family and friends down. Even if I returned home in time for the party I was unsure what state I would be in. I had already been told that there was no accommodation arranged at Newcastle and that I would be performing continuous duty until the job was done.

I went into work and retrieved my kit bag, which was packed with overalls, boots and hard hat, adding an extra set of clothes for the return journey home. On the morning of 30 December Pieter collected me from home and we drove the three-hour journey to Newcastle. By now there were two bodies confirmed as being in the rubble of the workers' club and possibly more. Excavation had been continuing twenty-four hours a day since the earthquake and we would be on standby to perform DVI when the bodies were eventually located.

As we entered the outskirts of the city I was struck by the total silence. We were waved through several roadblocks and given directions on how to get to the workers' club through the devastation. Many streets were blocked with barricades warning of gaping holes in the pavement or structures hanging precariously over the road. It was a strange sight; an abandoned city torn apart by nature. We wove our way through the streets until we came across a hive of activity centred around the workers' club. I saw the Salvos' mini tent city of food stalls where you could go to eat or drink at any time of the day or night.

We were ushered inside under a covered section of the car park adjoining the collapsed parking station and greeted by a couple of scientific colleagues, still wearing their filthy overalls; they were pleased to see us. We shouted above the noise of heavy earth-moving equipment, working below in the collapsed building site of the workers' club. After a debrief we were taken on a tour of the devastated city by Detective Sergeant Paul Horton. He pointed out the police station, hospital and morgue. As he drove I gazed out the window, amazed at the emptiness of the city. Barricades were blocking many streets and it was difficult to find our way around the damaged road system. As we drove along beside the railway line I saw a goods train in the distance weaving along the track in our general direction. It came closer as we approached a level crossing with lights and bells ringing. Paul drove straight up to the level crossing, accelerating towards the boom gates.

'No, stop!' Pieter yelled.

I hung onto the seat, frozen to the spot as I saw the train bearing down on us, horn blaring. Paul drove straight around the boom gates, weaving in and out as he crossed the tracks within seconds of the train passing.

'Fuck, what did you do that for?' I said, shocked that we were all still in one piece, as he continued to drive along the empty street.

'Don't worry, we had plenty of time.' His voice showed no emotion.

I thought he'd lost the plot. Whether he was dead tired or just not thinking straight I wasn't sure, but I wanted to get out of the car as soon as possible.

After pulling up in the morgue car park, Pieter and I followed Paul inside where we met the previous DVI team. We were given a rundown on the procedures they had put into place and handed blank forms in triplicate for later use when we returned to the morgue to identify any further bodies. I was glad to be given instruction because I had no real experience in DVI and I was eager to find out as much as possible before handover. The outgoing DVI team had finished their task and were now free to return to Sydney, their shift complete. After a quick tour of the morgue we returned to the car and headed back to the excavation site to watch and wait.

Pieter and I approached and introduced ourselves to the rescue squad guys who had been working tirelessly in an effort to find the two missing men crushed beneath the multistorey car park. As we stood beside the great gaping hole that was once the club car park, we strained to hear over the grinding sound of the excavation equipment revving and churning. The bucket dug up piles of rubble, depositing it next to the site. The smell of diesel fumes filled the air as they plumed out of the exhaust and filled the confines of the rescue area. Overalls, boots and hard hats had to be worn at all times as the site was unstable, with movement expected and the possibility of the building collapsing further during the excavation. Hanging precariously overhead was a huge concrete slab suspended by unstable steel reinforcing that was slowly breaking away. This was the entry point to the excavation site and the rescue guys warned us of the dangers of the area for anyone attempting to gain access to the ruins.

This was the most accessible point into the collapsed car park and we had to scramble down the piles of rubble to inspect any possible sightings of bodies. We had been instructed not to stand under the concrete slab but to quickly slide down the rubble and, under no circumstances, to linger in the vicinity of the overhanging slab. A siren would sound when a possible sighting was made and all excavation would cease so that the rescue squad personnel could take over recovery with hand tools. The siren was loud enough to be heard some distance from the site so all personnel could return to the scene and commence search and rescue as soon as possible. Pieter and I were joined by Chris, another member of the scientific investigation section, and we decided then and there who would do what when the bodies were located. I was to be photographer, while the other two members of the team were to be handler and writer.

Minutes turned into hours as I wandered around the site waiting for the siren to go off. I drank coffee and ate hot dogs supplied by the Salvos, chatting to the volunteer workers to pass the time. I sat in the police vehicle for hours on end as there was simply nowhere else to go to get some sleep but the constant sound of the excavation machines made this impossible. Pieter eventually found an old mattress which was in a dark room just off the excavation area and he tried unsuccessfully to get a little sleep there. When it was my turn, I too, attempted to lie down and get some sleep there, but the ground literally shook with the vibration of the earth-moving equipment just a stone's throw away. I gave up and instead wandered around the site, lit now by emergency lighting, trying to keep occupied until the time came for us to do our work.

Every couple of hours the siren would go off and we would all assemble beside the gaping hole watching hopefully as the rescue squad inspected the site. Each time it was a false alarm and, as the night dragged on, I was disappointed over and over when nothing was sighted and the machines started up once again.

At around 4 a.m. some cars were located and recovered from within the car park, lifted to the surface in the claws of the earth-moving machine, dangling precariously as they were swung over to the holding area. Each one was crushed beyond recognition, making it difficult to establish the make and model. With torches we inspected the cabin of each car in an effort to locate possible occupants and it was a relief that no one had been trapped inside the wreckage. Luckily, the owners of these cars had parked and left before the earthquake. After photographing and recording details of each vehicle, the information was relayed back to the station for the owners to be notified. It was a strange sight to see the cars lined up side by side, crushed beyond belief. The area resembled a junk yard of once shiny new cars which had been reduced to twisted metal.

Finally, just before daybreak, the alarm sounded once again

and we all scrambled to the edge of the scene to get a good look at what was going on. This time the rescue squad guys yelled out it was a find and we all gave a sigh of relief. The DVI team was now required to record the scene before further rubble was moved, so with my camera bag strapped over my shoulder, I struggled to clamber down into the cavity of the building site, stepping over exposed reinforcing and sliding down great slabs of concrete, stacked up like a collapsed deck of cards. At ground level the glare of the rescue squad lights was momentarily blinding until my eyes adjusted to the contrasting shades of black and white. Above me a single light illuminated the scene and a backdrop of poker machines teetering on the edge silently watched our every move. Through a small hole cut in the concrete slab, I could see the top of a human skull covered in dust with just a hint of short dark hair matted with blood. I took a number of photographs depicting the position of the body entombed between steel reinforcing, stone and concrete, while Chris took notes describing the position of the body and its surroundings.

From then on it was a painstakingly slow process as the rescue squad carefully cut away the concrete slab with a circular saw, removing each piece of rubble by hand so as not to disturb the dead man. Each stage was meticulously recorded until we uncovered the body of a second man lying directly under the first. He was curled up in a ball resembling the foetal position, his arms entwined around his mate, who was still holding a shifter in his hand. Both men were given an individual disaster victim identification number, which was to appear in every photograph taken at the sight and later at the morgue. It was testament to the wonderful job done during the excavation process that both men were found intact amongst the rubble and brought out of the scene in one piece. The men were each secured in a body bag, placed on a Stokes litter (metal stretcher) and then carried up the concrete embankment to a holding area where they were placed in a far corner. Here we conducted a further examination of the bodies and photographed them thoroughly before transportation to the morgue. It was now three days since the earthquake had struck and both men had started to decompose, filling the air with a putrid smell. I wasn't looking forward to spending time at the morgue in close proximity to them but was keen to get the job completed. I was tired and dirty and after waiting around with nothing to do for so long, eager to finally get it over with. The government contractors were called and the bodies ferried over to the mortuary with police in tow.

It wasn't until I got to the morgue and spoke to the attendant that I realised the police would be conducting the whole DVI procedure without assistance from the resident medical staff. There simply weren't enough assistants to cope with such an event, they explained, and the one morgue attendant on duty had to attend to all the usual admissions at the morgue as well. I had always been supervised by either the resident pathologist or morgue attendant on duty and I felt quite uneasy at first.

Pieter took charge and quickly got the first identification under way. We removed one of the victims from the body bag and together lifted him up onto the steel table. The smell was overpowering and that, together with the feel of his broken body as we lifted him, disgusted me. I momentarily turned away to gather my composure, hoping the others didn't think I was weak. Next we lifted the other body up onto the steel table so that we had them lying side by side in preparation for identification. I was having trouble breathing so I asked Pieter if we could wear some kind of mask to alleviate the putrid working conditions.

After consulting with the morgue attendant, three masks fitted with air filters and resembling something out of the *Planet of the Apes* were supplied and we all placed the cumbersome contraptions over our nose and mouth. It was difficult working with the masks in place as they were heavy and awkward to wear, but they did provide some relief from the stench in the air. It was difficult to speak with them on so we had to resort to sign language or yelling to be heard.

Back to the body of the first man and our task was to remove and document clothing worn and any other items found on the body. We found a wallet with driver's licence and personal papers inside his back trouser pocket. These items were placed on the end of the table and photographed together with the DVI number. Pieter then started with the removal of clothing after which the bodies had to be washed down with a hand-held shower and cleaned with a brush. This was a difficult task because of the state of decomposition and numerous injuries. There were multiple injuries and bones were exposed with flesh hanging from the protruding skeletal remains. It was difficult to pull items of clothing over protruding bones and Pieter struggled with a sock that he was attempting to remove. His teeth were clenched as he pulled the sock over the ankle bone in an attempt to free it. Finally it gave way, flicking him in the face. He stumbled backwards throwing the sock down on the table in disgust. He turned and walked out the door leaving it swinging as he left. It was time for a breather. We were all under enormous stress and although I wanted to get the examination over with, I simply couldn't go on. I needed to get out of that room and get some fresh air too, even if it was just for a minute.

I followed Pieter outside and placed my hand on his back as I approached.

'That sock was disgusting,' I said. 'When it hit you in the face it was too much.'

'Sorry, Ed, I couldn't take any more. I needed to get out for a minute,' he said.

Ed was Pieter's nickname for me. He often called me this when we were out working on a job together. What was he apologising for? It was a shit of a job. Most people wouldn't even be able to handle looking at a decomposing body, let alone undressing one. It wasn't a crime to be affected by what we were dealing with, because even with a professional approach it was hard to keep a barrier in place. Sometimes it all got too much and I really felt the strain. The smell had got right into my nostrils and I couldn't escape the disgusting odour. We decided to have a cup of coffee and as there was nowhere to sit, I squatted down in the gutter at the entrance to the morgue dock. Pieter and Chris wandered around aimlessly, sipping out of their styrofoam cups, passing me like a parade as they walked around in circles. I commented to Pieter that I could still smell the bodies and he agreed that he was having trouble getting the smell out of his mind too. I thought my senses were playing tricks on me until the morgue attendant approached and told me I was sitting right under the air-conditioning outlet and the smell from inside was being vented right into my face. I really was smelling the putrid air, it wasn't just in my mind. I stood up with a start, spilling coffee down the front of my overalls. I'd just spent half my break breathing in putrid air and I might as well have stood inside the morgue and drunk my coffee over the dead bodies.

Reluctantly we all filed back into the autopsy room and fitted our masks around our faces, Chris making no comment but silently getting back to work. Pieter picked up a pair of surgical scissors and this time started cutting the clothing away, making its removal much easier. Once the body was naked we washed it down with a scrubbing brush and it was now ready for identification photographs. I laboriously photographed each section of the body with the identification number in place, the body was rolled over and held at an angle to cover each section. At the completion of our examination we moved onto the body of the second deceased man and repeated the whole exercise. Part way through the task I felt something crunch under my work boots. I bent down to see what it was and discovered one of my garnet earrings lying on the wet, soiled morgue floor. I couldn't bring myself to pick it up, even though it was an expensive piece of jewellery, as it was now contaminated with body fluids. My former husband had given it to me as a Valentine's Day gift and it was now lost forever. I later threw the matching earring in the morgue bin convinced that not even sterilisation of the dirty earring would clean it sufficiently for me to feel comfortable about putting it back in my ear.

Pieter and I had now been working for more than twenty hours straight and we were both feeling tired and irritable with the knowledge that there was nowhere to rest. Now we were faced with the long drive home and neither of us was in any fit state to drive. We headed for the Newcastle police station to report to the crime scene office and inform them that the job had been finalised. After a short conversation with the section leader I went to the female locker room where I could at least get cleaned up and change my clothes. We then went to the meal room where breakfast was offered for the large contingent of police who were still working at the earthquake site.

Around 1 p.m. Pieter and I headed for home, but only got as

far as Belmont when the pager went off and we were directed to find a telephone and contact the duty operations inspector. Pieter was rostered as the on-call officer and it was apparent that there were jobs waiting for him back at Macquarie Fields. We pulled into Belmont police station where Pieter made a phone call and took down the details of the outstanding jobs to be completed upon his return to the office. I know how tired I felt, and the thought of having to continue duty after such a long shift was unbelievable, but Pieter had no choice. Instead of going home to sleep he was now forced to continue duty until he had completed all outstanding jobs. As I had driven the first leg of the journey Pieter now offered to drive back to Sydney and I settled into the passenger seat and tried to get some sleep. We were cruising along the Newcastle to Sydney freeway at Berowra Waters when I felt a sudden surge that woke me with a start. As I opened my eyes I immediately screamed out and punched Pieter in the chest – we were accelerating into the rear of the car in front and Pieter had slumped over the wheel. He had fallen asleep! Braking heavily, he slowed the car and pulled it back into the left-hand lane. We were pushing it to the limit and if we didn't stop and take a rest we weren't going to make it back home in one piece.

Pieter took the Brooklyn exit and stopped at a general store where we got out and had a drink, pacing up and down the whole time, trying to revive ourselves. There wasn't any time to stop as Pieter was needed back at the station and the longer we stuffed around by the side of the road, the later we were going to be. I took over the driving, insisting that Pieter try to sleep as it was the only opportunity he was going to get. By the time I arrived back home on New Year's Eve I had completed thirty-six hours of continuous duty.

Pieter, having dropped me off, headed into the office where he was to continue duties on and off until New Year's Day. Inside, I left the sliding door wide open, threw my kit bag down at the door and walked into a steel chair leg, breaking my toe on the way to the bedroom. Exhausted and with my toe throbbing I threw myself down on the bed fully clothed and fell into a deep sleep. Several hours later I was woken by the sound of the telephone ringing.

Still groggy from not enough sleep, I went about preparations for my New Year's Eve party – family and friends would soon be arriving and there was lots to do. I noticed a parcel sitting on the dining room table and discovered that a friend had visited earlier while I was asleep, and after calling out and not getting any reply, she'd left a note and a belated Christmas present. I hadn't heard a thing. I hobbled about getting things ready for the party and before long family and friends started to arrive. The party got off to a rowdy start and turned out to be a great night for everyone. It was a strange feeling – from digging out dead bodies under the rubble of Newcastle to celebrating the New Year. But my life seemed to be constantly swinging from one emotion to another and I believed I was taking it all in my stride. A few bourbons and Coke seemed to solve all my problems and before long, I was laughing and joking, the memories of the past couple of days seemingly far away. I finally got to bed at 4 a.m. and fell into a deep sleep until I woke with a start to the sound of the telephone ringing. I immediately felt the throb of a migraine headache and I could barely lift my head off the pillow. Grabbing the phone, I answered hoarsely and heard Pieter's voice on the other end.

'Happy New Year, Ed,' he said in his gruff voice.

'Yeah, happy New Year, Pieter. What's up?'

'Sorry to wake you but I've been up all night, firstly at a suicide and then at an arson, and I can't go on. I need you to come into the office and take over for a couple of hours so I can get some sleep.'

'Didn't you get any sleep last night?' I inquired.

'Nup. I finished up a couple of outstanding jobs after I dropped you off, then I went home and we had friends over for a New Year's Eve party and about 10 p.m. I got a fatal car accident and just as I got home from that I got a suicide shooting. This fool wanted to be the first person to die in 1990 so he walked down the middle of the road with a gun and shot himself in the head. After the dead'un, I got an arson and I've just finished the job and I'm absolutely stuffed. I can't keep this up. If another job comes in, you'll have to do it.'

It was supposed to be my day off. I wasn't expecting this.

'Oh shit, I don't think I can, I've got a migraine, I'm having trouble lifting my head up and my eyes are blurry. I don't think I could even drive.'

Pieter sighed and I really felt bad, as if I was letting him down. Then I had an idea.

'How about you bring the crime scene car over to my place, drop it here, take my car home and if a job comes in, I'll go and do it. That way I don't have to drive into the office and maybe I'll feel a bit better if I take a couple of Panadols and have a shower.'

'Great. I'll be there in half an hour.'

I hung up the phone, had a shower, got dressed, took a couple of Panadols and while waiting for Pieter to arrive fell asleep on the lounge. I woke up at 11 a.m., realising that four hours had gone by since Pieter had called. I began to worry. I rang the office number and the phone rang out, then I rang the station switchboard and inquired if anyone had seen Pieter. Nobody had sighted him, so I asked the switch operator to go and look in our office. She went upstairs and knocked on the door but all was quiet and no one answered, she rang back to give me the news. I was really worried now as she informed me that no new jobs had come in and Pieter didn't appear to be in the building. As I hung up, the phone rang again and it was Pieter.

'Where *are* you?' I asked.

'I'm in the office. I crashed on the floor after I rang you this morning. I've been asleep since seven. Someone knocking on the door just woke me up. I must have collapsed and fallen into a coma.'

'Are you okay?'

'I'm all right now,' he said. 'I'll head home and carry on. Don't worry about covering for me. I'll be right.'

'Same thing happened to me,' I said. 'I woke at eleven and thought, where the hell is he?'

'I hope I'm going to have a quiet day,' he said. 'I'll give you a ring if I need any help. You going to be home all day?'

'Yeah, I'm going back to bed. My head's pounding.'

I hung up and went straight back to bed where I spent the whole of New Year's Day in a blur, drifting in and out of a semi-conscious state.

Happy New Year. 1990 had arrived and I wasn't impressed.

# 14 Pheasants Nest

The weeks preceding 2 January 1990 were stinking hot and humid. In the office for the first time in the new year, I saw Whayne striding along the hall dressed in his overalls and boots.

'Where are you off to in this heat?' I inquired after our initial greetings.

'Bushwalking,' he grinned.

During our conversations over the Christmas break, Whayne had told me about the many hours he'd spent scouring the bushland around the Potholes swimming hole at Tahmoor, searching for the two missing teenage boys featured on the evening news. It was now seventeen days since they'd last been seen and the prospects of finding them alive were not good. By now, the search party were looking for two dead bodies and the most likely place to search was the bush close to where they had last been seen. A woman had told the investigating police that while driving south along the Pheasants Nest Bridge on 18 December, she had sighted two boys matching the descriptions of those missing walking along the southbound lanes. The bridge at Pheasants Nest is about five kilometres east of the swimming hole. This led police to believe the boys had stayed in this general vicinity but, despite an intensive search, they were unable to find any trace of them.

I had been following news reports every day since their disappearance and was hoping the boys would be located before I returned to work from annual leave. Whayne had been covering the day shift while Pieter was on call and now it was my turn to take over for the next seven days. With a sigh, I picked up the car keys and prepared to pack the car with my equipment in readiness for the crime scenes I'd be investigating over the next week. In the back of my mind I felt a lot of conflicting emotions about any potential discovery of the boys. By now, their bodies would be severely decomposed and any investigation into their deaths would be horrific. After my experience in Newcastle I was feeling anything but refreshed and ready for work. I even wondered if Whayne might be interested in taking over any investigation that arose in relation to the missing teenagers. He had already been heavily involved in the search and it was an unwritten rule that once you started something, you had the right to decide who saw it through. I was getting quite obsessed about being on duty when the boys were found and I was praying that Whayne might take the resultant crime scene on. I was grasping at straws as I felt the pressure of the looming investigation.

Whayne and I stopped to chat about the progress of the search for the boys. Clothing had been found on the river bank near the spot where they had been swimming on the day of their disappearance. A local rock spider (paedophile) had been named as a possible suspect in the case and a search of his house had turned up numerous pairs of boy's underpants.

Whayne had been recording any physical evidence that could possibly be linked to the boys' disappearance. So far, there was no concrete evidence that the rock spider and his stash of boys' undies were connected to the case, but the local detectives were following every possible lead, trying to solve the mystery. A large contingent of SES volunteers, along with the local bush fire brigade, had joined the police in the search of the dense scrub over the past week. The search had intensified further with the inclusion of Polair (the police air wing), the police dog squad, as well as local uniformed constables. Detectives from Liverpool and Campbelltown were also on site at the scene in the hope that any evidence that was found could be investigated to the full. In searing heat, teams of searchers spent hours combing the local area, sometimes going over the same area two and three times in case something had been missed.

Whayne complained about the heat and the prospect of spending another day tramping around in the bush in heavy overalls. It wasn't a pleasant thought but I agreed that I would come out to the scene once I had checked my mail and sorted through the mound of paperwork piled up on my desk.

Sergeant Helen Kirton from Picton police station had also been in close contact. She had been coordinating information between the police and the relatives of the boys and had been attending their homes regularly to keep the families informed. She was from the old school and had joined the force when women were relegated to working in the policewomen's room dealing with children and women's issues and were not permitted to work in the area of general duties. She was a designated detective and had performed general duties for the first time at Campbelltown police station when I was a constable there. She had initially copped criticism from the troops who had assumed she would be unable to competently perform general duties. However, she quickly proved them wrong and was highly respected by all who worked with her. When stationed at Macquarie Fields in 1987 we had often worked as partners on the truck and were affectionately referred to as the petticoat patrol. At the time it was probably one of the first car crews to be manned by women in the history of policing in NSW and was quite a novelty; now it is commonplace and no more remarkable than having two men working together on the car crew. Women like Helen paved the way for my generation; she was a true inspiration to young female members of the police force.

Around lunch time I arrived at Tahmoor, driving down the dirt track that led to the swimming hole. I was immediately struck by the large contingent of police, fire brigade and SES vehicles in the parking area. As I stepped out of the airconditioned car I felt the full force of the midday sun on my face and was instantly uncomfortable in the heat. It must have been close to forty degrees and the humidity was stifling. I wasn't looking forward to pulling my overalls over my clothes. I could hear voices echoing down along the river bank so I headed off along a sandy trail to meet up with the search party. It was hard going walking through the soft sand in boots but I soon met up with Whayne and a group of detectives scouring the river bank. I spent the next couple of hours picking through dense ti-tree and thick undergrowth looking for clues, but only managed to locate old items of clothing that had obviously been out in the weather for several years.

Finally we called it a day and headed back to the office. Over the next couple of days, Whayne would cover the afternoon shift leaving Shane and me to cover the day shift, so we would only meet at the changing of the shift. Pieter was now on much deserved annual leave and was looking forward to having a complete break. I was determined not to ring him unless it was absolutely necessary.

The following morning I woke to another steamy January day, the humidity attacking my skin as soon as I stepped out of the shower. At the office I sat poring over the heaped papers on my desk with the ever-present crackle of the police radio in the background. About 11 a.m. I heard something that made me stop and listen – the Picton vehicle call sign. The male voice sounded distressed: '35/17 to Campbelltown Radio, request for scientific to attend Pheasants Nest Bridge. We have persons deceased.'

'Campbelltown Radio copy. What is your exact location?'

'Would rather not specify over the radio. We have a bush scene, will meet scientific in the southbound lanes on the southern side of Pheasants Nest Bridge. We also need gloves, masks and disinfectant.'

'Copy that, 35/17, will contact scientific, standby for an ETA.'

Shane came to the doorway. 'Did you hear that?'

Leaning back in my chair I spoke over the shrill sound of the phone. 'Bloody hell. They've found those boys.'

It had finally happened on my shift. I swore, then answered the phone. 'Crime scene, Constable First Class Mckay.'

Shane leant against the doorway listening. The call confirmed it. The Picton car was requesting scientific to attend the Pheasants Nest Bridge. They had located two bodies, but it was not yet known if they were male or female. I knew who they were. I was asked to maintain radio silence. Once the media got wind of it, we'd have all sorts of trouble keeping the vultures away. Shane immediately volunteered to come out to the scene and give me a hand. I decided to ring Whayne at home and give him the opportunity to take the job on. Understandably he declined, although he did attend later, arriving at the scene an hour earlier than his shift required.

It was a foregone conclusion that this would be a major investigation, and if it was a double homicide it could take up to eight hours to process the crime scene. I would be needing all the help I could get.

Driving the fully laden scientific station wagon, Shane and I headed south along the Hume Highway towards Pheasants Nest. Along the way we heard a further request over the radio from the general duties constable at the scene for masks and disinfectant. Why the bloody hell were they asking for that? It was disturbing to hear this request as it could mean that they were tampering with the scene. There was no reasonable explanation why the constables at the scene would need masks and disinfectant unless they were in close proximity to the bodies and were unable to distance themselves from the putrid smell. We were both perplexed about this and discussed several possible reasons throughout the thirty-minute journey to Pheasants Nest. Again, the radio called us, asking for an ETA because the constables at the scene were impatient for our arrival. We advised radio of our location and Shane requested that the scene be roped off and a guard be put in place to keep the scene intact. So much for the radio silence. We soon crossed the large expanse of the Pheasants Nest Bridge and could see the police truck parked along the guard rail beside the roadway on the other side. I pulled up in front, and Shane and I went straight to the back of the wagon to pull our overalls on over our clothes.

The heat was intense, it was at least forty degrees, making me feel instantly uncomfortable wearing two sets of clothes. As we stood there, two more police cars arrived, pulling over to the side of the road. With my camera kit slung over my shoulder and Shane carrying the plano box, we made our way to the edge of the bridge. We approached a lone constable standing behind a guard rail at the top of a steep incline.

'Hope you brought your masks and disinfectant,' he said.

'Why?' I asked, my voice sarcastic.

'It's pretty bad down there – foul. You wouldn't want to go in without a mask on.'

'Go in where? Where are the bodies?' I asked.

'They're in the bridge, down the bottom of the pylon, over there.'

As he spoke he stood back and pointed to the bottom of the south-eastern supporting pylon. I was shocked, firstly because I wondered how the hell we were going to get to the bodies, and secondly that they were *inside* the bridge, not out in the bush as I had imagined. The constable pointed down the steep incline behind him which led to a rocky outcrop below the bridge.

'You can get in by sliding down there. The bridge has an access hole you'll have to climb through to get in but you'll need someone to hoist you up.'

As we spoke, a number of highway patrol constables came up and asked where the bodies were.

'Why?' I asked.

'So we can have a sticky, that's why.'

I turned to the young probationary constable and asked him to stand guard. He was not to let anyone pass unless they had a valid reason for being there. He wasn't impressed by my request but simply nodded his head in agreement, muttering, 'I'll try.'

Shane and I slid down the steep dirt incline on our bums, clutching the equipment to our chests with one arm and trying to steady ourselves with the other. At the bottom we found ourselves on a rocky outcrop directly below the concrete structure of the bridge. It was a large sandy area, peppered with rocks and debris left over from the construction of the bridge, and it enabled access under the south and northbound lanes. On one side I saw the remnants of a makeshift campfire. I walked to the edge of the outcrop and surveyed the rugged bush that led down into the shallow riverbed at the bottom of the ravine. The sound of cicadas and bellbirds echoed through the thick canopy of gum trees below, filling the steamy air with bush noise. As I absorbed my surroundings, I became transfixed by the enormous concrete pylon below. It stood beside its twin, part of a group of four massive pylons standing like stilts, reminding me of a giant praying mantis. Above, I was shadowed by the concrete expanse of the bridge stretching across the Nepean River.

I turned and walked towards Shane, who was standing underneath the bridge below an open manhole about one metre squared. Out of this hole swarmed a steady stream of blowflies. I peered up into the hole and saw a policewoman staring back at me through the darkness. It was Jodie David, one of the first uniformed constables on the scene.

'You'll need a hand to get up here,' she said, her voice echoing inside the bridge.

'Take the equipment up first,' I said as I passed her the camera bag and then the plano box. 'What's the lighting like in there?'

'Not good. You'll need at least one torch each. I can't even see my hand in front of my face,' she replied. 'And it's dangerous.'

I left Shane at the manhole and scrambled back up to the wagon, deciding not to make too many trips back and forth. It was a pain getting up the hill to the road and it was even harder doing it carrying the equipment back down. As I clambered to the top I passed a couple more uniformed police on their way down. 'What are you doing?' I asked.

'Checking it out,' came a sarcastic reply.

'You'll have to wait. I haven't even seen the crime scene yet and I don't want every man and his dog going in there,' I spat back.

The constables ignored me and continued down the hill. I yelled after them, 'Don't go walking around down there, it's part of the crime scene!' With a sigh, I continued up the slope and retrieved a couple of torches from the wagon. Overhead, I heard the dull hum of a helicopter approaching. The word was out and the media were on their way.

I was surprised by the number of police vehicles parked along the verge of the roadway and the groups of police standing around at the top of the bridge. I wasn't sure what to do about this. Although I had the probationary constable on guard, it appeared even at this early stage that there was going to be trouble with crime scene preservation. At that moment, I had more pressing concerns, but I did make a note to discuss the security of the crime scene with Shane. Because of our relatively low rank (constables first class), we could have a protocol problem with inquisitive police of higher rank. If Pieter was at the scene it wouldn't be a problem. As a detective sergeant, he was highly regarded amongst his peers. Calling him to the scene was probably the only solution, and it was typical that he would once again be disturbed from his annual leave. I reminded the young probationary constable standing beside the guard rail that he was suppose to be stopping anyone from going any further.

He shrugged his shoulders. 'What can I do? I'm just a pro. They won't listen to me.'

'Just do it,' I said, my impatience increasing.

I scrambled back down the hill, shoving the torches in my side pockets so I could steady myself with both hands. I was now covered in dirt and tried unsuccessfully to dust myself off when I reached the bottom. Looking back I saw the two uniformed constables standing under the bridge, one of them puffing on a cigarette.

'Put that out and get out of the crime scene!' I said, with as much firmness as I could muster.

'Calm down, we're not interfering with anything here.'

'Just put that cigarette out and don't stamp it out on the ground. This whole area is crime scene! Can't you understand that?'

'All right, all right. We just want to have a look. When can we see the bodies?'

'You can't, so I suggest you go back to your station.'

'We'll wait,' he retorted.

'No, you won't,' I said.

Turning my attention to the manhole where Shane was waiting for the torches, I passed them up and then he hoisted me up into the hole.

Immediately, I was struck by a sickly odour that invaded my nostrils and made me wince. It was an unusually putrid smell, and not one I had encountered before. This was a new version of death, attacking my senses in an overwhelming way.

I could hear a constant echoing of ba-boom, ba-boom as vehicles passed over the bridge's expansion joints; it was deafening. The smell combined with the booming sensation of the cars whooshing overhead gave the eerie impression that the bridge had a heartbeat. We were forced to yell over the noise. I shone the torch around in an arc and discovered that I was standing in a massive concrete cavity that ran the expanse of the bridge from one side of the ravine to the other. It was wide enough to drive a car through and gradually got higher as it progressed towards the pylon. I could just see a concrete doorway at the end of the tunnel, barely visible in the beam of the torch. Along the right-hand wall I could see the faint shadow of fluorescent lights at ten-metre intervals, giving the internal structure an eerie glow. Beside the open manhole at my feet, I saw a concrete plate, obviously the cover for the hole, its hinges intact, resting undamaged alongside the hole. The faint impression of a shoe was visible on its dusty surface.

As we made our way along the dark tunnel, I saw a number of drag marks, uniformly stretching along the concrete floor, together with clumps of what looked like ash from burnt paper. Jodie led us into the pitch-black of the pylon, darker even than the inner cavity of the bridge. She held her arm out to caution us to be careful where we stepped.

The room measured about five metres square and I stood in the doorway next to Shane as Jodie shone her torch over to the right. There in the darkness I saw a black hole in the floor, similar in size to the manhole we had climbed through to get into the bridge. 'They're in there,' she said, shining the torch over the black hole. What looked like a shirt lay nearby, partly over the manhole. 'If you shine your torch in there you can see the bodies.'

Shane and I approached the manhole cautiously, straining

to make out the hole in the darkened area of the pylon and mindful not to disturb the red-and-grey flannelette shirt lying over one corner. As Shane moved closer he stumbled in the darkness and instinctively Jodie grabbed him from behind, pulling him away from the open hole in the floor. Shane reared backwards in fright.

'Shit, I told you to be careful!' shouted Jodie. Shane had been a second away from falling down into the open pylon.

'Okay,' I said, straining to see Shane's face in the darkness. 'No one go near the hole unless someone is holding onto you.'

'Fuck,' Shane's voice echoed against the concrete walls, 'that was close.'

'Someone's going to end up down there with the bodies if we're not careful,' I said, dropping down onto the dusty concrete floor. Shane held my legs and I slid on my stomach to the edge of the hole. Then I shone the torch down into the darkness.

Lying face down, my head directly over the hole, I was overcome by the sickly smell of the decomposing bodies. I furiously swatted at the blowflies hitting me in the face as they made their escape. It was sickening to realise the flies were attacking me directly after gorging themselves on the bodies below.

'Get them off me!' I screamed as they flew into my mouth and nose. Shane swatted at them as they swarmed around my head before disappearing into the darkness, blindly trying to locate the way out beyond the light bouncing off the watery grave some thirty-five metres below. I refocused my attention. There they were, lying side by side in the torchlight, both bodies moving grotesquely with the infestation of maggots. I shone the torch around in an arc examining the crime scene, relaying what I saw to Shane crouched down behind me.

The opening to the hollow centre of the pylon was narrow

at the top before it expanded nearly two metres down from the top of the manhole. The boys lying at the bottom were entombed in the five-metre-square base of the pylon. From what I could see, they appeared to be lying in a couple of inches of water, water that was seeping in from the Nepean River flowing around the base of the structure. Two-thirds of the way down I saw two large pieces of reinforcing steel protruding from the inside of the pylon. In the torchlight I located what appeared to be a five-fingered death grip extending in a downward arc along the length of the narrow entrance. It looked like the concrete had been scratched by five fingernails. In another corner of the hole I saw two black scuff marks possibly made by the tread of a black-soled shoe. This small piece of evidence pointed to the fact that the boys were alive when they entered the hole. Scrambling back away from the manhole, I swapped positions with Shane, gripping his legs as he lay face down over the hole inspecting the distant scene.

'How the hell are we going to examine the scene down there?' he asked, shining the torch into the black hole.

'I don't know,' I said, shaking my head. 'How *are* we going to get down there?'

'Fucked if I know, mate,' Shane replied.

'Maybe we can get into the pylon from the outside, down near the river? There might be an inspection hole somewhere.' I hoped to God there was one.

'That would be the best way to get in. If there isn't, we'd have to be winched down from the top.'

'I'm scared of heights,' I said, trying to smile.

Shane turned and looked back at me. 'I'm claustrophobic, but if we have to get in there we'll have to do it. If you go down there, mate, I'll go in with you.'

If we had to be winched down inside the pylon to examine the crime scene, we would do it as a team. This was the first time I had attended a crime scene where I couldn't physically get to the bodies – the most unusual set of circumstances I had ever come across. The enormity of the problems of this scene was starting to sink in. I was anxious to get the job started.

Jodie mentioned that she'd heard Helen Kirton talking about access through the bottom of the pylon when she'd been at the scene earlier. Helen had left the scene to inform the parents that police had discovered what was thought to be the boys' remains. If anyone could find out about the access to the bridge it would be Helen. She was like a dog at a bone. Once she embarked on a particular inquiry she would not rest until she had uncovered the necessary information. I was hopeful because it would make a tremendous difference to our investigation if we could get into the pylon from ground level. I needed to view the bodies up close and do a proper examination of the scene, as distasteful as this might be. Jodie was pretty sure Helen would return to the scene as soon as she had spoken to the boys' parents and I hoped she was right. The sooner I could get the thought of being winched down into that hole out of my mind, the better.

Shane scrambled back from the manhole and we shone our torches around the room, locating a number of cigarette butts and a pink cigarette lighter around the manhole. The three of us stepped back out through the doorway and made our way back along the tunnel where we found the local area inspector, his sergeant and a Roads and Traffic Authority inspector heading towards us. The sergeant explained they were returning to the scene after taking a witness statement at Picton police station from the RTA inspector about how he had come across the boys. After the Newcastle earthquake, he had been inspecting a number of local bridges in case there had been any structural cracking. As it happened, he was friendly with the uncle of one of the missing boys and had been discussing their disappearance with him when he mentioned that he would be conducting a routine inspection of the Pheasants Nest Bridge. He had been asked by the boy's uncle to keep an eye out for any indication that the boys had been inside the bridge. He hadn't thought any more about it until that morning, when he was surprised to see the inspection cover was missing from the manhole.

Inside the bridge he noticed the foul stench and had followed the smell until he got to the south-eastern pylon where he saw that the inspection cover over the manhole leading down inside the pylon was also missing. It was then that he made the grisly discovery of the decomposing bodies.

The first thing I asked about was the lighting inside the bridge. It would be intolerable working in the darkness and I intended to call for the assistance of the police rescue squad to set up lighting. The RTA inspector told us about a master switch at the northern end of the bridge that operated the fluorescent lights positioned at ten metre intervals along the internal walls of both the north and southbound lanes. I inquired if they had been on when he accessed the bridge and he confirmed that they had been. This indicated that *someone* had made their way to the northern end of the bridge in the darkness and activated the master switch. This was unusual, I was told, as it was not normal practice for the lights to be left on. He agreed to escort us to the northern end of the bridge where we could examine the light switches and confirm if they had been tampered with. Someone had to stand guard at the entrance to the bridge so we left the two police to wait for us at the access hole while we inspected the light switches.

As we walked along the tunnel, the RTA inspector indicated a thin electrical channel running along the right-hand wall that carried cables linking the lights. Segments of it were covered in a grey conduit shroud, with other portions left exposed. At the time I wondered why parts of the electrical channel were visible but it wasn't until later that I discovered the importance of the missing conduit sections.

We stepped through an identical doorway leading into the north-eastern pylon, where we checked for the existence of an open manhole similar to the one we'd found in the south-eastern pylon. But in this pylon the floor area had been completely concreted in and there was no such open access hole. Along the way I found more traces of ash peppered along the floor at regular intervals, and larger deposits of burnt paper at the base of the master light switch. It was possible these were the remnants of a crude torch made from a rolled-up newspaper. After examining the master switches we made our way back to the southern end of the tunnel just in time to see the sergeant standing with one foot resting on the steel manhole cover, puffing away on a pipe, and completely oblivious to any crucial evidence he might have been destroying. I was furious. Though he was my superior, this man was acting in a totally irresponsible manner and I couldn't allow such disregard for crucial evidence nor any potential destruction of the crime scene. I tried to stay calm.

'Kindly remove your size eleven boot from the manhole cover. Can't you see there's a footprint on it? And put that bloody pipe out. The last thing we want in here is ash and smoke wafting about.'

He sheepishly removed his foot from the steel plate, slinking away like a ghost. Without a word, the inspector, no doubt feeling equally embarrassed, turned and followed him. Once on the ground, the inspector cupped his hands around his mouth.

'Don't suppose you need me here any more?' he called out through the hole. 'I'm off back to the station.'

'Wish he'd take the sergeant with him,' I said. 'What are we going to do about keeping every man and his dog out of the crime scene?'

'Better get Pieter here,' Shane suggested.

'I think it's the only way. It's only going to get worse, especially when the media turns up. We really need a phone. The rescue squad's the only section that I know that's got one so we better request they attend with lights and then we can use their phone. I'm going to call the Coroner, he needs to see this for himself. The last thing I want to do is use the radio though.'

Shane agreed.

'Once we've got the phone, I can call Pieter, photogrammetry and then the video unit. It might even be worthwhile ringing homicide. But if any of this goes over the radio, we'll have all sorts of trouble with the media.'

I had no idea how hard it was going to be to get hold of the telephone once it arrived. The detectives were on their way and later I discovered they had other ideas as to whom I was going to call and when. After scrambling out through the manhole I discovered more police milling around below the bridge.

'Can't you understand this is a crime scene?' I almost yelled at them. 'You have to stay up on the road! There's nothing for you to do down here except stuff up the scene. Just piss off out of here!'

I felt I was losing it. I was getting extremely agitated. Why wouldn't they listen and do what I asked? Finally, they grudgingly crawled up the slope. I'm sure they thought I was an absolute bitch but as far as I was concerned, I was just doing my job. If they made a complaint about my insubordination, so be it. Scrambling up the slope behind them I was really starting to feel the heat. I was filthy from all the dust and now I was sweaty as well. Things were deteriorating by the minute.

Up on the road I saw a helicopter trying to land on the roadway – the cavalry were about to arrive. Using the radio in the car, I called for the rescue truck and requested specific lighting to assist with the conditions inside the bridge. They had anticipated what I needed and it was already on its way. I also requested the use of a mobile telephone. In 1990 mobile phones were a rarity, restricted to hostage situations, and their use was strictly monitored. It was highly unusual for a telephone to be used in the field. It had to be a bloody good reason to request one, let alone make a number of calls, all of which had to be justified. This was to be yet another struggle I had to overcome. Passing the probationary constable on my way back down the slope I asked him to call me back up onto the road when the rescue truck arrived. It was now a matter of waiting until the rescue squad showed up because it was impossible to start our examination until adequate lighting was set up inside the bridge. We used this waiting time to map out a strategy that would best cover every aspect of investigating the scene. We discussed the sequence of examinations starting with photographing and videoing the entire scene followed by photogrammetry, sketches, note taking and then the collection of exhibits and trace evidence – all this before the bodies could be recovered.

It was going to be a hell of a long day. The sheer size and complexity of the crime scene would take many hours to complete and we had the added problem of waiting for assistance from various other police sections. It was frustrating that we would spend so much time examining the scene but not actually be able to get to the bodies. At this stage, I was still unsure of how we were going to get down inside the pylon and I was keen to discuss this with the rescue squad.

# 15 The retrieval

It was a relief when I finally saw the white overalls appear through the manhole. Constable First Class Lance Rice had a large hand-held light slung over his shoulder.

'What's that?' I asked after the usual introductions.

He slung the large torch forward, pointing it down along the tunnel and switched it on. 'It's a 700-watt hand-held light. Weighs a ton.'

I was amazed at how strong the light was, perfect to shine down into the hole where the bodies were. I went over the details with the rescue squad guys as we walked up the tunnel, working out how we were going to actually get down the hole to examine the bodies.

As soon as the rescue guys saw where the bodies were they were adamant it would be impossible for anyone other than a skilled abseiler to go down into the pylon, and even then they weren't sure exactly how it could be done.

'Looks like methane gas anyway,' one of them said.

'What do you mean?' I asked.

'With the advanced state of decomposition of the bodies, there's a good chance that hole is full of methane gas. The body produces it naturally as it breaks down, and in such a confined space, combined with the heat, the gas has nowhere to go. The air would be toxic down there and you wouldn't even think about going in without a self-contained breathing apparatus.'

I was instantly relieved. Shane and I were off the hook as neither of us were trained in SCBA or abseiling – there was no way we could go down inside the pylon. I was filled with conflicting thoughts, torn between wanting to get to the scene and do my job properly and knowing that I wouldn't be able to. It was a strange feeling, being at the scene and not being able to do the necessary work. I just had to do the best I could with what I had.

Even photographing the scene from such a distance was new to me and I hoped with what photographic knowledge I had that I'd get it right. I only had one go at it and if the photos weren't exposed correctly I would have no record of the scene.

With the hand-held torch illuminating the hole, I had a much clearer view of the bodies and their surrounds. The maggot-infested water had a bluish tinge, reflecting the light in a swirling pattern as maggots swarmed around the bodies. I could see two pieces of what appeared to be grey conduit lying over the bodies and I realised it came from the exposed electrical channel that ran the length of the bridge. What was it doing down there with the bodies? I could only surmise it went down with them or shortly after. I decided the best way to record the scene would be to attach my camera to a tripod, focus the camera and then, lying on my stomach with Shane holding my legs, push the camera over the hole and get the rescue squad guy to shine the light down the opening from the opposite side while someone held his belt. Using time exposure settings and zooming in on the base, I hoped to get a clear picture of the entire scene down below. Later, I also drew the entire scene lying on my stomach. The process was hampered by the constant need to turn off the hand-held light so it wouldn't overheat. Its heaviness tended to unbalance the operator. We were constantly plagued by the fear of falling in.

Lance inspected the area around the manhole looking for a possible anchor point for the recovery equipment but he was unable to find any suitable secure points. The rescue squad also got to work straight away, setting up lights on tripods at the entrance to the bridge and at intervals along the tunnel. I went back up to the road to use the mobile phone that had arrived with the rescue truck.

As I opened the door to climb into the front seat I was approached by a burly detective sergeant.

'What the hell do you think you're doing?' he asked.

I introduced myself and explained I was in charge of the crime scene and needed to use the mobile phone to make a number of important calls.

'I'm in charge here,' he spat, 'and if anyone is going to make any calls it will be me.'

After the morning I'd had I wasn't in any mood for arseholes.

'I was the one who requested this mobile and I'm going to use it,' I replied, determined to do my job.

'Who do you think you are, girlie? I'm from homicide and I'll be calling the shots!' Ignoring him, I stepped up into the truck, reaching for the phone. At the same time he ran around and dived in through the driver's side, grabbing the phone and trying to pull it from my hands. We arm-wrestled until he ripped the mobile phone from my grip.

'Now,' he said, smirking. 'Who do you want to ring and I'll ring them.'

'Give me the bloody phone!' I yelled. 'You can't explain the scene to the photogrammetry section. Anyway, they won't come out unless the request comes from the scientific section. They won't listen to you!' I realised I was yelling.

'What are you calling them for?'

'That's exactly why I need to call them myself. You haven't got a bloody clue why I need to speak to them. You're wasting time! I also need to speak to the video unit, and after that I want to call the Coroner.'

'Right then,' he said, '*I'll* call the Coroner. What's the number?'

'For God's sake, just give me the bloody phone! I have to speak to photogrammetry and video first so I can get the ball rolling, otherwise we're going to be here all night.' Reluctantly, he handed the phone back but remained by my side listening in. My constable first class status was obviously so lowly that, although he had no experience in my field of work, he felt he needed to watch my every move. At this point I decided to ring Pieter. I needed him at the scene more than ever and I just hoped he was at home to take the call. When he spoke, he was torn between his loyalty to the job and his commitment to his family. He told me later he felt compelled to rush to the scene. But he was burnt out and struggling with fatigue, and he desperately needed time off. The discovery of the boys' bodies couldn't have come at a worse time.

After making my calls I accompanied the detective sergeant and his partner back down to the crime scene, walking them through the tunnel so they could fully comprehend the scene. After talking with the rescue squad they satisfied themselves that everything was in hand and allowed me to start my examination. At this point it was likely we were going to need as many hands as possible to form a hauling party once the retrieval process got under way, so both detectives stayed right until the bitter end, watching and waiting until they were required to pitch in with the unpleasant task of recovering the bodies.

Shortly after my phone call, the Coroner attended the scene, having been ferried swiftly to Pheasants Nest by the highway patrol. With utter professionalism he made a painstaking inspection of the site. The photogrammetry and video units arrived and after a walk-through with Shane and me, the video guy started. After he finished, I helped the photogrammetrist conduct his survey. This was a tedious job because we had to place photogrammetry cones at regular intervals, mark them, position the lighting and then set the camera up on a tripod before taking each photograph. A scene of this magnitude required numerous photographs to be taken onto glass plates that had to be changed each time. These plates would later be developed back at the photogrammetry section and viewed through a plotting machine in order to produce a scale drawing.

With the photogrammetry survey finished, Shane and I started our examination, photographing the entire scene, including the trace evidence of the dust impression of the shoe print, sketching the bodies in situ, and finally cataloguing and collecting all exhibits.

It had been several hours since I had seen the light of day and having finally completed the internal crime scene, I was now facing a pile of paper bags containing exhibits that needed to be taken out and stowed in the wagon. I clambered down out of the bridge through the access hole into the harsh daylight and was confronted by an army of people milling around under the bridge. It was an absolute circus. I was furious. I couldn't comprehend the scene before me, there would have been at least twenty people standing around below the bridge including media and God knows who else. Some dickhead had been to McDonald's and got a large drink esky, propping it up on a rock so the thronging crowd could serve themselves cool refreshments as if they were at a rock concert. McDonald's wrappers were lying about on the ground where they had thrown the rubbish at their feet. While Shane and I had been sweating it out inside the bridge, these fuckwits were having a picnic outside. I couldn't control my temper.

At the top of my voice I shouted, 'Everybody fuck off out of here! This is part of the fucking crime scene!'

They all stood frozen to the spot, stunned expressions on their faces.

'Did you hear me? Just fuck off out of here! Everybody!'

I turned my attention to a uniformed constable who was smoking. 'Piss off out of here with that bloody cigarette! Can't you see this is the fucking crime scene, you dickhead?'

I was shaking with anger as I stood my ground until every last one of them left. From that point, not one unauthorised person ventured into the crime scene. It speaks volumes that I had to show such a display to get my point across. The constable on guard duty had long gone, having given up and returned to the station when he was ignored by the constant stream of people pushing their way past. Many of these people were in fact waiting for us to finish the scene so they could assist with the recovery process, but once a couple of people entered the crime scene others followed, oblivious to the fact that they shouldn't be there. Because of them, the media blended in with the crowd of emergency workers and were able to stand around under the bridge unnoticed. It was a bonus for them to be so close to the action. There was no way they were going to move without some strong language.

While Shane and I were below in the bridge completing the crime scene, members of the rescue squad were working out a plan of recovery up on the road. Constable First Class Kevin Higgins had now arrived and after checking the inside of the bridge, began discussions as to how to do the job and what equipment to use. There were no anchoring points inside the pylon, so they decided that the recovery team would be lowered through the manhole using a 22 mm manila rope, via a gantry and a hauling party. The sharp edges of the manhole would cause severe abrasions to the rope so it was necessary for an anchoring device to be constructed out of angle iron with two lugs welded at each end. Constable Higgins recalled that there was a wrecking yard nearby and set off to find the necessary equipment to make this. While he was away the remaining rescue squad officers viewed footage supplied by the video unit using a monitor inside a Channel 7 vehicle. Zooming in on the inside of the pylon, the rescue squad were clearly able to see two steel reinforcing rods protruding from the eastern wall near the base of the pylon. These rods would pose a risk to the abseiling members of the team and would have to be avoided during the final stages of the descent. Three rescue-squad members then climbed down through the bush to the base of the pylon and located a door-shaped access hole that had been filled in with concrete. Sergeant Helen Kirton was contacted and she told us that the RTA had been notified and were on their way to inspect the site. Shortly after examining the doorway, the RTA engineer announced that it would be impossible to remove the concrete doorway without the possibility of causing structural damage to the pylon, therefore rendering the pier unsafe. It was abseil in or nothing.

Constable Higgins returned with the pieces of iron and was standing up on the roadway with the other members of the rescue squad, who had been patiently waiting. With Shane I approached and told them it was now time to retrieve the bodies from their watery grave. Arrangements were made through an RTA foreman for the delivery of a small gantry to assist with the descent into the pylon. Each member of the rescue squad was assigned individual duties with Constables Higgins and Rice descending into the pylon to recover the remains. The two constables discussed a descent and recovery plan with special attention placed on the equipment used and safety precautions. A canister-type breathing mask would be used for the descent and then SCBA would be used at the base of the pylon because of the lack of natural ventilation. Each breathing set supplies approximately forty minutes of air to the operator, so timing was of the utmost importance. Under normal breathing conditions the air supply would last the whole forty minutes, but in situations of extreme stress the operator would be breathing more heavily, reducing the capacity of the air tanks much more quickly. They would have to deal with this if and when it happened.

About 5.15 p.m. the gantry was delivered and the rescue squad worked hard up on the road disassembling the apparatus, checking and double-checking its construction. Two steel, A-framed ends on wheels were joined at the top by a cross-bar supporting a shackled pulley. This would feed the rope used to lower the rescue squad operators and also to hoist the bodies up on a Stokes litter. The gantry was lowered from the road over the side of the bridge using a small crane attached to an

RTA truck. Then it had to be completely disassembled to allow access to the man-hole, and reassembled once inside.

Conditions inside the bridge had deteriorated. The hauling party – about ten police who had been waiting for hours to assist with the recovery process – was assembled and briefed outside the bridge before entering the pylon one by one. Inside, I handed out face masks and gloves but quickly ran out of both items. We would have to make do with what we had as there was no time to order more. A small bottle of Nilodour from my plano box was being used on the masks to try to stem the foul stench but it only added to the pungent mix. The rubber gloves and mask together with the heat increased my discomfort. I wanted the recovery over as soon as possible so I could get out of this stinking hellhole. The crew working on the gantry sweated, struggling under the heat of the lights. The booming and clanging of the tools echoing through the tunnel made it impossible to hear each other speak. We were joined by fire and ambulance rescue teams because it was anticipated that retrieving these bodies could result in serious injuries being sustained by any number of emergency services workers. Around this time Whayne showed up and I was relieved to have him there. Not only did he have crime scene experience but he was also a trained rescue squad operator. But unfortunately he was not trained in roping and rappelling, which would have allowed him to perform the retrieval process as well as the necessary crime scene examination.

After viewing the position of the bodies we discussed the methods of searching and recording the crime scene with the rescue squad people. Rice and Higgins were fully trained in roping and repelling which meant they could abseil down into the pylon, using the gantry as their anchor point. It was a dangerous procedure, and one that required the utmost skill and composure. The atmosphere inside the pylon had become tense as both men prepared for their descent. Shane, Whayne and I squatted down beside the rescue guys, giving them a last minute briefing of what they needed to focus on once they reached the bottom of the pylon. They would conduct a grid search to collect any physical evidence that lay at the bottom of the shaft, then any items would be brought up separately for identifying and cataloguing as exhibits. After speaking with both men I was confident they would perform a thorough search and I no longer felt uneasy about the possibility of vital evidence being lost.

Kevin squatted impassively against the pylon wall, watching the gantry as it was assembled while Lance, the less experienced of the two, checked his equipment. Finally, both men fitted on their breathing apparatus and after checking everything was in order, removed them, slinging them on their belts for later if the conditions in the base of the pylon were intolerable.

When he was given the go-ahead, Kevin stood by the gantry waiting for the signal to proceed. Kevin connected his descender to the abseiling rope and after a final equipment check by a senior officer, was given the thumbs up and disappeared inside the narrow opening. After descending approximately five metres into the shaft, Kevin locked off, stopping any further descent, and replaced the canister mask with the SCBA face mask. Things were bad down there. The interior of the pylon filled with the sound of his laboured breathing against the background hiss of the oxygen, each breath magnified through the oxygen mask as it bounced off the walls and ceiling, echoing back and forth. All focus was on Kevin as the tension mounted. Within seconds of his descent he encountered problems. He overbalanced backwards into a downward free fall, the weight of the oxygen tanks on his back toppling him over, and the line spinning him around head down during the thirty-eight metre descent. With absolute skill, calm and strength he righted himself, continuing the descent brilliantly. It was a relief when his feet finally touched the ground. He looked up through the glaring light above and gave the signal that he was okay.

Just as we all sighed with relief, the shrill sound of his oxygen tank warning whistle completely filled the bridge. Panic swept the rescue squad as they realised that Kevin's face mask was not sealing. Too much oxygen was escaping. Kevin was in grave danger. He told Cavanagh through the portable radio that he had less than twenty minutes air left in the tank under normal breathing conditions and that he needed to decant his second bottle of air. Otherwise, he would be overcome by foul air and face imminent death. A second oxygen set was required urgently and would have to be lowered down to Kevin. The order for quiet rang out as the team leader spoke to Kevin through the portable radio. Kevin's voice filled the bridge, echoing through the radio, urging them to hurry. Time was running out. The continuous screaming of the oxygen alarm combined with Kevin's urgent instructions created an unbearably tense atmosphere. In silence, we witnessed the drama unfolding. My heart was pounding, an overwhelming nausea filled my stomach. There was no way of getting him out alive unless he got another oxygen tank in time.

Like clockwork, the rescue squad retrieved, prepared and lowered the oxygen required, getting it down to him in record time. The warning whistle sounded again. Kevin was now faced with the dangerous task of changing his oxygen tank over. The deadly environment meant he couldn't afford to take even one single breath during the changeover without being overcome by the poisonous atmosphere and collapsing. Kevin was standing in inches of maggot-infested water in partial darkness accompanied by two of the most hideously decomposed bodies I had ever seen. His presence had disturbed the feeding blowflies and they swarmed around him constantly, bombarding him. Kneeling in the putrid water, he prepared to exchange the SCBA. Then he swapped the oxy tank without incident as all of us above held our breaths during the silent seconds. It was a welcome relief when once again his laboured breathing echoed through the tunnel. Kevin was safe. He gave the signal for the hauling party to haul the used set up to the top.

Immediately he ordered the Stokes litter and the body recovery gear to be lowered. Then he started the grid search around the bodies necessary for gathering crime scene evidence before preparing the bodies for the ascent. Kevin felt around in the murky water in the dark, relying on touch in order to find any items that might be there, then placing them in bags and storing them in the corner as he went. He found one of the pieces of electrical conduit cover that I'd noticed earlier lying across both bodies and placed it against the western wall.

The first body was lying face down at a forty-five degree angle between the northern and eastern walls, the head facing the northern wall near the feet of the second body. Kevin ran his eyes along the bloated and disfigured torso, looking for wounds. The Stokes litter was now hovering at his head and he reached up and guided it down into the filthy water. He opened the body bag, laying it out next to the body so he could roll it onto the bag. Once the body was rolled over, Kevin could see the severe compression injuries to the face, a result of landing face-down. Kevin had now been alone in the semi-darkness with the two bodies for twenty minutes and was beginning to stress under the pressure. Kevin checked the upper side of the body looking for injuries while Lance Rice was lowered to join him. With a buddy close by if needed, Kevin removed his face mask and leaving his air turned on, drew a breath. He was only able to continue breathing for thirty seconds in the foul atmosphere before he was overcome by either ammonia or methane, he wasn't sure which. He became short of breath and quickly replaced his face mask.

Lance stood in the murky water taking in the horrific surroundings. The squirming mass of maggoty water swirled around his boots as he waded around the bodies to give Kevin a hand. I was shocked at the state of the decomposed bodies. From above they had seemed intact, but now that Kevin had turned them over I could see that one of the bodies was severely decomposed from the waist up, the head was devoid of skin and the torso alive with an infestation of maggots. I watched as Lance turned his attention to the body lying in the body bag, assisting Kevin with the zipper and then attempting to drain as much fluid from the bag as possible. Kevin and Lance placed the body into the Stokes litter and tried to secure it with 12 mm rope but the thick rubber gloves they were wearing made it impossible to tie the ropes. They both removed their gloves and with their bare hands secured the ropes through the Stokes. Their hands and arms were saturated with the putrid water as it ran down their arms and dripped onto their overalls. The Stokes litter was attached to the hauling rope and after the all-clear the group at the top began hauling it up. As the litter spun above their heads the light from above cascaded down through the cage forming patterns of light dancing around the concrete grave below. Kevin and Lance were sprayed with dripping body fluids that rained down on them from the dead boy. There was no cover to take and they were forced to stand under the filthy grey waterfall. Kevin grabbed the portable radio from his belt and yelled into it for Senior Constable Cavanagh to organise the bush fire brigade to be up on the road ready to hose them both down as soon as they came out of the bridge. Using the portable radio meant that the fan-cooled light had to be switched off, which left the two men below standing in darkness, adding to the pressure they were already enduring.

I stood in the line of police and emergency service personnel as part of the hauling team, heaving on the rope. It wasn't long before the saturated rope began to drip, covering our hands in the foul liquid. We found it difficult to get a firm grip. Those that were wearing gloves began to throw them off as the rope was impossible to haul with the rubber gloves slipping on the saturated rope. Hand-over-hand, we continued pulling on the rope. The pylon became suffused with the smell of rotting flesh.

'It's splashed onto my face! Get the hexifoam! Get the hexifoam!' Shane yelled. Someone grabbed the can of body disinfectant sitting by the pylon wall and threw it across to Shane. He spat onto the floor as he tried to clear the filthy substance from his mouth and eyes. We were all now exposed to the body fluids as the putrid water ran down our arms.

My overalls were dripping at the arms even though I had rolled the sleeves up as far as I could. I struggled to work with the mask and finally threw it off, discarding it in the corner with a pile of used rubber gloves. Sergeant Rob called for the hauling party to stop as the Stokes litter entered the narrow mouth of the shaft. The stretcher had caught and had to be lowered again to get it in the right position to manoeuvre it through the narrow opening. With the command to continue, the litter finally appeared through the top of the manhole.

Those standing at the opening pulled the stretcher out and laid it beside the hole. I approached the body, now my responsibility. I decided it would be best to examine both retrieved bodies outside as the pylon was now filled with the foul stench of death and after eight hours in the bridge, I felt I had waited long enough to carry out my examination. After all the ropes were removed, Whayne, Shane and I carried the Stokes litter along the tunnel, laying it down at the entrance hole while Shane and I climbed out of the bridge to prepare for the Stokes to be lowered into our waiting hands. Reaching out for the stretcher Whayne pushed it through the hole and Shane and I took its weight. A gush of liquid ran to the lowest point and like a cascading waterfall the fluid ran down my arms hitting my armpits and then running down my sides onto my stomach and down my legs. My skin was saturated with rotting, maggot-infested fluid. It was a hideous feeling. Shane and I struggled with the awkward load, dragging the litter through the hole while Whayne steadied it from the top and clambered through the hole, half-kneeling as he tried to hold up his end. Outside we were met by the government contractor who had been patiently waiting for the bodies to be brought out into the light of day.

As John approached us, Shane flicked his hands as he tried to shake the excess fluid from his hands and arms onto the sandy ground. We both stood with our dripping arms outstretched by our sides while we decided where to lay the body out. I was surprised to see that the heat of the day had turned into dusk and instead of flies buzzing around our heads we were now bombarded with mosquitoes. It was just before 7 p.m. and within an hour the day would turn into night. John indicated a flat area under the bridge, protected from the media view. Several helicopters flew overhead and I didn't want them zooming in on the bodies, getting gruesome footage for the evening news. We placed the body in the protected spot and left John to stand by it while the three of us went back into the bridge to help haul the second body out. Barry had now joined us and set about taking photos of the area below the access manhole outside the bridge. I was glad he could help out at this point. It was getting dark and I needed the surrounding area recorded photographically before the sun set.

When I went back inside the bridge, I was alarmed to hear the shrill sounds of Kevin's and Lance's warning whistles. Both men had been breathing at an increased rate and their oxygen tanks were running low. The hauling party lowered two new breathing sets and waited while Lance and Kevin changed their breathing gear in the semi-darkness. Kevin changed to new bottles first so he could give Lance a hand. Lance knelt down beside Kevin in the water, removing his bottle from his back but leaving his face mask in place. Kevin placed the new set on his back and told Lance to take a deep breath and hold it while he disconnected the hose using an in-line connection. Kevin's hands were slippery and he fumbled with the hose as Lance stood holding his breath. It was no good, he couldn't get it connected, telling Lance to take a breath of the foul air. Lance removed his mask and took one deep breath before Kevin was able to connect the new line and give him the all-clear to start breathing through his mask. The Stokes was then lowered and both empty breathing sets were attached to the rope and hauled to the manhole. Kevin and Lance resumed their search of the murky water, placing exhibits in plastic bags and storing them against the wall. The remaining body was lying face up at a forty-five degree angle between the western and northern walls with his legs bowed at the knees. The upper torso was extremely decomposed with severe maggot infestation to the head, shoulders and upper arms. They unfolded the second body bag and placed it beside the dead boy, Lance grabbing the lower part of the body and pulling it over to the body bag as Kevin warned him that he was worried the hands might fall off. If the hands should break free he told Lance to pick them up and put them in a separate sealable bag. Later, Lance told me that he had an overpowering urge to vomit; he hoped the hands didn't come off because he feared he would be sick into his face mask and choke. They struggled to move the body in one piece, dragging it out of the filthy water. The hands stayed intact but the skull broke away and later had to be scooped up and placed into the bag separately. The bag was zipped up, drained of fluid, then placed and secured in the Stokes litter.

For the second time, Lance and Kevin were covered in body fluids as the body disappeared over their heads on its way up to the top of the manhole.

Lance grabbed the radio. 'Is the fire truck ready? Make sure they're ready with a hose to wash us down, make sure they're ready when we get out.'

His hands were covered in rotting flesh, maggots were on his arms and body fluids soaked through his overalls. The blowflies hadn't let up as they swarmed around and he swatted them away furiously. After the bodies were removed Lance and Kevin made a final inspection of the base of the pylon, collecting a steel pipe and pieces of conduit. In the murky water Lance found pieces of the dead boy's chest and, not wanting to leave any of the dead boy behind, he collected it in a separate bag. Lance strapped the exhibits and body parts onto his belt. Holding the conduit pieces separately, he waited for the hauling party to lower the rope in preparation for his ascent. His warning whistle sounded again and he switched onto his second air bottle. He was relieved to finally receive the signal to be hauled up, attaching his harness and leaving Kevin behind to wait his turn.

As Lance was winched up he collided with the protruding steel rods, which broke the controlling knob off one of the oxygen tanks. Then, as he was dragged through the narrow opening at the top, a bag containing body parts was punctured by a protruding bolt, showering Lance with its contents. Sergeant Robb leant down into the opening and grabbed the leaking bag and pieces of conduit Lance was holding, then dragged Lance free from the hole. He lay on his chest and slid along the concrete floor as all hands pulled him away from the open manhole. The pylon filled with the chorus of voices.

'Well done, mate, well done, you did a great job.'

I touched him on his shoulder, 'Well done, Lance.'

He looked up with strained relief, his face black with perspiration and dirt. He somehow looked older with dark circles under his eyes. He didn't speak but there was no need, words could not convey how he felt. The most pressing thing on his mind was to get out onto the road and under the fire hose; he needed to erase the smell that was torturing him.

The rope was sent down for the last time to bring Kevin up. He had been down there too long, it was nearly 8 p.m., and I was worried. Kevin had done one last search of the murky water to be absolutely sure all exhibits had been collected. He found a number of items and attached them to his harness using a tape line. He connected himself to the rope and gave the signal, he was ready to be hauled up.

The hauling party got to work. As Kevin approached the surface and finally negotiated the access hole we pulled the rope slowly, giving him time to stand straight as he passed through the small opening. As he surfaced from the manhole he was greeted by a chorus of cheers.

'Good on ya, mate, well done, well done, mate, you did a great job.'

Some of the party began to clap and one by one they stepped forward and patted him on the back. Kevin removed his mask and attended to his breathing set. His white overalls were now a filthy grey colour, saturated and stuck to his body. His hair was wet with perspiration. Without a word he disappeared along the hollow tunnel to join Lance out on the road.

Lance stood stripped to his undies under the pressure hose when Kevin emerged. With hexifoam they scrubbed and scrubbed, firstly fully clothed and then naked as they tried to erase the stench that had attached itself to their bodies. Their clothes lay in a pile on the side of the road to be destroyed later. Soon Kevin and Lance were joined by members of the hauling party as they tried to wash themselves under the hose. It was a strange sight, men standing semi-naked under a pressure hose on the side of the freeway as cars sped past. The holidaymakers, completely unaware of what had transpired in the hours before, cupped their hands to their eyes as they peered into the setting sun and wondered what was going on.

Shane, Whayne and I carried the second body from the bridge in the same manner as the first, this time anticipating the gush of fluid when it passed through the manhole. Outside John, the government contractor, helped lay the litter down so the bodies were side by side. Shane re-entered the bridge and set about cataloguing the exhibits. I turned to John and asked if he could unzip the body bags so I could examine the contents. It was now 8 p.m. and the light was fading. The setting sun was a huge ball casting shadows below the bridge as far as I could see. The vivid blue body bags looked strange on the sandy ground, a stark contrast with the natural bush tones.

Whayne interrupted my thoughts as he approached. 'Why do you want to examine them here? There's no need,' he said.

'I've been here for nine hours and I haven't even looked at the bodies! I can't leave the scene without examining them. I haven't even photographed them yet.'

There was no way I was going to be swayed. Whayne argued that we should wait until we got to the morgue, but the bodies were going to the Glebe mortuary and it could be a couple of days before the post-mortems were done. I couldn't wait until then. It was part of my job to examine them then and there.

Suddenly, the nightmarish reality of this whole job overwhelmed me. It was a real-life horror show – the deaths of two young boys, the pressure, the danger, the stench, the foul liquid, the heat. Whayne had had enough. He'd reached his limit.

Without a word, he moved to a rock, sat down with his back to me and put his head in his hands. I stood looking at him for a minute before turning back to John, who was standing by one of the bags waiting to open it.

'Just hang on a minute, John, I'll get my camera ready.'

I bent down to open my camera bag and connected the flash to the camera body while he stood and watched. I stood up with the camera strap slung around my neck, steadying it in my hands. 'Righto,' I said. 'I'm ready.'

John unzipped the bag as his partner stood by and watched, then bent down and pulled the plastic sheet back. As the body was revealed, the head rolled off the litter and hit the ground with a thud.

'Good one, John,' said his partner.

John scuttled around to the side of the litter and scooped the head up off the ground, placing it back in situ. I approached, my face screwed up in distaste, photographing the boy as he lay beside his mate.

I got to work, taking a number of photographs before examining the boys' clothing, which was intact except for a small tear at the waist in the front area of one boy's shorts. I made a note to further examine this at autopsy. I then examined the second body, which was as badly decomposed as the first, the torso area exposed to the bone with parts of his ribs and spinal column visible. His clothes were also intact and both boys had their shoes on. I noted they were black soled. It was amazingly quiet and serene as I completed my examination. Everyone else was either up on the road or attending to the dismantling of the gantry inside the bridge; it was a contrast to the crowd who had been by my side from the instant I had arrived nine hours earlier. Any curiosity about the scene had faded long ago and the smell of the two bodies had cleared the area in an instant. This final task was sickening as I struggled with the overpowering smell at close quarters.

'Righto,' I said to John. 'Zip them up. You can take them now.'

I packed up my equipment and Whayne and I scrambled up the dusty incline to the road where I could hear the guys laughing as they cleaned the gear above. One lone helicopter circled overhead in a last-ditch attempt to get footage. Shane, Whayne and I were the last ones to wash our hands under the hose. After cleaning my face with hexifoam I went over to Lance and Kevin, who were sitting in the dark by the side of the road wearing borrowed overalls slung around their hips. Not having brought clean undies they were forced to go without. We talked over the job and what they'd found down inside the pylon. I made notes of where each exhibit was located and thanked them for doing such a thorough examination of the crime scene.

'You guys going to the pub for a drink?' Lance said. 'We're meeting at the Imperial. The press are there.'

A drink was tempting – I hadn't had a drink or eaten in hours – and I was starving.

'We'll give it a miss,' Shane said. 'Still got paperwork to finish. At this rate we'll be lucky to get home by midnight.'

'Enjoy your drink,' I said, as I walked away.

At the wagon we were met by Pieter who had just arrived and we stood talking by the side of the road. Even though it was late he'd decided to come to the scene and check how we were going. It was great to see him but all he could do was listen to the facts and reassure me and Shane that he was satisfied we had done a thorough job.

It was a relief to finally get the overalls off and remove my boots. Everything stank so I put my dirty gear in paper bags and loaded them into the back of the wagon. For a while I sat talking to the homicide team. We went over the evidence and agreed to be in touch again after the post-mortem results were known. Shane and I left the scene, one of a stream of vehicles, and headed back to Macquarie Fields. We were both utterly exhausted, I had a splitting headache and I couldn't get the smell of the bodies out of my mind.

'Can you still smell them?' I asked.

'Yeah, this car stinks.'

'I bet it's the exhibits in the back,' I said, looking over my shoulder.

'Reckon that's it. I can definitely still smell the bodies,' Shane said.

I opened my window and sucked in the clean, fresh night air for a minute. Then I slumped back into the bucket seat.

'Can't *stand* that smell,' I said.

I complained all the way back to the office.

In the darkness we unloaded the wagon and stored the exhibits in the dock. I didn't want them up in the office – it was bad enough putting up with the stink in the car. It was 9.30 p.m. and Shane and I still had plenty more work to do. I'd had a gutful. I wasn't in the mood for going over the events of that stinking day. I just wanted to get home and have a shower.

I fell into the chair behind my desk and got to work sorting out my notes and starting a précis sheet. It was 11.30 when I finally completed my notes; time to go home. I wasn't bothered about dinner – I didn't feel like anything now – I was past eating.

'See ya, Shane,' I yelled as I disappeared down the back steps to the car park. 'Just another day at the office,' I said as the door slammed behind me.

I sped away in the scientific wagon, mindful that I was still on call. I hoped there wouldn't be any more deaths tonight.

'Can't stand that fucking smell,' I said to myself. I stopped in surprise.

'Did you hear me?' I yelled. 'I can't stand that fucking smell!'

At my doorstep I stripped off my clothes and kicked them out onto the verandah. Wasn't having those stinking items inside. I stepped straight into a steaming shower and stood under the stream of water, washing myself furiously until I felt clean. Afterwards, I poured myself a strong bourbon and sat down by the light of a candle. Images of the boys danced before my eyes through the flickering light. I stared out into the darkness of the bush, but I couldn't erase the bridge from my mind. I was still there.

# 16 Bare bones

The alarm woke me with a start. At least I'd managed to get through the night without a recall. I dragged myself out of bed. Stepping into the police car I was immediately assaulted by the smell from Pheasants Nest, the pervasive odour had somehow impregnated itself into the wagon. I'd have a good look in the back when I got to the office. Perhaps fluid from one of the exhibits had leaked onto the carpet.

At the office, I got straight to work sorting out papers and preparing files to the constant ring of the telephone. As soon as I hung up it would ring again and I scribbled notes with the telephone stuck under my ear and tried to do ten things at once. The staff downstairs were trying to fob the media off, but they were persistent. I took a couple of the calls from local press but I explained it wasn't my position to give out information, they should speak to the detectives in charge from Campbelltown police station. Foremost on my mind was to get my film ready for processing and conduct a formal examination of the exhibits. I managed to locate Doctor Peter Bradhurst at the city morgue, who would be conducting the post-mortems. He had already viewed the bodies and made mention of the poor state they were in. Both bodies would be X-rayed and screened for HIV and hepatitis B in preparation for the autopsy the next day. Shane came in, and leant against the filing cabinet on the far wall.

'How you going, Esther Mary?' he said.

'Getting there. You coming to the PMs tomorrow? I could do with a hand.'

'Sure, no worries,' he said.

'How'd you sleep, last night?'

'Shithouse, how about you?'

'Not too good, I was all keyed up, took me ages to get to sleep,' I said. I didn't tell him how I'd talked to myself.

'I went and sat on my back step for a while and had a couple of drinks. I couldn't believe that job yesterday,' he said.

'It doesn't get much worse than that. I don't know what I would've done without you and Whayne.'

'No worries, mate. You know I wouldn't let you down. I'm making a coffee, want one?'

'Yeah, thanks.' Shane disappeared along the hall to get the coffee.

As I went about my work I felt keyed-up, sort of rushed and nervy. Each time the phone rang I jumped, aware of feeling tense. But there was no time to analyse it. I found myself rushing around the office, tripping over myself trying to do too much.

That afternoon on my way home from work I was still haunted by the filthy odour in the wagon. I'd spent ages searching the back of the wagon for the source. I emptied all the equipment out onto the bitumen but couldn't find anything that could be causing it. I'd have to have another look tomorrow. I was almost home when a call came over the radio.

'Campbelltown radio to Scientific 180.'

'Scientific 180 to Campbelltown radio,' I replied, picking up the radio handset.

I was asked to attend a death in a house in Rosemeadow. I turned the car around and headed for the address.

Outside the house I was met by the general duties constable from Campbelltown police station. She told me a seven-year-old boy had been electrocuted in the bath. His three-year-old sister had thrown a hair dryer into the water and killed him instantly.

'Where's the mother?' I asked, dreading seeing her.

'She's down at the station.'

I turned and went to the rear of the wagon, pulling out my camera kit.

Inside I scanned the scene – a two-storey townhouse. I immediately focused on a damp bath towel lying at the top of the stairs. A wave of panic swept over me. I felt shaky and ill at ease, nervous just being in this house. I wanted to run, to get out. All of a sudden, the whole incident flashed before my eyes: the laughter of the two children playing in the bathroom, the sound of splashing water, the mother outside bringing the clothes in off the line, the hair dryer lazily hanging from the cord attached to the wall, the child throwing it into the bath, the splash, the scream, the terror, the stiffening of the little boy's body, the mother running, the horror, the blood-curdling shriek, the mother cradling the wet body in her arms, the phone call for help, the morgue . . .

*I can't do this*, I thought.

Don't be stupid, I told myself. Get on with it. Don't be an

idiot. I pulled my camera from the bag, focusing on the job. I took my photos, examined the bathroom in all its innocent pinkness, and looked at the hair dryer lying on the floor. What a stupid, dumb thing to do. Why would *anyone* leave a hair dryer plugged into the power socket near the bath? I packed up and headed for the morgue.

The morgue attendant led the way in and there he was, lying on the steel trolley, a beautiful little boy, blond hair still wet from the bath, little toes pointed. Serene, as if sleeping in the cold. No, I reminded myself. He was *dead.* I went about taking my photographs in silence as the morgue attendant stood watching over his charge.

At home that night I felt down. Perhaps a drink might pick me up. I had always made it a rule not to drink alcohol when I was on call but I didn't care any more. I found myself preoccupied, brooding over the events of the last couple of days. Frightful images of what I'd seen inside the bridge and of the little boy's pale dead body gave me no peace. I saw them over and over in my mind.

Finally I realised – I couldn't think of anything else.

Next day, the trip to the morgue was slow as we battled peak-hour traffic. Dressed in our overalls, we anticipated the day's events. Shane was at the wheel while I sat exhausted in the passenger seat. Neither of us had slept much over the last forty-eight hours, and we were both looking the worse for wear.

'That smell is still making me sick to the stomach,' I said, whinging at Shane once again.

'Could be in our heads, you know,' he said, looking straight ahead as he drove.

'You reckon?' I half believed him.

'I can *definitely* smell the bridge,' he said. 'But we've stripped the car so where could the smell be coming from?'

'Dunno. But it's getting to me.' I scowled. 'And what about all those dickheads trampling through the scene?'

Once I started talking about Pheasants Nest I couldn't stop. At the same time, Shane was talking to me. I wasn't listening to him and he wasn't listening to me. I could hear Shane's voice under mine but I couldn't stop. I had to tell him what was on my mind. The images were torturing me. The whole scene out there. It wouldn't go away. And Shane was doing the same thing. Whether I was listening or not didn't matter. Shane pulled up outside the morgue but we were both still talking as we arrived. I came to my senses.

'Do you realise we've been talking over the top of each other the whole way here?'

'Sorry, mate,' he said. 'I didn't realise.'

'No, *I'm* sorry. I should be listening to *you*. I promise I'll listen on the way home.'

'Don't worry about it. I'm only talking shit anyway.'

'Yeah, right. Me too.'

We climbed out of the wagon and went round to the tailgate to get the camera and our kit bags containing fresh clothes. We were still talking over each other when Shane slammed the tailgate shut.

'Shit,' we both said. He'd locked the keys inside.

I waited by the wagon while Shane went inside and got a piece of packing tape. Within a few minutes he'd opened the door and we retrieved the keys.

Stepping inside the morgue I was immediately hit by ozone. I hated its insipid odour. It was supposed to take away the putrid smell of death but, to me, it made the smell worse. I screwed up my nose as I slid a white hospital gown over my overalls and slipped a pair of cloth booties over my boots.

I scuffed in through the big plastic double-doors, past the weighing machine, making a mental note to weigh myself on the way out. I did this whenever I visited the city morgue. Shane and I stood talking to one of the morgue attendants, who had been assigned to assist with the double autopsy of the boys, and he told us the bodies were now ready, lying side by side in the dirty necropsy room.

I prepared my camera, slinging the camera strap over my head and holding it in my hands as I waited by the double doors. Shane handed me a face mask.

'Good morning,' Dr Bradhurst greeted us, then strode through the doors, beckoning us to follow.

The room was pure hell. The stench from the bodies was overpowering. I strained to take each breath. As I walked between the two tables, I felt the crunching of maggots under my boots. I turned to see Detective Tony Maher come in.

'Listen to the maggots crunching under my boots,' I said.

At this, Tony ran from the room and vomited violently.

'Are we ready to proceed?' Dr Bradhurst asked, looking at Shane and me.

'We're ready.'

We had agreed that I would photograph the first body and Shane would photograph the second. That way, the horrendous task would be divided between the two of us. I started work, standing up close to the body in order to focus. But I found myself breathless and overcome by fatigue, straining to get enough oxygen into my lungs.

Dr Bradhurst commenced his examination, removing body parts, examining particular points of interest. He set the boy's clothes out on a table to the side and I stepped over to photograph them, paying particular attention to the small tear down the front of the shorts. It was difficult to tell what colour they had been. Maggots squirmed about in the slimy grey matter that coated the fabric.

The morgue attendant walked around the table, crunching maggots like rice bubbles under his shoes. The first body was grey and slimy, with rotting flesh draped over protruding bones. I was startled by the maggots wriggling through the exposed torso. The incessant movement gave the impression that the corpse was 'alive'. The morgue attendant picked up the backbone and held it in the air so I could take a photograph. The thick slimy backbone horrified me. Ignoring my breathlessness I tried to focus on the job. I looked around the room. No one seemed to notice I was struggling to breathe. My eyes were getting heavy, they felt glassy, and I could feel my eyelids swelling and puffing up. I tried to focus but I couldn't breathe. I felt panic. I couldn't go on. But I was terrified of collapsing on the maggoty floor. I didn't want maggots on my shoes. The panic grew. I had to get out of there.

'Shane,' I called, 'can I see you outside?'

Desperately I turned to Dr Bradhurst. 'I need to speak to Shane outside. I won't be a minute.'

Outside, I ripped my mask from my face and fought to breathe. With tears in my eyes I pleaded with Shane to help.

'I can't do it,' I said, 'I'm totally fucked. You do the first body. I just need to sit down for a minute. I felt like I was going to choke in there.'

'Take it easy, mate. Don't worry.' He took my arm and guided me into an old black chair sitting by the far wall. 'I'll do it. It's okay.'

'I'm sorry, mate,' I said. 'I've let you down.' I shook my head, staring at the floor.

'No way,' he said. 'You'll be right in a minute. Just sit here for a while and you'll get over it.' He left me and returned to the dirty necropsy room.

I took in my surroundings. I was sitting alone, my head in my hands, among a row of steel trolleys parked against the wall. I was consumed by this hideous situation. *How the hell did I end up here?* I willed myself to get it together and pull myself out of this hole. I realised I couldn't. Something had snapped. I wanted to rip my hair from my head. I clenched my fringe in my hands and pulled until I felt pain. Then I looked at my hands, shocked to see them trembling uncontrollably. My heart was pounding hard in my chest. What was *wrong* with me? Why couldn't I carry on? I sat there trembling, horrified and despairing. I wanted to scream. I was weak. I was a failure.

Senior Constable Steve Mackinnerney startled me as he came through the double doors and strode over to me. 'There you are!' he said, 'I've been looking for you all over the place.' He shoved a wad of papers into my hands.

'What's this?'

'Need you to do an urgent statement for court,' he said.

'You've got to be fucking kidding, haven't you? What do you think you're doing following me to the bloody morgue?' The words burst out of me. I couldn't control them. 'I've had the worst couple of fucking days of my life! There's no way you're going to get your bloody statement!' I was shaking with anger. 'Have a look in there.' I pointed to the autopsy room. 'If you want to see what I've been doing! See how *that* compares to your piddly prang!'

'Shit, I didn't realise.' He was immediately contrite. 'Are those the bodies from Pheasants Nest?'

'Yes. That's why I haven't done your statement.'

'Sorry, mate,' he said as he exited through the clear plastic doors, 'I can see you're having a rough time. I'll catch up with you later.'

About an hour later, Dr Bradhurst came out of the post-mortem room and asked if I could take samples of maggots collected from the two bodies to the Department of Entomology at Rydalmere for analysis. It was extremely important that we get a precise time of death as the boys had been missing for sixteen days and we needed to ascertain if they had died on the day of their disappearance or some time later. So it was crucial to the investigation that I get the live maggots to Rydalmere immediately. There, they could be accurately categorised and measured to ascertain at what stage they were in their cycle.

'Pull over to the side of the road every ten minutes or so and take the top off,' he said, indicating the plastic jar of samples. 'Give them some fresh air.' He handed me the specimen jar containing parts of the dead boy's liver seething with feeding maggots.

I was mindful that Shane needed to be relieved but I still wasn't sure if I could go back into that room. Then Shane himself appeared through the swinging doors, stressed and tired, dark circles under his eyes.

'How's it going?' I asked, already knowing the answer.

'It's bearable,' he said, focusing on the jar of maggots in my hand.

'Dr Bradhurst wants these taken over to Rydalmere,' I said.

'Would you rather continue here with the PM or drive to Rydalmere?'

'You go, mate.' he said. 'I'll keep going here.'

I really appreciate that,' I said, trying not to let my relief show.

Shane could see I wasn't able to keep up my end of the bargain. What he was doing was horrendous, but he never complained.

I stripped off the gown and headed for the car with my precious saving grace – a jar of maggots. The irony of it made me laugh out loud as I sat at the traffic lights in bumper-to-bumper traffic, unscrewing the lid off the maggots every now and then to give them fresh air. If the people driving beside me only knew what I was doing! The pungent odour filled the car. I must have reeked when I finally entered the laboratory at Rydalmere with my specimen jar.

Dr Garry Levot greeted me at the door.

'You look like you need a drink,' he said.

'Do I really look that bad?'

'Put it this way. You don't look too good.'

'I reckon if I had one drink I'd collapse,' I said.

'It might do you good to sit and have a rest for a minute,' he suggested.

'No. I've got to get back to the morgue. My partner's still doing the post-mortem and I've got to get back there in time to drive him back to Macquarie Fields.'

I looked around the room. It was obvious they were still in Christmas mode here. There were Santa decorations on the walls and a sense of cheerfulness filled the room. I felt a pang of jealousy. These people were happy and cheerful, enjoying their work. They were winding down for the day, taking it easy. It was a far cry from my working environment, the morgue. I just had to keep going so that the job could be finished.

I headed back into the city. Garry had asked me to contact the Department of Meteorology for a printout of the minimum and maximum temperatures over the past couple of weeks. Apparently it was vital to compare the ambient temperatures when calculating the stage of maturity the maggots had reached. I promised to ring him the next day with the information he needed.

Shane was packing up the camera gear when I arrived back at the morgue. He was too exhausted to drive so I slid into the driver's seat and we set off for the hour's journey back to the station. The mood in the car had changed. Unlike the morning's incessant talking, we now only communicated in short outbursts. Even though I could still smell the bridge, I was too tired to complain.

'I really appreciate what you did at the morgue, Shane,' I finally had the grace to say. 'I don't know what happened to me today. I just lost it.'

'You would've done the same for me,' he said. 'I don't think I could've driven to Rydalmere in the state I was in, anyway.' He leaned back and closed his eyes.

At home that night I went straight for the bottle of bourbon and poured myself a stiff drink. I needed to relax, calm my nerves, try to block out the images from the morgue. I longed to completely obliterate myself but I was still on call and the prospect of the phone ringing at any minute never left my mind.

The evening news mentioned the deaths of the two boys, asking was it an accident or murder. The item went on to suggest that drug barons operating in the Pheasants Nest area were responsible, or perhaps the deaths were related to a local paedophile ring enslaving children, killing them and then dumping their remains. The report was just as inaccurate as the articles I'd read in the local paper. The reporters had no idea, they were just trying to beat up a good story. It pissed me off. I poured myself another drink and turned the TV off. Then I sat and stared out the window. I knew I should eat something but I couldn't be bothered. I still had the stink of the morgue on me. I couldn't erase it, it lingered on my skin, impregnating my pores. I showered and went to bed, calmer now that the alcohol had taken effect. But I lay there for hours unable to drift off; my mind just wouldn't stop. Finally, exhausted, I fell asleep.

The next thing I knew was the blackness that surrounded me. I was gripped with terror. Some unknown horror confronted me. Four walls of blackness with no way out, just murky darkness mingled with the smell of dust, choking dust in the air and on the floor.

I try to shout, *Who's there*? But how can I speak? My throat is dry, constricted, my voice is gone. I'm all alone and I'm scared. Where's the light? I can't see through the thick darkness, only those black walls surrounding me with their heavy evil. Something very bad is there, I'm not sure what, but I know it's bad; I need help but I'm alone. I'm struggling to move but my body won't work. Every part of me is broken. I can't move. I can't help myself and I'm scared of those black walls. I want to scream, 'Get me out, help me, help me!' but I don't know what is there, waiting in the evil darkness. I want to run, get away, escape this evil world but I can't, it's too late. There is no way out and I'm dying –

With a start I sat bolt upright, choking on each breath as I struggled to control my breathing. *Where am I?* My eyes staring into the darkness, heart pounding with fear, I could see the moonlight through the bedroom window. It was just a dream, I told myself, I'm not dead, I'm all right. I lay back in the darkness, still too scared to move until finally the first rays of the morning sun shone through the window.

Each day seemed worse than the one before. I'd somehow changed over the past few weeks. I felt I had become another person. Life didn't seem so simple any more. I wasn't interested in food, I was racked with stomach pains. I'd lost weight and I had a constant headache. A red rash appeared on one eyelid and below my lip. My eye was swollen and I constantly rubbed it. Even now, as I write, the rash has reappeared. I struggled to be happy about work. In the past I had always loved my job and was an energetic team member but now I felt defeated. For the first time, I felt I couldn't be bothered. What was the point any more? There was nothing good about my life. I could only expect bad news and I was becoming tired of it all.

I became cranky and short-tempered, the office pissed me off and I had no time for anyone. I felt very much alone and misunderstood. I felt paranoid but I didn't know why. At all costs I had to hide my despair. I was obsessed with Pheasants Nest, I wanted to dissect the incident, go over it at every opportunity. I couldn't let it go. Shane was the only one who understood. Like me, he was feeling the strain. My work suffered, Pieter could see I was different. He knew something had changed and he put it down to burnout. It was to be expected, said everyone, and nothing out of the ordinary for police doing crime scene work. Pieter was worried but felt it best not to make a big deal of my present state. It would pass, he hoped. Time would put it right.

A couple of weeks after Pheasants Nest I was finally able to pinpoint the source of the foul odour in the wagon. A small bolt had come away from a metal pipe that was recovered from the base of the pylon. It was covered in body fluids and had been rolling around aimlessly under the back seat filling the car with its foul stench. I was very glad to find the bolt. I was beginning to believe the smell was all in my head, but when I realised there really *was* a source, I knew I wasn't going mad after all.

On the same day I was sitting at my desk when Whayne came into the office waving a bundle of photographs around in the air.

'I've just seen the most disgusting photos! They're so putrid I don't even know what they're suppose to be. Anyone recognise these?'

'They can't be that bad,' I said. 'Bring them here, show me.'

'I really mean it, Esther. These are filthy.' As he waved a couple of them under my nose I got a glimpse of that grey slimy backbone being held up with a rubbery gloved hand. Also shots depicting maggot-infested decomposed bodies. Immediately I knew what they were. I had forgotten that Whayne hadn't seen the dead boys close up, and that's why he didn't recognise the photographs.

'Get them out of here!' I almost screamed and pushed his hands away, knocking the pictures to the floor. 'Get those pictures away from me!'

'Why, what are they?'

'Pheasants Nest! Just get them out of my sight! I don't ever want to see them! Shred them! Throw them in the bin! Do whatever! Just get rid of them!'

'Don't be stupid,' Whayne started to say. 'You can't shred them. I'll put them in the brief.'

'No! Don't put them in my brief!' By now I really was screaming. 'I don't want them in there! Get rid of them!'

Whayne realised I was deadly serious.

'I'll put them in a paper envelope, that way you won't have to look at them, is that all right?' he said calmly.

'Okay. But just get them away from me. I can't look at them. They make me sick.'

I was shocked at my outburst. It was ridiculous to suggest he shred the photographs. They were vital evidence, required for the coronial inquest. What was I thinking? But now that the photos were back from printing, I knew I had to go over the whole incident again. I was filled with a sickening dread. Pheasants Nest was never going to go away.

My private life was also suffering.

Just before the new year I had started a new relationship. Paul was also in the police and under pressure from his job. He was attached to the accident investigation squad and had the sad task of informing relatives when their loved ones had been killed in motor vehicle collisions. Around Christmas time, he realised he couldn't take it any more, and had decided to quit the force. He was now away from the constant reminders of death but I was engulfed in it and needed someone to talk to.

A couple of weeks after Pheasants Nest I prepared a dinner for two and placed the meals opposite each other with a candle in the centre of the table. We sat and talked over our rack of lamb when suddenly I saw in the flickering candlelight the image of the dead boys' ribs at the morgue. I instantly pushed the plate away, knocking the candle over.

'Get it away from me!' I screamed, pushing my chair back from the table. The slimy rib cage was right there, on my plate.

Horror filled me. 'Get it away from me!' I screamed again and burst into tears.

I sobbed uncontrollably with my head in my hands. My tears falling through my fingers to the floor, soaking through the seagrass matting. Once I started I couldn't stop crying. It went on and on. My whole body was racked with grief. I was hysterically sobbing through outbursts of incoherent speech. At that moment every death I had encountered came flooding out. I felt like I was standing in the middle of a graveyard, not knowing which grave to mourn. So many lives senselessly lost were caught up in my subconscious, and they were all finally bursting out.

'Just leave me,' I begged. I wanted to be alone.

The rest of the night was a blur. Somehow I managed to get to my bed. Alone, I sat hunched up, alternating between hugging my knees and rocking back and forth, and then tearing at my hair as the tears streamed down my face. I cried all night until I realised it was time to get ready for work.

Looking in the mirror I saw a hideous sight – I couldn't go to work looking like that. My eyes were red and swollen with black circles underneath. My face was swollen and pale. Suddenly I looked ten years older. I rang Pieter. When he heard my voice he knew instantly something was very wrong. I told him I'd been crying all night, that I couldn't face the office. He told me I was having a nervous breakdown, the very thing he'd warned me about a couple of years earlier. It was to be expected, he said. He himself had done this same thing. He told me I had two options – either take a week's annual leave and try and get over it, or he could contact the superintendent in charge of the scientific section and see what he wanted done with me. But, he warned me, if he told the boss, he would have to contact the welfare section and any counselling I received would go on my personnel record like a black mark against me, and could cost me a promotion later on. When I realised this, I begged him not to tell anyone. I would arrange a holiday in the next couple of weeks. I would be all right, I assured him. We made a pact that if I was okay after my break we wouldn't mention it again and I would just go back to duties and get on with my job as before.

With Paul, my mother and her partner I went to Tasmania and stayed with relatives. It was a peaceful trip and I took in the serene mountains and fresh air. Away from work, I felt calm and at ease. I thought blocking out the images I'd seen would somehow make it all go away and at this point the numbness took over. After my break I felt ready to go back to work but the enthusiasm had gone. My heart wasn't in it as it had been before.

Back in the office again, I set to work preparing the brief of evidence for the coronial inquest into Pheasants Nest. Shane and I spent hours poring over the evidence and moulding it into a chronological account of our findings. My photographs clearly showed the internal structure of the bridge. I was particularly amazed at the zoomed-in shots of the bodies shown in unbelievable clarity, and I had ordered an enlargement of one of the photographs showing the boys lying at the bottom of the pylon with the hand-held light illuminating the scene. When it came back from the photographic section there was a note attached to it from one of the operators at the photographic unit.

'Congratulations,' it said. 'A brilliant shot.'

Considering the unusual lighting conditions, I had managed to get the best possible exposures and the court would get a good understanding of the scene as we found it. As I mounted the enlargement I thought how sad it was that I'd taken such a good photograph of something so tragic and, unlike the morgue photographs, which I couldn't face, I viewed this distant picture as a clinical piece of evidence. Shane and I had managed to get hold of a Wang computer and we were becoming computer literate. Even though using the Wang was far better than using an electric typewriter it was still frustrating, and we spent a lot of time fiddling around with the formatting. After finishing the lengthy joint statement we both signed it, even though I would be the one who would give evidence. I numbered and labelled the photographs and drew sketches depicting the boys as they were found. As the inquest drew closer I worked at home in my own time to get the brief completed. Finally I wrapped the enlarged photograph in brown paper so the parents wouldn't be confronted by the state their sons were in during the proceedings at court. I was mindful that the photograph would be sitting on the barrister's table. I got a whiff of the bridge when handling the paper bags containing the plastic conduit pieces and had to turn away. I hoped the smell wouldn't invade the courtroom. But what if it did? Why did I feel I needed to protect the relatives from the reality I was faced with? It was more their reality than mine – why shouldn't they know the full details? Why did I feel that they would be better off being blissfully unaware of the facts. Perhaps it would provide closure if they knew the truth. I realised that reality was what *they* were faced with now, not the former happy family life they'd had before their sons' deaths. Death *is* the reality.

On 2 July 1990, I entered Campbelltown Coroner's Court, handed over my brief of evidence and sat at the side on the hard wooden benches that were slightly elevated from the rest of the gallery. The parents of the boys sat to my right at the back of the court waiting for the inquest to commence.

'All stand,' came the familiar call from the sheriff. 'This court is now in session.'

Coroner Michael O'Brien entered the room. I bowed and after the usual ceremony returned to my seat.

The sheriff continued, 'I now open the inquest into the deaths of Jaymie Egner and Matthew Kelly at Pheasants Nest Bridge on or between 18 December 1989 and 3 January, 1990.'

The first matter to be addressed was the scurrilous reporting by a particular journalist, who had consistently written articles that the two boys had been murdered. He was summonsed to the court and directed to sit through the evidence by the presiding Coroner. His unsubstantiated criticism of the police investigation was subsequently put to rest.

A steady stream of witnesses then gave the court a picture of the boys' movements before their disappearance. We heard from a number of people who had been inside the Pheasants Nest Bridge in preceding years. One witness described how he had found the open hatch underneath the bridge. With a number of companions he had entered the internal structure and explored it at length. He had first entered the bridge in 1985 and seen that the hatch cover to the south-eastern pylon was in place but noticed it was missing when he entered the bridge in early 1989.

I was called to the witness box. I stepped up, gave the oath, and proceeded to give evidence over the next three hours. My evidence was straightforward and precise. I read my testimony and handed up the photographs and drawings. When asked what my opinion was I reconstructed the scene. It was my view that the boys had voluntarily climbed into the bridge. In darkness they had lit a newspaper and used it to make a paper torch as they walked through the tunnel to the master switch where they operated the internal lights. They then walked back along the tunnel, stopping at the south-eastern pylon where they sat around the open manhole and smoked cigarettes. The boys then pulled pieces of conduit from the nearby electrical channel and played with them, possibly using them as swords, poking them at each other until one of the boys accidentally overbalanced and fell into the hole, grabbing the second boy by the waist of his shorts and causing the rip down the front. The second boy was pulled down by the weight of the first and tried to grab the sides of the manhole, hence the five-fingered death grip and black scuff marks from the soles of his running shoes. I believed that both boys fell to their deaths with the pieces of conduit, one of them hitting the exposed steel rods on the way down. They were both killed on impact. After being asked a number of questions I was excused.

We heard evidence from Dr Bradhurst as to his findings during and after the post-mortem examinations. An amount of alcohol was found in the boys' blood samples, however, this was interpreted with caution because of the advanced state of decomposition. All injuries sustained were consistent with severe impact caused when falling from a great height. Entomology evidence estimated that the boys had most likely died on the day of their disappearance, 18 December 1989.

In summing up, the Coroner directed the RTA to install locked covers immediately and have these covers inspected regularly. He found that death probably occurred on 18 December and was due to sustaining multiple traumatic injuries as a result of falling 35.8 metres into the base of the south-eastern pylon of the Pheasants Nest Bridge. He accepted my evidence in its entirety and commended both Shane and me on the presentation of the brief of evidence. He recommended we both be commended to our senior officers. In turn, the Police Prosecutor, Sergeant McMurray, also commented on the high standard of the scientific brief of evidence and stated he would bring it to the notice of the district commander. The Coroner's closing words to the court were: 'I find it was a tragic day in the lives of two adventurous boys. I cannot find that any person or persons were involved or in any way directly responsible for their deaths; they died by misadventure.'

I was pleased with the Coroner's findings, I had believed all along that the boys had entered the bridge to explore. I reflected on my own childhood, exploring the bush with my brother. My brother would have got up into the bridge and I would have followed. It was, indeed, a terrible tragedy. In the now empty courtroom, I approached the barrister's table. He stepped forward and shook my hand.

'Well done, a beautifully presented brief of evidence,' he said, 'Who trained you?'

'Detective Sergeant Pieter Strik,' I replied.

'I've never seen such a comprehensive scientific brief of evidence. I've worked at the Glebe Coroner's Court for years and have never seen a brief of this calibre. I intend to recommend you be commended for your professionalism.'

'Thank you, it's nice to be recognised occasionally. This really was a difficult job and I'd like to say I had a lot of help from my colleague, Shane Potter. I'm just glad it's all over.'

On 27 July 1990, at the Goulburn Police Academy, Shane and I watched as Constables First Class Kevin Higgins and Lance

Rice were awarded the Commissioner's Valour Award for Bravery. None described it more aptly than Sergeant Greg Smith from Green Valley police station when he said: 'The operation required courage, compassion and skill, regardless of what experience and training these two police may have had, I cannot think of a more upsetting and heart-wrenching task.'

On 26 February 1991, Shane and I were awarded a Commissioner's Citation at a ceremony held at the Liverpool office of the South-Western Region Command. Chief Inspector Gilligan made the presentation in front of a crowd of family, work colleagues and friends. Shane and I stood side by side reflecting on the day that had brought us here.

As I stepped forward to accept my award, my old boss from the foot patrol and mentor, Senior Sergeant Lloyd Morrison, leant over to my mother and whispered, 'I hope we don't lose Esther and Shane over this incident. It's jobs like this that lose us good police.'

# 17 Burnt out

The thought of suicide first crept into my mind in early 1990. I had always believed suicide was a cowardly act, but my perception of it had changed. Now, the idea seemed to draw me in. I began to think of suicide often, mostly when I was alone at night and lay sleepless, mulling over the day's events. I felt such a mix of mental and physical exhaustion and there seemed no end to the sadness encroaching on my life. My former happy nature was gone, my work continued to drag me down. And my new relationship was ending before it began. My boyfriend, Paul, was a wreck, he hadn't coped well with leaving the force and seemed to be on an emotional rollercoaster. I believe his instability was caused by policing, yet away from it he was lost. Unbeknown to me he was a drug user and secretly muted his sorrows with amphetamines. Later, when I discovered the truth about his drug use, I was horrified. I didn't know it at the time but I was extremely depressed.

I carried on at work, trying to hide my true feelings, but I suspected Pieter was worried and keeping an eye on me from a distance. The workload was as heavy as ever and there was no time for slacking off, or having a break. If one member of the team didn't pull their weight it meant the other members suffered and we were all acutely aware of each other's stress. It was paramount that I carry on and do my shifts, which meant being on call every two to three weeks. It was during these call-out periods that I really felt the strain. The phone ringing in the middle of the night was becoming unbearable and I found myself shaking and short of breath when I picked up the receiver. On one occasion I found myself crying in the car on the way to a fatal car accident. I had convinced myself that the deceased would be someone I knew. When I arrived I yelled at the constable standing by the road, demanding to know who had died. Once I realised it wasn't anyone I knew, I pulled myself together as if nothing was wrong. I became extremely good at hiding my emotions and could turn myself off emotionally as soon as the need arose, but when I was alone it was a different story.

The nightmares became a part of my life and I often woke in the middle of the night sitting bolt upright, screaming and crying. I started having recurring dreams, sometimes a couple of times a week. In one particular dream I was lying naked on the morgue table. A familiar pathologist was performing an autopsy on me while my colleagues stood by taking photographs and mumbling what a terrible tragedy it was. I would wake just as the doctor sliced into my rib cage; the pain was excruciating as the knife cut into my skin. I could feel this pain as I sat up in bed sobbing and holding my side. In other dreams I was working in the morgue. I was always wearing a drab green lab coat, which was covered in blood. I was surrounded by bottles filled with human organs floating in a bloodied fluid. There were bodies lying in rows on steel trolleys in various stages of autopsy with body cavities cut open and limbs missing. I could always smell the blood in my dreams and would wake with a dry mouth, tasting the foul odour.

In the morning I was exhausted and felt like I'd been up all night; I could feel the bags pulling on the skin under my eyes. But I never mentioned the dreams to Pieter at work. At the time, I thought they were a normal response and, anyway, it was police culture that you didn't talk about it. In fact, I barely gave the dreams a thought, they just became part of my life. And then there was that previous conversation I'd had with Pieter, that if I wasn't coping he would talk to welfare. There was no way I was going to jeopardise all the effort I had put in, only to be told I was being transferred to a desk job.

The constant sleep deprivation was taking its toll and I was exhausted all the time. This worried me as I was often on the road late at night feeling the strain. Eventually the inevitable happened and one night I fell asleep at the wheel. I slumped forward and hit my head on the steering wheel as the car veered off the road and hit the dirt verge at 100 kph. I woke with a start, slammed on the brake and pulled the car back onto the bitumen. By pure luck the road was empty and I had survived this time, but how long would it be before it happened again? I really didn't care. On these occasions it would be all too easy to just run off the road and hit a tree. I would play out this scenario many times over when I drove home from a job in the middle of the night. It was desolate out on the unlit roads that led to my home, no one would witness the accident and I really thought that no one would care. I couldn't bring myself to discuss these thoughts – even with my mother to whom I was very close. In a sense I was ashamed of the person I had become.

There were lots of ways I could kill myself. I could hang from the wardrobe door, that would be easy, but then I could also take an overdose or use my service revolver. It crossed my mind all the time but there was always one nagging problem – I couldn't do it to Pieter. It just wouldn't be fair to call him to the crime scene. I would have a twinge of regret about putting my workmates in the position of having to attend my death. That would sober me up and bring me out of my macabre thoughts. As quickly as I had organised my exit from this world I would forget about it and get on with whatever it was I had to do. My emotions were swinging like a pendulum.

Things really started to come to a head one night when I was on call. I was staying with my brother and his wife because I was in-between houses and needed somewhere to live for a couple of weeks. I found myself lying awake in my usual anxious state. I was feeling down and unsettled, and I realised I was focusing on my camera bag, which was sitting by the bed. I usually stored my service revolver and handcuffs in the front zipper pocket of my camera bag when I was on call, as I was required to have my 'appointments' (gun and handcuffs) on me at all times. A powerful force was pulling me towards the bag. The gun was fully loaded, and the only thing stopping me from shooting myself was that inner voice telling me it wasn't fair on Pieter. In my mixed-up state I hadn't even considered my brother or any of my family. I lay frozen to the spot trying to comprehend the crazy state I was in. I realised that the only thing to do was to get up and get rid of the gun, get it out of my sight. I pulled on some clothes over my pyjamas, slung the camera bag over my shoulder and walked outside into the cold night air. I unlocked the police car, threw the bag in the back and slammed the door shut. *That's it*, I thought, *now I've got no choice but to go against police procedure and leave my appointments in a police vehicle.* If the gun and handcuffs were stolen I knew I'd be charged with neglect of duty. I didn't care any more. I had to get the gun away from my side. I crawled back into bed and lay awake staring at the ceiling.

It was 1 a.m. and the pager went off. Attempted murder in Macquarie Fields. I went into crime scene examiner mode, and the rest of the night was spent out in the cold, combing the road for clues. The injured woman had been chased from the local pub by an angry mob of women and hit on the head with a wonjee stick (Aboriginal weapon). She was later to die in hospital.

Around mid-1990, I felt particularly down after attending a job with Shane one morning. No sooner had we walked into the office at the start of the day when a job came in. It was a cot death of an eighteen-month-old baby. Shane looked at me sadly as he anticipated the scene at the house. I offered to go with him for moral support. We were both struggling after Pheasants Nest and it was jobs like this that made coping with our work all the more difficult.

We entered the house to the sound of the mother sobbing. The general duties officers led us to the bedroom and indicated the baby lying in a cot against the opposite wall. Shane photographed the scene and then we examined the baby and the cot. We found that it was not a cot death but an accidental death. The baby had somehow managed to dislodge the steel pins that held the lower portion of the moveable railing in place. Once the pins were out of their mounting, the lower portion of the railing could swing free with the top portion anchoring the top of the rail. The baby had tried to crawl down and out of the cot through the small gap and become trapped between the lower portion of the rail and the mattress. The baby had choked to death.

It was a terrible scene. We both struggled to keep our composure, examining the little innocent boy with his teddy bear pyjamas on. He wore an all-in-one romper and I can still remember his little feet encased in the soft material. While we were examining the scene the father had rushed home from work and been given the bad news by his wife. When Shane and I had completed our examination we walked out of the house and I was shocked to see the parents holding each other on the front porch. I guess they sat outside because we were inside and they needed to distance themselves from the investigation, but it was terrible to see them sitting there. I paused for a minute and they both looked up and met my gaze. Their strained faces were wet with tears. I couldn't bring myself to say anything, just gave them a sympathetic look and walked away.

In the car Shane and I sat and talked for a minute as tears welled in my eyes and rolled down my face. I was not crying alone. Shane was also distraught and struggling to hold back tears. I honestly felt I hadn't done enough. What really got to me was the fact that the parents thought the child had died in his sleep. I asked Shane not to drive off but to wait a minute, I needed to ask him something.

'Don't you think we should go back and explain to the parents how their baby died?'

Shane put his head in his hands and paused for a minute before speaking. 'Mate, I don't know if I can do it.'

'They think it's a cot death, they really should be told what happened. If it was me, I'd want to know,' I said.

'I don't know how I'd handle talking to them,' he replied.

'If you'll come with me, I'll tell them, you don't have to speak to them, just come and stand with me while I explain what happened; I think that's the right thing to do,' I said.

'Okay, do it,' he replied.

Together we approached the couple who were still sobbing in each other's arms on the front patio. We introduced ourselves and then I explained our role and what we had done inside the house. I described the problem with the cot and how it had caused the death of their baby. It was a relief to see the look of comprehension on their faces. They told me that the cot had been the mother's when she was a baby and this was the second generation in her family to use it. I think the realisation that it was an accident at least gave the parents a reason instead of going over and over that unresolved question of why. They now understood what had happened and that the baby had most likely woken earlier that morning and tried to get out of the cot when the accident occurred. It was no fault of theirs, just one of those freak things that inevitably lead to safety recalls and furniture design modifications.

The young couple simply said, 'Thank you.'

It was yet another blow to our battered emotions and I brooded about the death for the rest of the day. Shane wasn't faring too well either as he had a daughter of a similar age and knew all too well how painful it would be to lose a child in such circumstances.

Still, day after day I turned up for work and did my bit to serve the community. I was quite convinced that my declining mental state was perfectly normal for someone doing crime scene duties. After all, it was part and parcel of the job. I hoped it would pass.

Around this time Operation Transplant was underway.

A number of detectives from various squads had been seconded to form a task force operation and were conducting surveillance on an organised car theft racket. Cars were stolen in Melbourne and brought to a predetermined location in the south-western suburbs of Sydney. The motors were removed, then the cars sent to a wrecking yard nearby to be dismembered and used for parts. The engine and chassis numbers were ground off, new numbers stamped on, then the cars were re-birthed using compliance plates taken from a wreck. These cars were then registered and sold in Sydney. The stakes were high and there was a lot of money changing hands; it was also a political football as crime statistics were forever hitting the media. The Minister was outraged and demanded the racket be stopped. Pieter was asked to supply one scientific constable to the task force – it would be a secondment for six months and meant working on stolen cars full time. Both Shane and I were struggling and Pieter knew it would be a break from the pressure of crime scene work, which would do both of us a lot of good. I was nominated to take the secondment but for Shane this was a bitter blow. We would both be an asset to the task force but there was only one position and I guess Pieter felt that I was closer to the brink than Shane.

Initially I was woken in the middle of the night on a number of occasions and given covert addresses to attend. Throughout the surveillance stage I took aerial photographs and under the cover of darkness marked suspect stolen cars so we could later track their movement. It was a dangerous job, darting from our undercover police vehicle into service station yards and crawling around on the pavement trying to get under the vehicles to place our marks on them. The crooks involved in this job meant business – they put out a contract on the lives of two of the detectives involved in the operation. I was paranoid about my identity being revealed but the crooks didn't suspect a woman was involved in the investigation, so I found some consolation in that fact. After the search warrants were executed I was responsible for recording and cataloguing the stolen cars and their parts before embarking on the long and tedious task of forensically examining hundreds of suspect stolen cars. I spent six months working in a wrecking yard amongst the filth and squalor of abandoned vehicles and parts. It was a dirty, rat-infested environment that was unbearably cold at times. I worked alone, turning up for work each day with my camera and etching kit, and systematically examined every corner of the place. After a couple of months I became accustomed to my new environment, there was no need to get dressed up for the occasion, overalls and boots were the order of the day. I didn't realise it at the time but I was being exposed to myriad dangerous chemicals and their fumes. The sleeves of my overalls were covered in holes where the chemicals had eaten through the material. I was not warned to wear a mask or cover my skin when I used the chemicals and I often suffered slight burns on my hands and arms when acid dripped on me. I also suffered from headaches and blurry vision; later I realised this was due to the fumes I was inhaling. But still, I didn't complain, I was naive about the long-term physical effects. Eventually, I prepared a ninety-eight page statement for court.

Although I was off call and away from the death scenes, I was still feeling down and alone. The many hours spent alone in the eerie atmosphere of the wrecking yard began to play tricks on me and I became jumpy at signs of the slightest movement. I hated the rats that often showed their pesky faces when I was clambering over piles of tyres or springs. It was always a relief when one of the detectives or local general duties police turned up to check on me. It was a miracle that the crooks didn't send one of their hit men over to the yard during the day and simply blow me away. One of the familiar faces I was always happy to see was Constable First Class Gary Howes, from the vehicle examination unit at Zetland. I had developed quite a rapport with him and was always grateful for his assistance. He was a mechanic by trade and had the luxury of carrying a lot of equipment in his four-wheel drive. He would call in and see how I was going, lending a hand when I needed an engine part removed or supplying the equipment I so greatly needed. While working together we would discuss the state of affairs with stolen vehicles in New South Wales and we were both passionate about doing something worthwhile to tackle the problem. Gary had the foresight to suggest we start a scientific squad called vehicle identification and he was keen for us to work together. I wasn't too sure about working solely on vehicles, but as time went on I began to see that this would be a much more stable career path than my crime-scene work.

After finishing my stint with Operation Transplant I slid back into the gloom of crime-scene work. Once again I found myself on twenty-four-hour call and dreading the sound of the phone ringing. I came to the realisation that I absolutely had to leave Macquarie Fields. I felt it was killing me and, much as I wanted to continue in my chosen profession, I needed to get out. I decided to apply for a transfer to the Sydney district crime scene unit. This seemed a good compromise as I had heard that the city office had twice the amount of staff with half the workload, and they also had the luxury of working in pairs. I could continue my work with more support and fewer jobs. I was sure this would be a better working environment and I would be more able to cope. But I felt defeated when I finally broached the subject with Pieter. It was like I was abandoning ship. I was no longer strong enough to stand and take what was dished out. Pieter was disappointed that I was leaving but supported me in my transfer because, as he put it, he only wanted what was best for me.

Finally we got word that there was to be a debrief at the Sydney Police Centre for all scientific staff who had attended the three disasters – the two bus crashes and the Newcastle earthquake – the previous year. Pieter, Whayne, Shane and I dutifully turned up on the day and sat in a lecture room surrounded by about twenty colleagues. John Merrick, the grief counsellor from the city morgue, stood before us and listed a range of symptoms that occur when a person is psychologically traumatised. Included on the list were: sleeplessness, irritability, fearfulness, avoidance, nightmares, anxiety, headaches, stomach complaints, lack of appetite and so on. He handed out a sheet of paper listing those symptoms and asked us to fill it out. Glancing around the room I noticed there was a lot of ticking going on but no one was prepared to openly admit what was on their sheets. John then asked members of the group to raise their hands if they had suffered any of the symptoms. Not one person in the room was prepared to put their hand up but I suspected that, in varying degrees, every one of them suffered from some of these symptoms. At the conclusion of the meeting John wrote his phone number on the whiteboard and offered counselling, albeit unofficially, if the need arose. As I jotted the number down in my diary I was almost certain I would need his help in the future.

After the meeting I met the officer in charge of the newly named physical evidence section, Superintendent Henry Delaforce, and requested a transfer. He was accommodating and told me he would be happy to have me as part of the city team.

On 17 November 1990, I began duties at the Sydney district crime scene section. However, I was rostered on afternoon shift alone. I felt nothing had changed. Instead of reaping the benefits of more staff, I was used for my experience and often rostered alone on afternoon or night shift to cover the whole Sydney district. I was now living on the fifteenth level of a high-rise apartment block in Surry Hills. It was a huge contrast to my former life on acreage surrounded by bush. My relationship with Paul was over and with few friends and no family close by, I spent much of my spare time alone staring at four walls. I was lonely and sad but I was good at hiding my true feelings, and I kept turning up to work each day and carrying on.

Still, the nightmares continued, I felt constantly exhausted, and I suffered severe headaches that nearly drove me insane with the pain. I would lie awake night after night brooding on the latest murder or death I had attended. I spent a lot of time crying and was shocked at the sight of my puffy eyes when I looked in the mirror in the morning. I did my best with make-up and hoped nobody at work would ask any questions.

One night I felt particularly agitated and stressed as I lay awake with a pounding migraine into the early hours of the morning. I had been crying over a drug overdose incident and double stabbing I had attended the day before. At the scene I was reminded of Paul's drug habit and feared he would end up dead just like the person before me. As it turned out, many years later he did die of an overdose.

As we drove away from the drug overdose scene, my colleague, Lyle, and I heard a signal one over the radio. It was an urgent call for assistance a couple of streets away. With lights and sirens blazing we rushed to assist the local Glebe general duties officers. We ran into the foyer of an old block of units where we found a policewoman and a man covered in blood wrestling on the floor. We assisted her to restrain and handcuff the offender before following the blood trail into apartment number one. Inside I saw a young couple covered in blood and suffering from horrendous stab wounds. The young man held a towel to his face and I asked to see what his injury was. He had lost his entire nose, it had been severed with a large carving knife that lay on the floor at his feet. He asked for a cigarette and I lit him one but when he took a drag on it his face turned green. He had a punctured lung. The woman had a huge laceration to her thigh, exposing the muscle and bone, and had almost lost her arm, which was severed except for a tendon holding it in place. We did our best to calm them and attempted to stem the flow of blood until the ambulance arrived. It wasn't until one of the ambulance officers asked my partner to pick up the victim's nose that the injured man realised it had been severed. After the two victims left for hospital we set about examining the crime scene. There was a lot of blood and I struggled with the sickly smell as it dried and filled the room with its pungent odour.

Lying awake that night going over the scene in my mind, I could still smell the blood, it seemed to fill the room and I couldn't escape its odour. I felt confused and disorientated. It was a feeling I hadn't experienced before. I couldn't think straight, my pulse was racing and I could actually see my heart pounding in my chest. I wondered if I was going to have a heart attack. I had to get something, anything, to help the pain in my head. I searched for Panadol but couldn't find any so in my delusional state I got in my car and started driving around the city aimlessly. It was midnight and I drove to Bondi, then through Kings Cross until I finally ended up in Macquarie Street in the city outside the hospital. I sat in the car crying. What should I do? Should I go in and get help, or drive away? Something told me not to go in. Looking back on the state I was in then, I'm sure if I had gone in I would have been scheduled and placed in a psychiatric hospital. I was on the brink of collapsing and completely losing it. As I stumbled in the door of my unit, I had a thought – where was my cross? When I was ten years old, my parents had given me a small gold cross on a chain with a tiny ruby recessed into the centre. As a child I had worn it everywhere but had discarded it when I became a teenager. I rushed into the bedroom and ripped open the drawers of my dressing table furiously searching for it. I threw items out onto the floor and scattered treasured memories of my childhood about until I came across a small plastic box. I'd found it. I was elated. I fastened the cross around my neck and a sense of calm swept over me. I was all right now, my cross would protect me. As the tears rolled down my face, I said the Lord's Prayer. Holding the crucifix, I vowed I would never take it off and to this day it still protects me. But it would be another ten years before I realised that there *is* life after dealing with death.

# 18 Choosing life

'What are you looking at, you skinny bitch?'

My eyes were fixed on my plate as I sat at the dining table. Not daring to look up, I shuffled my chair forward to let the enormous woman pass.

'Sorry,' I said, still avoiding eye contact. 'Just trying to make way for you to get through.'

'I used to be a model once you know!' she said. 'You're not the only skinny person in this world.'

'Good for you,' I said, managing a smile and hoping she would go away.

She turned and stormed off leaving me to realise that this was where my career had taken me – the loony bin. I couldn't believe I had ended up in this place. I was no longer a detective senior constable of police, but an inmate in the nut house. Looking around the room I was engulfed with sadness to think of what I had been reduced to. My career had ended here in this hospital. How had it come to this?

After finding my little cross in 1990 I no longer thought about suicide. My faith in God gave me strength. In 1991 I met Suzana, who had recently joined the crime scene unit. Together we talked about ways of dealing with death and she suggested reading a passage from the New Testament. Turning to the back page I chose a particular verse from the index that related to how I felt. This, combined with prayer, gave me peace and enough strength to carry on. I renewed my passion for running and hit the city streets whenever I could. I pushed myself to the limit, which I found relieved the pressure of work. I believe now that faith, combined with physical fitness, was what kept me going, despite having been to hell and back.

In March 1991 I bought a decrepit Edwardian terrace house in Womerah Lane, Darlinghurst, and threw myself into restoring it. I developed a new circle of city friends and took up sailing at the Cruising Yacht Club at Rushcutters Bay. Sailing on *Sho'gun* with its crew gave me a new direction, and living within walking distance of the club helped make sailing a convenient distraction from my working life. Always happy when facing a new challenge, I concentrated on learning to sail and spent at least two days a week hauling the sails on the multicoloured yacht I came to love. Midweek we raced in the twilight series and we spent Sundays 'booze cruising' on Sydney Harbour. The feeling of freedom out on the water gave me a sense of belonging and I began to embrace city life. Mark, a drug squad officer I had known when working at Macquarie Fields, became my flat mate and we forged a special friendship built on mateship and humour. So now my life took a new, positive direction.

For the next twelve months I continued crime-scene work in the city and found myself settling into the new routine. Midyear the section changed from call-out roster to shift work, which meant I went back to working three shifts as I had when I first joined the force. A couple of times I was rostered to work alone on night work. It was eerie working in the large crime scene office alone but I did my shifts and by this stage I was competent at examining complex scenes. By now, the service had addressed the increased risk of HIV. We were finally offered a lightweight paper suit to wear, though I now realised it was impossible to be totally protected from the dangers of infection. One afternoon I was called to a stabbing at Central Railway Station. After examining the scene I began to collect a number of exhibits which included a blood-soaked item of clothing. As I dropped it into the paper exhibit bag blood splashed into the corner of my eye. With city work came many HIV positive drug overdoses. These victims were usually skeletal as a result of being in the last stages of the disease. At first I was very concerned, but after examining many such scenes I realised I just had to be extra cautious. Over time I developed a strong sense of compassion for the victims. Talking to friends and relatives who had just lost their mate to HIV gave me a better understanding of the disease and I became much more accepting, judging people for who they were rather than for what I perceived them to be. At a drug overdose I found myself scraping bloodied vomit into a paper bag with a tongue depressor to spare the relative the job of cleaning it up. The general duties officers thought it was funny when I ran to the window and dry retched from the thirty-sixth floor. I was angry at their immaturity, but then, why would they understand my reasoning for cleaning up after the dead? They just didn't know what it was like to be faced with death day in, day out.

Later that year I accepted the offer to set up the new vehicle identification team at Zetland, an industrial suburb just south of the city. I jumped at the chance of transferring to the vehicle examination unit. It was a good compromise. I would still be attached to the physical evidence section and working in the area of stolen vehicles in a forensic sense, but away from dealing with death.

It was a little daunting when I arrived at the vehicle examination section with my goods and chattels to find I was the first female police officer to be attached to the all-male domain. In the past it had been a prerequisite to be a qualified mechanic to work in this section and it was a new phenomenon to have a non-mechanic, who was also a woman, working in this area. After the initial shock to the troops I was accepted and worked very well alongside my male counterparts.

Although busy at work and away from the pressures of being on call, I still found it disturbing dealing with the aftermath of death. Sometimes, cars came in to be examined with the remnants of dead occupants inside. Blood, skin, bone and brain matter could be seen inside the mangled wrecks and invariably gave off an unpleasant odour. The latest road fatality was a constant topic of conversation amongst my work mates in the lunch room and it was here after work that I began a regime of drinking. At least a couple of days a week I'd stay back with some of my work mates and have a couple of drinks.

At home I was still spooked by the sound of the phone ringing. The nightmares continued and I struggled with bouts of insomnia, lying awake for hours. At times I felt down and lonely, but couldn't put my finger on what the problem was. My drinking had escalated to the point that I suffered a stomach ulcer and high blood pressure. My doctor was quite critical of this and warned me I would be risking permanent liver damage if I continued to drink to this degree. I was worried enough to make an appointment with John Merrick, the grief counsellor at the morgue, who did a wonderful job listening to my fears. There seemed no end to my torment but I always walked out of his office with a renewed strength to get on with things. After my doctor's advice I decided to give up drinking for six months. I did feel better after this break, however I always regressed when I felt stressed or under pressure.

In January 1993, I crewed a yacht while the owner entertained clients who had sponsored the boat during the Sydney to Hobart yacht race. I was helping rig the boat when I caught a glimpse of the clients walking down the pier. With a laugh I announced I recognised one of them – it was the tall, fair-haired detective I had worked with at Campbelltown who'd said I looked so young on my first day in the job. As Ken stepped on board he immediately recognised me. After talking to him I realised that he had spoken about me on and off to our mutual friend, Bob Berthally. Ken, who was recently separated, was living at Brighton-Le-Sands. It had been eight years since he'd resigned from the police force and he was now working as a chief executive officer with a shipping company. He had a close-knit circle of friends, with whom I got along well, and that was the beginning of a wonderful friendship that culminated in our marriage in 1995.

Over time, Ken was able to draw out the hidden feelings I harboured from my crime-scene days. He was extremely sensitive and comforting when I expressed how I had felt at many of the grotesque scenes. He mentioned the nightmares but I would always pass it off with a shrug. Sometimes I drank to get to sleep and this would hide my inability to drift off as I slumped into bed in a stupor. Ken would comment that he couldn't understand how crime-scene examiners handled their job and it was becoming obvious to me that I had myriad underlying problems associated with my past. What I came to realise later was that I was reliving, over and over, the horrific details of my past experiences. It was inevitable that eventually I would collapse under the burden of what I held close to my heart. Without therapy it would continue to build up and then subside before building up again. Drinking only served to numb the pain temporarily. Eventually I realised that my seemingly unnatural reactions to everyday occurrences were in fact normal responses, given that I had worked in an area filled with trauma for five years without a break, little training and no support. In a sense I was set up for what was about to unfold – it was only a matter of time.

In 1993, forensic services began to take a new direction. No longer was on-the-job experience enough, academic qualifications were now essential and all staff were informed of the implementation of the Diploma of Applied Science in Forensic Investigation (NSW Police). I was accepted in the first intake and found myself surrounded by books. Finally the department was making an attempt to train its members but, for me, it was too late. This was the training I had desperately needed before I was thrown into the job alone and untrained in 1987. It wasn't until I began studying that I fully realised how inadequate my training had been. Looking back at the complex scenes I had examined without any formal qualifications, I felt horrified. The pressure of studying also began to take its toll and I felt unable to cope. Again I rang John Merrick and he counselled me through it. Somehow my body recognised the old feelings of having too much to do and not enough time. The feeling of working on overdrive resurfaced and I became flighty and nervous. All of a sudden I had trouble organising myself and the workload got on top of me.

To add to the pressure of study, I was nominated to write the subject 'Vehicle Identification' for the Diploma of Applied Science, and was transferred to the forensic services training and research unit. I had no formal training in writing and absolutely no idea where to start. I began by researching the subject and then wrote it in six weeks. After this I was given other projects to write for the diploma, including the initial draft of forensic medicine, and assisting with final editing on several other subjects. In all, I spent fifteen months working in the area of training and research before being transferred back to the vehicle examination unit in late 1994.

My job now included running the subject vehicle identification for the diploma, marking papers and running residential training courses. This was on top of my basic duties working on vehicle theft rackets where I was responsible for examining multiple stolen vehicles, fielding vehicle inquiries, maintaining the vehicle data base and giving expert evidence in court. Eventually an additional untrained constable was assigned to help but at the same time we lost the officer in charge who had gone off sick with stress. Warren had become a great friend and colleague and I missed his leadership as I witnessed the section slowly failing as staff deserted the ship. Suddenly, there seemed no direction and I felt I was sinking under the weight of all my responsibilities. I was back to feeling incredibly frustrated that there was not enough time in the day to get the job done. I also felt the stress of the many crime-scene examiners I spoke to every day. The phone rang incessantly with vehicle inquiries from around the state, and during the course of these calls the crime-scene officers would unload the details of their latest horrific job into my understanding ear. I began to suffer hearing problems in my left ear which I attributed to the pressure of the phone as I clutched it tensely, listening to my colleagues. The pounding in my ear was unbearable at night and I wondered what the hell was happening to me.

In 1994 I sold my terrace at Darlinghurst and, with Ken, I purchased a new terrace at Newtown. Ken's eleven-year-old son, Chris, was now living with us and we felt the house at Darlinghurst was too cramped. But the move to Newtown was a disaster. We cowered in our home feeling under siege from the locals who wandered past our front door drunk and abusive. Our cars were damaged in the street. I hated everything about the area. I felt unsafe and began to feel extremely paranoid about break-ins and being attacked when I walked from my car to the house after dark. After less than twelve months we sold up and bought a house at Bonnet Bay, forty minutes south of the city.

My horrific nightmares, where I would sit bolt upright in bed screaming out and crying, continued. I was morbid and thought about death often. I knew I needed help and made an appointment to see Stan O'Brien at the police welfare unit. I saw him several times over the next six months and expressed my concern at how much I was drinking. His reply to this was that a couple of drinks wouldn't hurt, and, in fact, if it relaxed me, it would be okay to drink in moderation. During these discussions the death of the two brothers at Appin and the job at Pheasants Nest surfaced and Stan offered to perform Rapid Eye Movement (REM) therapy. The counsellor moved his fingers across my line of vision rapidly in order to induce a relaxed state of mind in which alpha waves induce a semi-conscious or semi-wakeful state. This was supposed to allow decision making or planning and help the recipient relax. What he didn't mention was that this method would be of most benefit if performed regularly. It all seemed like hocus pocus to me and I felt no benefit whatsoever. But what could I do? Even the so-called experts at the welfare unit didn't seem to know what was going on, so how was I supposed to know what to do? It seemed each time these morbid thoughts would surface they would melt away just as quickly. During one of our sessions Stan advised that the job at Zetland was adding to my stress and that I should seek a transfer, preferably out of forensic services. I was shocked and disappointed. My expertise lay in forensic work, it was all I knew and I was to graduate shortly with my diploma of applied science. I had worked hard all these years to become an expert and now it seemed like I was being told it was a waste of time and I should get up and walk away. I resisted his advice and instead looked at other avenues within forensic services where I might continue my career.

In 1996 I transferred to the document examination unit and embarked on learning the science of forensic document examination. I was disappointed to leave Zetland but it was time to desert the sinking ship. In mid-1996 Ken and I planned a family and I soon became pregnant with my son Robert. During the pregnancy my anxiety levels rose to new heights. I was now preoccupied with all things morbid and was terrified about something happening to Ken. I was especially anxious when he travelled overseas with his job and could only sleep at night after saying a prayer for his safe return. I was horrified by my reaction when Ken brought home a cane bassinette for the baby. It looked to me like a tiny white coffin and I struggled to convince myself that the cot would be safe for the baby. Was it a sign or was it all in my head? I was becoming confused and distraught. I struggled daily with my fears to the point where I became incensed at the realisation that I was being robbed of the happiest time in my life by my fear of death. During my pregnancy I gave one of the best performances of my life as I acted the part of the happy expectant mum, when all the time I was terrified.

On 22 June 1997, Robert was born. For the first time in my career I was on extended leave and now found a new and exciting meaning to life. The experience of motherhood brought me great joy, though I struggled with my fears daily. I worked hard to push them into the back of my mind although I did allow myself to check the baby constantly when he slept to see if he was still breathing. I kept my fears to myself but it was apparent to Ken that I was suffering some form of over-protectiveness with my paranoia over the baby's safety. It wasn't long before Ken and I decided to have another baby and Alice was born two years later on 8 May 1999. Other than a short stint back at work part time, I had been on maternity leave since March 1999 and I was now on extended leave and living in Brisbane.

I had persuaded Ken to seek a transfer with his job. I had convinced myself Sydney was unsafe and that it would be far better to get away. Later I realised that no amount of running away would alleviate my mental state. Shortly after Alice's birth Ken began to notice I was grinding my teeth in my sleep. He had also seen the re-emergence of the frequent nightmares. My anxiety level had risen to a critical peak as I struggled to maintain an even keel with the two children. I was on high alert, always at the ready for impending danger, and was extremely over-protective. Finally Ken fronted me with it and asked, 'What the hell's going on?' At first I denied there was a problem, but after brooding on it for a couple of days I admitted he was right – I needed help.

I contacted police welfare and was told I could see a psychologist of my choice for five sessions before my situation would be reviewed. I found these sessions extremely confronting as memories and experiences long buried in my subconscious began to emerge. One of my nightmares – of being trapped in a dark room – was compared by my psychologist to my experience at the bridge at Pheasants Nest and also my inability to escape from a caravan where I was trapped with a dead man many years before. The simplest of daily routines became unbearable, to the point where I had extreme difficulty bathing my little boy because of the scene where the child had been electrocuted in the bath. I was dealing with constant flashbacks where the simplest trigger would remind me of a distressing scene. Slowly I began to address these situations and work on alleviating them from my life. It was the start of a long recovery that saw me back in Sydney in September 1999.

After visiting my GP I was referred to a psychiatrist, Doctor Selwyn Smith. With his help and guidance I began the long and difficult journey back to health that continues today. It had taken many years for my true feelings to surface but after being diagnosed with post-traumatic stress disorder (PTSD) by Dr Smith, I finally began to face the demons that had plagued me over the past ten years. Facing my fears in group therapy was a major step towards recovery and I was determined to see it through and come out the other side.

Dr Smith initially prescribed Zoloft, an antidepressant, but after taking it for two weeks I wasn't responding and was subsequently prescribed Ativan, an antianxiety agent. This drug is taken only when required, which works well for me. I am happier dealing with my emotions without the intervention of drugs. But there are days when I find taking the medication beneficial.

Next I had to face the long and stressful process of applying for my illness to be classified as Hurt on Duty. It was difficult filling out the forms as I was re-living the traumatic scenes. Sitting at the kitchen table, tears streamed down my face as I wrote about Pheasants Nest and other deeply distressing scenes I had attended. Suddenly I was back in time and could smell the dead boys and hear the booming sound inside the bridge. These responses were completely overwhelming and I had no idea how to deal with them.

With my doctor's support I tackled the police issues that were in themselves a contributing factor to my stress. This process included assessments done by independent psychiatrists who would then report back to the police service. Each time I endured these interviews I was at the mercy of the doctors' opinions. I waited in the hope that my circumstances would be seen as the direct result of my exposure to traumatic events in the course of my duties as a crime-scene examiner. The psychiatrists probed into my childhood, family life and schooling and I was forced to go over and over the same details each time. The process was bound in red tape and communication was all but nonexistent. I was advised by a colleague to attend the police medical officer (PMO) and did so in hope that he could advise me in relation to medical discharge. When I saw the PMO I hadn't yet decided whether I would return to work but it seemed that the best course of action would be to distance myself from policing altogether. I took the paperwork with me, thinking we would discuss it step by step during the meeting. I couldn't have been more wrong. The doctor strode into the waiting room and called my name at the top of his voice. Then he spun on his heel and marched back to his room, me in tow like a naughty schoolgirl. Inside his office I was met with contempt. He demanded to know why I was off sick and accused me of moving to Brisbane so I could join the Queensland police. I tried to answer his questions honestly but he constantly interrupted and threw further questions at me until I became confused. I could feel my anxiety rising and the emotion building up.

He said, 'You're a police officer first and foremost, before anything else, and you should get off your arse and get back to work.' I pleaded with him to listen. I tried to explain what I'd seen during my crime-scene work but he spat back, 'Anything you've seen at a crime scene is no different to what you see on television!'

I couldn't believe this was coming from a doctor, a person I had thought I could go to for help. He became increasingly aggressive towards me and I could see his distaste as he snarled back at my every answer. He told me I should go back to general duties and that my experience in forensic work was of no consequence. As far as he was concerned I could just go back to mainstream policing and that would solve everything. I burst into tears and sobbed hysterically. When I looked up blurry-eyed, he glared back at me with a satisfied look.

'Give me the paperwork,' he demanded, stretching across the desk and gesturing for me to hand it over. I was paralysed and clutched it to my chest. Through my tears I told him I wanted to keep it, I didn't want to give it to him, he was unreasonable and I was sure he would not support it.

He said, 'Not necessarily, go get another doctor's report from your psychiatrist, he knows the ropes, I'm sure he has all the right answers.' Now he was openly criticising my psychiatrist; I couldn't believe it. He went on to criticise St John of God and the PTSD program. 'It's a waste of time! It will only make you worse, in my view it just makes people like you feel sorry for yourself. You just have to get on with it.'

I ran from the office and went to the ladies toilet where I cried hysterically. It was some time before I could compose myself enough to leave the building.

At home that night I repeated the story to my mother and husband. They were both horrified that I had been abused at that level. My husband rang the doctor's immediate superior and I rang the police association and made a formal complaint. I was told that I wasn't the first police officer to be abused by the doctor, there had been several before me, but not one person was prepared to put their name to a complaint for fear of reprisal. I wasn't concerned, I hadn't done anything wrong and I wanted this doctor stopped. I felt he was a bully. Eventually my complaint was processed through the health care complaints commission but the doctor was merely spoken to and not reprimanded. I was surprised when eventually the doctor supported my application for medical discharge, and wondered what had changed his opinion?

I continued seeing Dr Smith, who listened to my fears and helped me come to terms with my symptoms. In the early stages I had trouble performing the simplest of tasks such as grocery shopping, or walking along the street with the children in the pram. I was in constant fear of an impending disaster – being run over, say, or being shot. I feared for the children's safety constantly and was extremely nervous when out in crowded places. I was fearful of walking over grates in the pavement or roadway in case they collapsed and would immediately feel threatened when I heard the sound of a helicopter overhead or the sound of a siren. I had many phobias about food which made preparing or enjoying a meal very difficult. I would peer into my meal looking for maggots or other foreign bodies that could be hiding amongst the rice or pasta. I couldn't eat rack of lamb and found it intolerable to look at it on my plate, nor could I stand the sight of blood running out of undercooked steak. In the midst of all this doom and gloom I completely lost my sense of humour, which had always been a big part of my life. It had simply slipped away over the years until it was almost nonexistent.

Dr Smith immediately made application to the police service for me to be included in the next PTSD course at St John of God hospital. Along with my Hurt on Duty application it was approved swiftly and I felt lucky to be one of only two constables to be admitted. Beforehand I found a babysitter to come and take care of Alice and Robert. This was a very difficult step as I had feared leaving them. I found a wonderful caring lady who talked me through my fears and in time became part of the family. Having to do the course and leave the children forced me to deal with my fears; I worried constantly but I managed to cope one day at a time.

At St John of God hospital during the PTSD course I realised that my perception of life had become distorted. I was determined to rediscover my old self and worked hard every day during the six weeks towards resuming my old identity. Admitting my phobias during group discussions allowed me to realise that I had lost all sense of reality. Slowly I accepted I was worrying about things that would most likely never occur. Believing this was true was difficult but I worked hard to convince myself that I was worrying unnecessarily. I learnt to deal with the mixed emotions, memory loss and lack of concentration, all of which are slowly returning to normal. I was tearful and at other times numb and couldn't express myself. I learnt to bring these emotions back into line with reality and to identify when I was reacting in these ways and immediately work on controlling them.

Each person in the group had a turn at telling their story. This was a confronting experience as the group sat in silence while I recounted my story. I will never forget their looks of acknowledgement. It was a profound experience both to tell my story, and in turn to hear each individual harrowing tale. I learned in group therapy not to judge others and to avoid negative people.

Physically, I looked drawn and tired. Fatigue showed in the bags under my eyes, and the lines on my face showed the strain of dealing with death. St John of God believed in healing not only the mind but also the body. I was given an exercise regime that got me back into running. Going right back to my academy days I had always enjoyed the physical challenge of long distance running and had used this as an outlet over the years. It was a good feeling to put the running gear back on, step out onto the road and push myself to the limit. I found myself gritting my teeth and yelling out loud at times when I needed to get the stress out; it was pure relief after pushing myself physically. It is still my regular regime to take time out and run myself into the ground.

With a counsellor I tackled my food anxieties. Each week I worked on one issue, starting with an attempt to cut up raw meat. Next, I cut one chop from a cooked rack of lamb, ate it, then two, then three until I was comfortable with it. I reaffirmed to myself that it was not a human rib but a piece of lamb. I worked hard to overcome these anxieties with food to the stage where I can now cope with the sight of blood running from a steak; I'm not happy about it but I can stand it.

The issue of alcohol consumption was addressed during the course and I was shocked to see the damage excessive drinking does to the human body. The depletion of thiamin causes memory loss and in severe cases brain damage. Other organs like the kidneys and liver are affected too, and the cycle of drinking to relieve stress damages any hope of recovery. We were asked to make a pledge of abstinence from drugs or alcohol during the course and although I haven't cut it out altogether, this was the beginning of my conscious decision to limit my alcohol intake. I no longer feel the need to drink to relax but it has taken a lot of hard work to get to where I am, and along the way I have slipped back plenty of times.

Towards the end of the course we were invited to bring our partner in for counselling where we dealt with the pressures on the family of living with a loved one who suffers PTSD. Ken was asked how he copes with my illness and it was a chance for him to feel part of the whole process. What it taught me was the power of love and support. We talked about patience and care and how to identify when our partner is suffering. He expressed his concern at my inability to show affection and that he wanted me to work on this issue. It was true that I felt numb at times and did have difficulty showing my feelings. I promised I would work on this. The fact that support was also available for our partners made them feel part of the healing process and gave them the acknowledgement they deserved. After each partner had spoken we all had a better understanding of how individual families coped.

An incident shortly after I returned home demonstrated how important family support can be. One morning when I was using the hairdryer the electrocution warning tag fell to the floor. Looking at it I was paralysed with fear. I could neither pick it up nor throw it away. I managed to hide it in the bottom of the cupboard, but for three days in a row the tag fell to the floor when I pulled the hairdryer out. I sank into a deep depression until finally I sat crying one evening. Ken asked what was wrong and I tried to explain my fear of the tag. Robert, then aged five, stood listening, then disappeared into the bathroom and pulled the tag from the cupboard and threw it in the bin. When he returned he put his arm around me and said, 'It's all right now, Mummy, I've thrown it away.' This was such a wonderful gesture of understanding and support. I cannot express the importance of family and friends in the recovery process. Not so long ago, I sank into a deep depression that lasted for two weeks. Robert simply said, 'Are you sad, Mummy?'

At such times the love of my family brings me back to reality and helps me to focus on what is really important. During this same period I shared my fears with Ken. I told him I didn't think I could carry on and that I needed to go to hospital. He put his arms around me and pledged his support. 'We can get through this together,' he said. And with his support, and that of my mother and my special close-knit circle of friends, I could. At times we take advantage of the generosity and encouragement of the people who are closest to us but I have learnt that this is the best medicine. To have someone sit and listen to you without judgement is one of the best remedies.

Looking after our health was a strong message delivered throughout the course and afterwards I sought medical help for the pounding in my left ear. I discovered I had a displaced jaw due to the constant effects of teeth grinding. The ear pounds louder when I am stressed, but with massage and lymphatic drainage it has improved. I underestimated the value of massage for sufferers of PTSD. The combination of exercise and massage works wonders in relieving tension and I wish I had discovered it earlier. Even the belief that you should take time out to care for your own needs was only instilled in me during group therapy. I now know that there is a whole range of wonderful caring people who are there to help and I am no longer afraid to ask.

After the PTSD course I discovered I was still burdened with grief for the people who had died during my career in the police force. I was silently grieving their loss even though I didn't know them. The grieving process, or lack of it, was the most challenging aspect of my illness and it became painfully obvious that I needed to learn how to let go and move on. It was like I had hit a mountain. I had started to climb, but just couldn't get over the other side to finish the journey and get to another place. This was only possible after I returned to St John of God and participated in a week-long bereavement course. Just being able to cry and express my pain during group therapy alleviated the burden and allowed me to deal with each death individually. I was finally able to dissolve the grotesque pictures of the dead I had in my mind, let go and grieve.

The stop technique works well for me. When a flashback occurs and I feel myself drifting back in time I say *stop* and focus on whatever is in my direct line of vision. This technique gets more effective the more it's practised, and I have mastered it to the point where I rarely allow myself to be drawn back into distressing scenes. As time goes on I have more control over my emotions and can think things through rationally. Some days are better than others and I am now aware that the triggers are always going to be anniversaries such as Father's Day and the New Year period when the boys were discovered in the bridge. It is difficult dealing with these dates but with medication I can get through it. I still suffer nightmares that leave me exhausted for the whole day but now I understand why I feel the way I do and just knowing the cause helps with understanding the process. I am careful not to expose myself to news items, which can trigger dreams, and I am better at distancing myself from distressing television footage or stories about tragedy. I am much more positive about life as a result and don't dwell on the negative things that I cannot change. Each day I find one thing that I enjoy, whether it be a colourful bird or beautiful sunset or seeing my kids smile; I appreciate all that I have.

I am still recovering and I take one day at a time, being mindful not to put unnecessary pressures on myself. I am painfully aware of my limits and try to acknowledge when I'm not coping and just take time out and slow down. It is a daily struggle but one I feel I am winning and I hope in time I will be better able to cope with the day-to-day pressures of life. I still wear my little cross, and there are times I rely on it when I think of death, but I can now take it off for short periods without the fear I once felt.

I regularly see Dr Smith, whose encouragement and wisdom never cease to amaze me. He is a wonderful caring doctor who is totally committed to his profession and I don't know where I would be today without his strength and support. Through this ordeal I have come to understand that it was inevitable that I would eventually crash and burn. It was an impossible load for an untrained young person to carry without support and follow-up. The damage was done right at the beginning of my scientific career and for the police force to throw an untrained young constable out on their own twenty-four hours a day, seven days a week to examine complex scenes of crime involving multiple traumatic deaths was to impose an impossible burden. The emotional overload would eventually crush the spirit.

When I realised this I filed a civil claim which eventually culminated in settlement out of court. But not before they fought the one loophole that could destroy my chances of a claim, that being the time extension required when an injury has been sustained more than three years earlier. I went to court and gave my sworn evidence during which I proved that I was unaware I was suffering a psychiatric illness until my doctor diagnosed me with PTSD in 1999. I felt it showed my true spirit and love of policing that I was able to work for as long as I did. After giving evidence I sat in the back of the court listening while the barristers argued points of law. The tears streamed down my face as I looked around the court and realised this was my final testimony. The judge gave a long determination during which he read out the list of crime scenes I had investigated. He paused at the end and then stated, 'These are not incidents, they are tragedies.'

It was a bitter blow to realise I was no longer fit to continue police work. On 8 March 2001, I was discharged, medically unfit, Hurt on Duty, from the NSW police force. My papers state that I am incapacitated for police duty due to the infirmity of 'Post-Traumatic Stress Disorder with a gradual onset'.

Writing this book has been a long and sometimes traumatic experience. I have written with tears rolling down my face as I recounted some of my experiences over my seventeen years of service, but I am proud of the job I did and I know that there are many equally proud forensic police out there doing the job today. We need these highly trained professionals and depend on them to bring justice through our courts. I can only praise them for serving the community and hope that the police service, with the benefit of hindsight, will look after its members' welfare and recognise the needs of emergency workers. We have learnt a lot about PTSD over the last couple of years and we continue to learn. I sincerely hope that the next generation of forensic police will benefit from what we now know of the effects of exposure to numerous traumatic events.

I took the oath, I've served the state of NSW and I've survived – for that I was awarded the National Police Medal for Service during a ceremony held by the Forensic Services Group at their Westmead laboratory. Commissioner Ken Moroney stepped forward and shook my hand. He inquired after my health and whilst pinning the medal to my lapel said, 'I am proud of you today, as I'm sure your family and friends here today are equally proud. You were a credit to the service.'

# Epilogue

On a wet winter's day in 2001, I was driving through Thirlmere, a small village not far from Pheasants Nest. Suddenly it occurred to me that the two boys were buried at the cemetery there. Should I go and visit their graves? I was undecided but instinctively drove to the cemetery and pulled over to the side of the road. It was dismal outside. I hesitated, watching the raindrops fall onto the windscreen through tear-filled eyes. The scene at the bridge flashed through my mind. I could not get out of the car. Eventually I drove away, glancing at the headstones in the rear-vision mirror.

After that day I thought of the grave sites often. I didn't tell anyone that I'd been to the cemetery. I wasn't sure if it was the right thing to do. Over the next couple of years I also toyed with the idea of going back to the bridge. I felt I needed to see it again. One morning in March 2004, I was driving south along the M5 and, rather than turning off at Wilton, I drove on. I could see the bridge looming up in the distance and I felt strong and composed. The time had finally come.

I went back to Pheasants Nest and I stood by the memorial at the side of the road. On the plaque were the words: 'Jaymie and Matthew: Always together, mates forever'. I bent down and wiped the dust from the plaque, then replaced the plastic flowers in their vase. I stood and reflected for a moment as cars sped past, their drivers utterly unaware of what had happened there all those years before. Then I clambered down the slope and stood under the bridge, looking out over its wide expanse towards the pylons below. The access hole was securely locked. The bridge looks much smaller now.

# Afterword by Dr Selwyn M Smith

Police officers are frequently exposed to human suffering, violence and death. Studies have shown that police experience high job stress, physical illness, alcohol abuse, impaired lifestyles and family problems as a result of their work. They are also more likely than the general public to commit suicide.

Police officers are trained not to show weakness. Indeed, many believe that discussion of emotional problems or the demonstration of feelings is a sign of feebleness. Stress reactions in police officers are often compounded by unsupportive attitudes of superiors, who reinforce the idea of keeping 'a stiff upper lip' in response to traumatic situations. This is based on the false belief that police stress is an employee problem and has nothing to do with police organisational structure.

Police officers are an occupational group at high risk for the development of Post-Traumatic Stress Disorder. Their families also often experience significant distress. This is linked to their fears of the death, injury or kidnapping of their loved ones. The unpredictable nature of police work, shift work, and the frequent inquiries when the police service is in the news also disrupt relationships within the family.

The essential features of a Post-Traumatic Stress Disorder include a cluster of personal symptoms that follows exposure to extreme stress. This includes feelings of fear, helplessness and horror. Avoidance and numbing of responsiveness are added features of this disorder. The traumatic event is often re-experienced in various ways, including recurrent and intrusive distressing recollections, recurrent distressing dreams, and flashbacks. Persistent symptoms of anxiety or increased arousal, hypervigilance, startle responses and impairments in sleeping also occur. Sufferers often experience irritability and are prone to outbursts of anger. They may resort to alcohol or drugs of addiction as methods of coping.

Esther Mckay has written a remarkable book. She describes in riveting detail the work of a police officer in general and of a crime scene investigator in particular. Her descriptions are both crushing and heartrending. *Crime Scene* is also a significant contribution to the literature of police work because it outlines the insidious nature of the traumatic effects of crime-scene work. Over the course of many years this work has taken a tremendous toll on Esther, and she describes her emotional responses with rare and moving frankness. The chapters devoted to her work at Pheasants Nest leave an indelible imprint on the reader.

Esther Mckay has been bold and imaginative in seeking ways to improve the working conditions of those dealing daily with extreme trauma. Her dedication and contributions in the face of adversities are worthy of acclaim. I am sure this book will provide inspiration to others in seeking to prevent the onset of Post-Traumatic Stress Disorder, not only in police settings but also in other hazardous working environments.

*Selwyn M Smith, consultant psychiatrist*